STAN

STAN

TACKLING MY DEMONS

STAN COLLYMORE

with OLIVER HOLT

CollinsWillow
An Imprint of HarperCollinsPublishers

First published in hardback in 2004 by
CollinsWillow
an imprint of HarperCollins*Publishers*
London

First published in paperback in 2005
and fully revised and updated

1

A CIP catalogue record for this book is
available from the British Library

ISBN 0 00 719807 8

Set in Linotype Sabon by
Rowland Phototypesetting Ltd, Bury St Edmunds, Suffolk

Printed and bound in Great Britain by Clays Ltd, St Ives plc

The HarperCollins website address is
www.harpercollins.co.uk

*To Mum, quite simply the best,
and to my babies Tom and Mia.*

PICTURE ACKNOWLEDGEMENTS

All photographs supplied by the author with the exception of the following:

page 9: top left Sporting Pictures/Rex Features, top right Action Images, bottom left Nick Kidd/Rex Features, bottom right Phil O'Brien/Empics; page 10: top Mark Leech/Offside, middle Getty Images, bottom Getty Images; page 11: all © Action Images; page 12: top Rui Vieira/Empics, bottom Nottingham Evening Post; page 13: top Chris Lobina/Rex Features, middle Roy Beardsworth/Action Images, bottom Action Images; page 14: top left Anton Want/Allsport, top right David Kendall/Empics/PA, middle Rex Features, bottom Nottingham Evening Post; page 15: top John Giles/Empics/PA, middle Liverpool Daily Post, bottom Action Images, page 16: top Steve Morton/Empics, middle John Giles/PA, bottom Tony O'Brien/Action Images; page 17: top left Chris Moore, top right Richard Young/Rex Features, bottom left Martin Legge/LFI, bottom right Nils Jorgensen/Rex Features; page 18: top Darren Walsh/Action Images, bottom left David Kendall/Empics/PA, bottom right Action Images; page 19: top Reuters, middle David Cannon/Allsport, bottom Rebecca Naden/PA; page 20: top Darren Walsh/Action Images, middle Chris Lobina/Rex Features, bottom Matthew Ashton/Empics; page 21: top Richard Young/Rex Features, middle Owen Humphreys/Empics/PA, bottom Tim Ockenden/Empics/PA; page 22: top right Richard Heathcote/Action Images, middle Tom Honan/Empics, bottom Paul Marriott/Empics; page 23: top Michael Regan/Action Images, middle Nick Potts/Action Images, bottom Ross Kinnaird/Allsport; page 24: top Rex Features, middle right PA Photos/EPA, middle left The Sun newspaper, bottom right Sky One/Andi Southam.

CONTENTS

ACKNOWLEDGEMENTS

Estelle, thank you for being there for so long. I will always be grateful – I love you. I would also like to thank the following people: Simon Kennedy and Oliver Holt for keeping everything on track with this book; Lynne, Bev, Andrea and families – I don't see you that often but I love you nonetheless; Paul Bellamy, Paul and Caroline Haddaway, Steve Neuchterlien, Mark Davis – I couldn't wish for better friends; Mac Bellamy (the 4x4) – without your intervention there would be no career, no book; Jatta Farley my surrogate mum – I miss you loads, thank you for looking after me for two years; Michelle for being such a great mum and giving me my beautiful boy.

To Stuart Ayres, Trevor Cooper, Colin Murphy, Barry Fry, Frank Clark and Martin O'Neill, for being true advocates and teachers of this beautiful game of OURS and Dr Mark Collins for his work and support for people struggling with depression. Finally, thanks to the following for their constant support: Ed Stein and the Claw, Andy Gray, Tony Finnigan, Jonathan Crystal, Paul Mase, Rachel Cluley, Rob Davis, Hannah Wareham (Maverick spirit), Zara Reed (lovely lady),

Alan Westwood (Terry), Alison Barker (I ain't crying), Anita Smith (my favourite Yorkshire lass), Babushka; all the straight and talented people at Five Live including: Charlotte, Mike, Greeny, Richard, and Tim the engineer; Audra Lamoon, Jamie Moralee, Diane (the Mackem), Emma Shaw, Hepburn, Isobel (miss you loads), Mark Bright (the Latch), Gary Shaw (thanks for the memories – my true inspiration to be a footballer), and everyone at Cannock baths back in the day.

Please accept my apologies for any key people who I have inexplicably forgotten from this list. It's 4.18 am, I'm in Miami, and my agent Simon is on the phone telling me the book is being printed today and I have to finish.

CHAPTER ONE

IN THE BEGINNING: AN UNWANTED LEGACY

I wish that my first memory was kicking my football for hours against the perfect wall of the swimming baths in Cannock, where my mum, Doreen, worked as a receptionist. I wish it was playing endless games of football on the patch of consecrated ground round the corner from our two-up, two-down. The cemetery's claimed that grass now. There are gravestones where we used to play.

I wish it was going for a drive with my mum in her light blue Beetle, the car I made her keep for years and years, right up until I was playing for Liverpool, long after it ceased to be roadworthy. I made sure it was left parked on the drive of the house on the upmarket suburban estate where I lived when I hit the big time with Nottingham Forest and Liverpool. I used to entertain a steady stream of girls at that house when I was at the height of my philandering, four or five a day, every day, every week. The front room of that house saw some action. One girl would leave and a few minutes later another one would arrive. I operated them on a rota system. One time, I came home and the Beetle was gone. My mum had given it away.

You know what, I even wish my first memory was being made to ride my bike naked around the green off to the side of our little house by one of the local lads. I'd be five or six, I suppose. His dad was a miner at one of the local pits. They had come down from the northeast. I was the only black kid in Cannock and I used to get picked on. This boy liked to lock me in the coal-bunker at his house, too. He'd leave me there for hours while I shouted and begged and screamed.

Later, during the miners' strike in the mid-1980s, he kept working. He was a scab. When all the pits in the South Staffordshire Coalfield closed and 30,000 jobs disappeared into the ground with them, most people in Cannock started up mini-cab companies. There were hundreds of taxis everywhere and no one to ride in them. The shops were all boarded up. The place was a ghost-town. He became a window-cleaner then. Once, he asked me to help him on his rounds. I did it for a few weeks.

But my first memory is of crying and pleading in our small red-brick house. It is of looking up and seeing my dad standing over my mum, gripping some sort of heavy brush in his hand and beating her with it. I remember trying to intervene, trying to stop him, and I remember being pushed away. I remember looking at her face and seeing blood and tears and I remember being very scared.

That was standard behaviour for my dad. He used to beat my mum up regularly. He would drag her up the stairs by her hair, into their bedroom, and subject her to prolonged attacks. Hours on end, sometimes. And my mum put up with it. She didn't think she had any choice because she had left her first husband for him. She had made her bed, she said, and now she had to lie in it. But her life with him was one long torment.

Even though Cannock is close in geographical terms to multicultural areas like Wolverhampton and Birmingham, it was, and still is, very ethnically pure. Maybe because it was a mining town, I don't know. Normally, the only black faces were the ones that were covered in coal dust. Ones like mine, mixed-race faces, weren't tolerated very well. A neighbour of ours used to hang out of his upstairs window yelling 'you little black bastard' at me every time I went out. Back in the late Sixties, a white woman leaving her white husband and white kids for a younger black man was about as shocking as anything could possibly be in a conservative working class community. We used to get all sorts of racist abuse from the neighbours. They put signs in our garden, saying 'Blackie Go Home'. My mum's own brother refused to speak to her for 25 years after she hooked up with my dad. Uncle Don got in touch when I became a famous footballer. Funnily enough, he wanted to manage my financial affairs. I gave that the swerve. The separation between him and my mum was never mended. He died a few years ago. She didn't go the funeral.

I think I blotted a lot of that out until recently, until I actually sat down with my mum and talked with her about it. She cried, and it made me feel angry all over again about the legacy of fears and insecurities my dad bequeathed me: the way I daren't be alone; the way I have an almost psychopathic desire to be loved; the way I need constant reassurance from a string of women; the way I can't make any relationship stick.

My dad was an incorrigible womaniser, just as I have been. When my mum went into labour with me on 22 January

1971, he was on the phone in a call box down the road, chatting up a girlfriend. Mum went up to Stone hospital by herself, and when he eventually showed up he was so abusive to the staff that they threw him out. He went off and registered my name anyway, without consulting my mum. He named me after him: Stanley Victor Collymore.

He was from Barbados originally, somewhere near St Andrews and Bathsheba, on the Atlantic side, an educated man who at one time had hoped to become the first black announcer on the island's national radio station. He was in the RAF when he met my mum at a dance and charmed her off her feet. She left her first husband and three daughters and they flew to Barbados, but she missed the girls too much so they returned and made their lives in Cannock.

They were married in a church in Chadsmoor, on the outskirts of Cannock. Five people there, that's all, on Christmas Eve 1969. No fuss. Just a short ceremony. Somewhere close by, there was a Methodist college where Arthur Wharton, the first black footballer to play professional football in England, studied when he first arrived from Ghana. I've tried to pin down where that Methodist college was several times, all without success.

I don't remember much about my dad. We finally freed ourselves of him when I was four. I went for a few visits up to his house in Rugeley after that. His idea of light entertainment was playing me educational tapes about sugar cane cultivation in Barbados. We would lie on the carpet in the front room of his house, just listening to someone's dull voice and watching the tape whirl round on its spool.

Sometimes, when I was playing at my mum's home – my

home – in the side alley, I'd suddenly be aware of a presence and I'd look up and he'd be there, staring at me. He always seemed very sinister and cold to me on the rare occasions he took me back to his house for a visit. He scared me rigid, and with good reason. I don't recall him laying a finger on me but my mum said he smacked me so hard when I was a six-week-old baby that she thought he had broken my hand. Mostly, though, all I remember is a cold, immaculately dressed man who brought terror into my life. It's achingly predictable, but a few years ago he started writing letters to my mum, asking her whether I could give him £25,000 for a deposit on a new house. No answer required.

So much of my life since then has been affected by what he did to us and by the fact that there was just my mum to bring me up. It is much, much more than the mere fact of not having had a male influence to guide me. It is the deep, deep fear I have always had of being left alone; the compulsion I have to make sure there is no dead time in my life, that every minute is filled, with either women or with football.

I often think of myself sitting alone in that red-brick house at night, perched on a chair by the front window and staring out towards the main road. My mum worked all the hours God sent at the swimming baths to try to make ends meet. Most nights, after the short walk back home up the hill, she would get back about 10 p.m. If she was just a few minutes late I would start to panic, really lose it. I was petrified that one day she wouldn't come back and I would have nobody.

My mum seemed old to me. She was 40 when she married my dad. He was 27. I thought she was so old she might pop her clogs any day. When we were going off to football matches, all the other kids had a father and a mother and they all seemed youthful compared to my single parent. However, she did more than her fair share of driving me about to places when I was a kid playing football in the local leagues, and she bought me everything I ever needed. She scrimped and saved and made sure I had the latest football boots and plenty of food on the table. My half-sisters said she spoiled me rotten. But sometimes, I would do something and she would say 'you're just like your dad'. It would send a chill through me, even though I knew that she often didn't even mean it as a criticism, just a nod to genetics.

When I hit my girlfriend Ulrika Jonsson that night in the Auld Alliance pub in Paris during the 1998 World Cup, those words seared through my brain again. *Just like your dad. Just like your dad.* I knew my mum would be devastated. I knew I had let her down in the worst possible way. The thought of hurting her, as well as the guilt of what I had done in six seconds of madness to somebody I had fallen deeply in love with, was almost too much to bear.

That night in Paris was the start of the death of my football career. It destroyed me. After that night, everybody had an excuse to get rid of me when things got tough, and pretty much everybody did. Except Martin O'Neill. After that night, I knew for certain the pipe dream I'd harboured of being an upstanding, halo-ringed Alan Shearer or Michael Owen figure and to make my mum proud, would never be realised. I knew that the third England cap I had won in the 4–0 win against Moldova in September 1997 would be my last. Even that was only eight minutes at the end of the game as a substitute for Les Ferdinand. I had played two other games for my country, both friendlies against Brazil and Japan, but I had missed out on the festival of the 1996 European Championships in England even though I was playing the best football of my career. Terry Venables chose Alan Shearer, Teddy Sheringham, Robbie Fowler and Ferdinand as his four forwards for that tournament.

I missed out on the World Cup in 1998, too. That was why I was free to go on that tortured trip to France with Ulrika in the first place. I had been in Glenn Hoddle's squad for the qualifying game against Italy the previous October but my form had collapsed by the following summer and I was injured anyway. Apart from that, Hoddle didn't really fancy me, even though I had agreed to go and see Eileen Drewery, the healer he put so much faith in, with a few of the other lads.

In the autumn of 1997, before the qualifying tie in the Olympic Stadium in Rome, Hoddle had said he felt I would benefit from a trip to see Eileen. I went with Ian Wright and Paul Ince in Les Ferdinand's Range Rover to her little bungalow somewhere near Reading. I was last in. Eileen laid me down on the bed and put her hands on my stomach and my head. 'Do you drink a lot?' she asked. I said I didn't. 'Do you smoke a lot?' she asked. I said I didn't. 'Have you slept with a lot of women?' she asked. I said: 'Well, yeah, actually, I have.' She nodded her head in a kind of knowing way. She seemed happy then.

I felt a bit worried about openly admitting such a thing, even though I had managed to keep my trap shut about the times I had sneaked out of the England team hotel at Burnham Beeches to go over to nearby Cookham Dean and shag Ulrika. I mentioned the questions Eileen had asked me to Les in the car on the way back. He just laughed. He said he'd given her the same answers.

Hoddle seemed pleased. In fact, he was more friendly to me than he ever was before or since on the day after I had been to see Eileen. 'It's much better having you around now,' he said. 'Eileen told me she'd cleansed your chakras. I can sense a more positive aura around you now.' Bastard still never put me in the team against Italy. Or in any squad after that, for that matter. And I never got close again.

In another era, I would have won more caps. I scored 41 league goals in 65 games for Nottingham Forest and my only reward was a couple of appearances in the Umbro Cup in the summer of 1995. Think of how few goals Wayne Rooney has scored and how many caps he has got. Think about my pal Darius Vassell and his comparatively spartan returns for Villa and how many caps he has got. I'm not knocking Rooney or Darius. It's just that England caps seem easier to come by these days. If my career had started three or four years ago, I would have had 40 England caps by now.

I had one glimpse of what might have been. In my debut, against Japan at Wembley, Shearer burst through in the first five minutes. There was a defender between him and the goalkeeper but I was free on his left. If he had squared it, I could have passed the ball into an open goal. What a start that would have been. Of course, the greedy bastard went for goal and missed by a mile. On such moments, international careers stand and fall, especially if you are pigeon-holed as a maverick, as I was.

I knew in my heart that my £7 million move to Aston Villa from Liverpool in the summer of 1997 had been a step down for me, and that my career was starting to slide. When I had joined Liverpool from Forest two years earlier, they had paid £8.5 million for me, a British transfer record at a time when the popularity of football was exploding in this country. Shearer usurped that, too, when Newcastle paid £15 million to take him from Blackburn to Newcastle, and in the years after the 1998 World Cup I started to live my life in football's shadows.

The Ulrika thing. The thing in Paris. I can never quite bear to say 'the night I hit Ulrika'. I think it's a device I use to spare myself the full horror of the recollection. Whatever euphemism I use to refer to the moment when I hit her, it can't disguise the fact that that moment and its repercussions nearly killed me. I know some people will say that's my fault, that I am just reaping what I sowed, and I will never ever seek to suggest that I did not do a terrible thing that night. But it was six seconds of madness, something I have never done before and something I will never do again. And yet it has stayed with me. It has stuck to me more than anything I ever achieved for Forest or Liverpool or Villa. It has blighted my life from that moment to this.

When I was trying to build a new career in broadcasting, doing some summarising for Five Live and presenting a few shows of my own in the Midlands, it gave me intense satisfaction, a real buzz that was as good as the buzz I got from football. But, even before they dropped me like a hot potato when *The Sun* revealed I was involved in dogging activities, I still felt obstacles were put in my way because of that terrible night in Paris that had happened six years previously. The truth is, some people still remember it as if it was yesterday.

I'm not complaining about the criticism I got at the time. Even if it was all a bit bewildering, even if it felt as if I was about to be ripped to pieces by a lynch mob, I accept that what I did was an appallingly stupid, misguided and awful thing. I had built myself into a state about various things surrounding our relationship. I was jealous. I was deeply in love with her. But those are not excuses. They are just meant as statements of fact.

I realised how hard the struggle to rebuild my reputation was going to be one Saturday night before the 2002 World Cup when I was doing the *606* phone-in show with the radio commentator Alan Green on Five Live. We had got to the last few minutes of the programme when a punter rang in and said he thought I should be in Sven-Goran Eriksson's World Cup squad. England were due to face Sweden, Argentina and Nigeria in the group phase but this was obviously a set-up because I had retired by then. Anyway, like an idiot I gave the guy his cue and asked him why he thought that. 'Because you're good at beating Swedes,' he said. I was embarrassed. In fact, I was mortified. Greenie got rid of the guy straight away but it was awkward. Afterwards, the producers said not to worry about it and I did my best to put it out of my mind.

I was due to do a third consecutive *606* the following Saturday, too, but some time in the middle of the week, I got a call from Peter Salmon, the BBC's Head of Sport. He said there had been a change of plan. They weren't going to give me the show because there was no time delay and they didn't want to risk any more dodgy calls.

I was desperately, desperately disappointed. And I was angry. I just felt so insulted. I was doing the job well, but because this thing reared its head they just caved in and took me off the air. I thought that was the end of it. I thought I wasn't going to be able to broadcast. I thought if people were going to knock me at every opportunity, what was the point. I thought that if I wasn't even going to be allowed to get past 'Go', what was I going to do?

For a while, I had tried to be whiter than white. When I was summarising for the BBC, I made sure I got to the game two hours early. I behaved like Mary Poppins, basically, which didn't give me too much scope for having a bad day or coming down with the flu or something like that. I was professionalism personified, but even before the dogging scandal I was still blackballed by the BBC governors for a celebrity *Come Dancing* programme they were putting on. The programme-makers wanted me but the people higher up put a veto on me. They binned me and chose Martin Offiah, the former rugby-league player, in my place.

I know I did wrong that night in Paris, but sometimes the punishments that I am still suffering seem out of all proportion. Look at people like Johnny Vaughan and Leslie Grantham who have been rehabilitated after crimes they committed many, many years ago. My crime was to hit a woman, a woman who happens to be a very popular and attractive television personality. It was wrong and I will regret it bitterly until the day I die. But I didn't put anyone in hospital. I didn't kill anybody. I didn't run somebody over when I was drunk behind the wheel. And yet, sometimes it feels that some people treat me as if I had.

The fresh bout of depression the 606 incident plunged me into led me to the brink of suicide. I had lost the joy I used to get from football long before that, and from the time I joined Liverpool right through to when I went into the Priory and beyond, it felt like I was having to endure on a weekly basis the kind of crises most people only have to deal with once or twice in their lives.

Perhaps that sounds self-pitying. Maybe it is. But it felt like I was having to put up with a lot. The media impinging on my private life. All the shit that went with that. And I knew I was barely dealing with it. I knew I was barely keeping a lid on everything. I had to do something about it or I knew I wouldn't see 40. Ending it all was starting to seem increasingly tempting. But I also thought about all the things that would be a waste if I ended up topping myself.

I thought about my son, Tom, my child from a relationship with a Cannock girl called Michelle Green. Tom was born in 1996 while I was away with England at Burnham Beeches. You want to know how I met Michelle? I saw her washing her car in the driveway of her parents' home. I was driving past but I stopped my car, wound down the window and asked her out. We only had a brief relationship, but she got pregnant and we had Tom.

The relationship with Michelle hasn't exactly been plain sailing either. I suppose with my attitude towards fidelity, plain sailing is never really going to be too high on the agenda. I had a blazing row with her about access to Tom just before Christmas in 1997. It ended with me storming out of the house I had bought for her and slamming the door hard on my way out. I drove my car round the corner to talk it all through with my mates Paul and Caroline at their house and parked outside.

Half an hour later, the police arrived and arrested me on suspicion of assault. Michelle had called them and claimed I had knocked her out cold and kicked the door off its hinges to get to her. I was released and then re-arrested on Christmas Eve. The second time, you could have been forgiven for thinking they'd just found Osama Bin Laden. I walked out of the door and there was one black maria parked on the pavement to my right and another to the left. Both full of coppers. The only thing missing was a sniper on the roof and a helicopter circling overhead.

I pleaded not guilty and the case went to Crown Court and a two-day trial. We both gave evidence and the jury found me innocent. There was no evidence against me because I had not done any of the things she said. There was no damage to the door and there was certainly no damage to Michelle. The judge said there was no stain on my character and I could go. However, when Paris happened people remembered the false charges Michelle had made and wondered whether there had been some substance to them after all.

Michelle and I don't talk about any of that now. We treat it as if it never happened. We have a good relationship. I pay her Child Support and I see Tom, who is eight now, whenever I want. Tom was one of the reasons I decided to quit playing football and move back to Cannock in 2001. I wanted to see more of him. I resent the years I missed when he was growing up. I had him a lot when he was a baby, but then, as what was left of the relationship between Michelle and me degenerated into wrangles about pay-offs and maintenance, I hardly saw him again until he was five.

More than that, I resent the years my mum missed because she was caught up in the bitterness between us. Michelle used to say my mum could see Tom as long as she didn't take him anywhere near my house. So she used to push him around Cannock in his pram in the pouring rain just to snatch a few precious hours with him.

Tom's growing up fast now and I love him to bits. He plays for one of the kids teams at Cannock. I think he might have the talent to make it as a professional if things go his way. When I was thinking about suicide, I didn't want to leave him. I thought about Tom, and about my mum who had suffered so much and sacrificed so much. I thought about my wife, Estelle. For some of the time when I first began what has become a recurring flirtation with suicide, she was pregnant with our daughter, Mia. Estelle had stood by me for so long and weathered so many storms and tolerated so many indiscretions.

From the time I went into the Priory in January 1999 until the beginning of 2003, I was so low generally that thinking about suicide actually gave me a lift. It was a way out that was a clean no-brainer. I think that's why a lot of people do it. Part of me wanted it because I knew that if I did it I wouldn't have to think about the things that were torturing me any more.

I was a total mess back then. I couldn't get out of bed. I couldn't structure my day properly. I'd be sitting in bed in the morning watching *Trisha* and all these people with their problems. I couldn't face having a shower or getting dressed. Those all seemed like major events I didn't want to confront. And, of course, Estelle was growing increasingly exasperated with me because I was sitting around the house like a zombie.

I came close to doing myself in a few times in that period. Estelle found me sitting in my flat in Birmingham with a belt round my neck. I was just sitting there like a fucking dick, my hands tightening this belt, the telly flickering in the corner. On another occasion we had a row about something, she walked out and I slit my wrists. I didn't do it big. I didn't want to go the full way. I just wanted to give myself the option to do it. It wasn't even really a cry for help because I didn't tell anybody about it, but it bled badly enough for me to have to bandage myself up.

Mostly, I used to think about hanging myself. I thought that would be the best way. In fact, I was reading a lot of stuff about quick ways to die at that time. It was all the stuff about making sure the length of rope was right for your weight.

But when it came to it, I didn't have the bottle for that either. Not then, anyway. Now it's not bottle that's stopping me. I'm not sure what stops me now. Sometimes, especially since the dogging was exposed and I was ridiculed again and my relationship with Estelle finally crumbled, I still think suicide is just around the corner. But back then I used to sit there thinking about what would happen if I was on a fucking tree branch 30 feet up and I'm just stuck there dangling and I can't breathe but I don't die. If it had been a case of just doing it so it would all be over and done with, then great. But it never happened because I think more than anything the mere thought of suicide was just this release valve. Rather than staring into space thinking about ways of dragging myself out of this depression, rather than taking tough decisions, I could just go out into the garden or into the woods and it would all be over. How I got through that time, I don't know. I just kept telling myself to grind on through it. But there were plenty of days when I thought the only way out was to pull the chain on it.

Perhaps I didn't do it because my mum never pulled the chain on me. Perhaps it was because when I thought about what she had been through, it seemed somewhere in the back of my mind like cowardice to take an easy way out. Perhaps it was because when I asked her about what her life with me and my dad was like, the realisation of how strong she had had to be gave me some strength, too.

It wasn't easy for her talking about it. When other families go through their photo albums, they see happy, smiling faces staring back out of them. But one of the pictures we remember best is one of my birthday parties. She's there with a birthday cake, gazing into the camera with a black eye that my dad had given her. She wept when she talked about those days in my early childhood:

I made a dreadful mistake when I left my first husband. He was a really nice fella. He was a director of a small firm in Cannock and he worked hard. When he worked in Wolverhampton, he would cycle all the way there and all the way back. But we married when I was 19. We had three kids. I suppose there wasn't much glamour in my life.

Stan's dad was a charmer. He was a good-looking fella, tall and handsome. Everyone liked him. Particularly women. I had a blonde beehive hairdo back then and I caught his eye. When I left my first husband, we went to Barbados for a few weeks and stayed in a kind of shack amid the sugar cane where he had been brought up. I started to realise I'd made a terrible mistake when I saw him smash that shack up in a fit of anger.

I tried to leave Barbados without him but he followed me back to England. By then, my first husband had found somebody else so Stan's dad and I moved back into the council house I had been living in before. He was 13 years younger than me. He went to work in the tax office in Cannock and pretty soon Stan was born. But everything had already gone terribly wrong by then.

When I was seven months pregnant with Stan, we had an argument about something and he put a telephone cord around my neck and tried to strangle me. I called the police, obviously, but in those days they were far more blasé about domestic violence. They just said, 'Have a cup of tea and talk it over and everything will be all right after a good night's sleep.'

When Stan was a few months old, his dad began to teach at a college in Birmingham. I was called in one day to be told that one of his students had had a nervous breakdown because she had got entangled in a love affair with him. She was just the first. Soon after that, I got a phone call from a woman who said she and my husband were getting married and who then asked when I was moving out of the house.

One of his girlfriends was the daughter of the manager of the Co-op in Cannock, and that poor girl even bought a wedding dress. She was so convinced that she was his sweetheart. I don't know if it was because he was frustrated at not being able to be with these women more, but he began to hit me regularly then and things got worse and worse.

During the four years we were married, I had to go to the hospital several times. He broke my jaw with a punch once. On another occasion he cut me over the eye when he clouted me with a heavy brush. That was the time Stan tried to intervene; that is Stan's first memory. I went up to the hospital to have it stitched because the cut was bleeding dreadfully and they found the bruises on my arms and stomach. I told them I had fallen off a ladder.

Mostly, he would drag me up to our bedroom by the hair and beat me there. I think his logic was that the bed sagged when he was hitting me so the punches wouldn't bruise me as badly and it wouldn't be so obvious what he was doing. The lady that lived next door to us always knew when there was a problem, because when I knew I was going to get a beating I would beg Stan's dad to let me close all the windows first so the neighbours wouldn't hear. I'd plead with him not to shout, so the neighbours wouldn't know I was being beaten up.

He was such a strange mix, Stan's dad, very formal and always immaculately dressed to the point where he might change his shirt two or three times a day. He would ring me from work and tell me when I could go shopping but that I mustn't be away more than an hour. And I would have to be back, because if he rang and I wasn't there he would come and look for me and I would get knocked about again at home.

And then, of course, there was the abuse we used to get as a family, the racial abuse that almost hurt more than my husband's punches. Jeff's mum was one of the worst. It was always stuff about how I should move away because I had married a black man. The things she said to me were so dreadful that once, when she had said something particularly cruel to Stan, I went round and asked her to come out into the garden so I could give her what she deserved. I'm ashamed of that now. I wonder if she's ashamed. She wouldn't come out into the garden anyway.

Stan won't talk about it much but they used to do terrible things to him, too. One day, I was walking over to the garages at the other end of our circle of houses and I saw a group of boys coming across the field, making another boy crawl through the grass on his hands and knees. The boy on his hands and knees was Stan and they were weeing on him, actually weeing on him, as he crawled.

Stan used to get it from his dad, too. Not physical abuse, but he would do really strange things. He bought Stan a toy cat once and then one day when he came round he took the cat upstairs with him and disappeared for ages. When he had gone, I went to look for it and he had cut it up into tiny pieces and left it scattered across the bed.

People always wonder why I didn't leave him earlier but where was I going to go? My mother lived with us and by that time she had Alzheimer's disease. There was nowhere to go. They didn't have refuges for battered wives then. And

I felt I had made my choice and I had to live with it. I'd lost a lot of my friends, too, because they were too ashamed to come round and see me any more. I found out afterwards he had been visiting a few of them and they . . . well, they liked him.

Eventually, though, I just couldn't put up with it any longer. He started hitting one of my daughters, too, so I got a divorce and got him kicked out. Even after that he would prowl around on the land at the back of the house. He rang me and threatened to cut my throat, and I had to make Stan a ward of court to keep him away. Sometimes, I could just sense his presence outside. I just knew he had come to watch us. They stopped him coming into Cannock but he never disappeared. He kept writing to me, kept saying he knew that I had never married again because I still loved him.

Stan isn't like him. Just because he has been a womaniser doesn't mean he is like him. Stan has got friends. Stan tries to do his best for others. I was ashamed of him when he hit Ulrika but that's the only time I have been ashamed of him. I had always pleaded with him, 'be kind to ladies'. But that one incident doesn't make him like his dad. Not by a million miles.

I know wives who have been victims of violent husbands sometimes say this, but in many ways I blame myself. You see, I never loved Stan's dad. Even my first husband, I never missed him after I left him. I think that's just my way. Perhaps it's just that I never met the right fella, but I don't think I'm capable of loving anybody apart from my kids.

I've never tried to find my dad. But just after Christmas last year, he found me. He sent me an e-mail after I'd written a piece in the *Daily Mirror* touching on some of the abuse he had handed out to my mum. He said that he considered I was lost to the black side of my family and that I had been corrupted by white ways of thinking. He said that if I ever criticised the black race as a whole, I had better keep looking over my shoulder because he would be coming for me.

It made me laugh really. Partly because he hadn't wasted any time trying to renew my acquaintance ten years or so ago when he suddenly realised I might be earning a decent wedge at Nottingham Forest. Funny that, isn't it? Him and my Uncle Don, who'd combined to make life so difficult for my mother, united by a love of money that conquered all their hostility towards my mother in a trice. What a pair of sad bastards. Pathetic specimens of humanity.

I laughed, too, because my dad's threats made me think of the time when I was at Forest and I had my hair dyed blonde. I looked like a right twat, to be honest with you. Frank Clark, the Forest manager, said I should spend more time on the training pitch and less at the hair salon and I might improve myself as a player. Point taken.

A couple of days later, I opened a newspaper to see a picture of my dad staring out at me as large as life. I hadn't seen him, even a picture of him, for more than 10 years. He had a handsome face and he was wearing smart, elegant, Seventies-style clothes. He wasn't being very complimentary about me, though. It was the same sort of stuff. How I was trying to turn myself into a white boy. How he had always wanted me to play cricket for the West Indies, not be a common footballer. What struck me most was that I did not feel a thing. No hurt. No hatred. No despair. Why should I after what he had done to us? Why should I after the legacy he had bequeathed to me? If he had a soul left, my dad had just sold it. And I didn't feel a thing.

CHAPTER TWO

WALSALL: A MIXED BAG

Everybody thinks I underachieved as a footballer. Everybody always says I could have done so much more. I could have been one of the greats. I could have had 80 caps for England instead of three. I could have been a stalwart of the national side. I could have won a hatful of medals and the admiration of my peers. They say it's such a shame it turned out the way it did and that I walked away from football when I was 30, when I should have been in my prime, not burned out, my mind frazzled.

Well, I want to nail all that. I didn't underachieve. I overachieved. I had a great career. I played for Aston Villa, the club I had always wanted to play for. I played for Liverpool, one of the most famous names in world football. And I played for my country. I scored the winning goal in the best match of the 1990s, Liverpool's 4–3 win over Newcastle at Anfield in 1996. I scored goals that got people up off their seats. I was an entertainer. The fans of the clubs I played for loved me. That will always mean more to me than any one of the medals that public opinion has deemed the arbiter of success in a footballer's career.

I don't agree with that criteria. Alan Shearer has never won a winner's medal in all his time at Newcastle, and yet the enjoyment and the satisfaction he has provided for Geordie supporters who worship him is worth a million medals. You don't have to have little bits of silver hidden away in a bank vault somewhere to convince you that you were a success. All you need are memories that make your chest puff out and your eyes glisten when you think of them. That's why I count helping to keep Southend United in the First Division in my season there as one of my finest achievements. That's success to me.

But that's not the main reason why I look back at my playing years with pride, and not with regret. If you want to understand me, if you want to put what I did in its proper context, you need to know what I was up against. You need to know what was going on inside my mind. You need to know about my thought processes and how they tortured me. You need to know about the mental illness I suffer from and how I have struggled to overcome that all my life. You need to know how I'm fighting Borderline Personality Disorder. And how, essentially, that often feels like a losing battle.

When people talk about me and how I wasted my talent, there are usually two favourite themes they trot out. Firstly, they talk about how, wherever I went, I never got on with my team-mates. They talk about me being a loner. They recall apocryphal stories about team-mates not celebrating goals with me. They repeat rumours about players not talking to me in the dressing room at Nottingham Forest. They say I was arrogant and aloof and that I was bad news for team spirit wherever I went.

The other strand is my attitude to training. The common perception is that I damned myself by being an incorrigibly lazy twat. The stories go that I left behind a trail of infuriated managers who had grown increasingly exasperated by my reluctance to fall into line on the training pitch. It's almost like football was the fucking army and I was guilty of serial insubordination. Failing to obey some fuckwit officer who never had a tenth of my talent as a player and who catered his sessions to the lowest common denominator. Well, I'm not a 'yes, sir, no, sir' person. I don't respect automatons and drones.

If clubs failed to get the best out of me, that is their failure. Not mine. If they paid millions of pounds for me and then tossed me into the general pile of players, if they treated every personality alike rather than catering for individual needs, then why should they be surprised if someone like me doesn't react well? Man-management isn't rocket science, but because I was fragile mentally I needed loyalty and care. When I got that, at Southend, Nottingham Forest and Leicester, I flourished and the team prospered. When I didn't get it, I withered.

Training and I have always been strange bedfellows. Part of that stems from the fact that my first experience of a professional club was mutilated by a horror of a human being called Ray Train, who was the youth-team coach at Walsall when I joined as an apprentice on £29 a week at the age of 17. Being an apprentice under Ray Train was like a baby coming out of the womb and the first thing it sees is people firing guns or battering the fuck out of each other. This was my first taste of professional football and training at a league club.

The man terrified me. It's a strong word but I use it intentionally. He inspired terror in me. My first day under his tutelage set out the pattern for the rest of my career as far as a distaste for training goes. It was a template for cynicism about training. I still associate training with him. Even when I'm sitting in my car today outside the health club I use in Great Barr, I start to sweat and get the shakes before I go for a work-out because I associate working out with him.

That first day at Walsall was a beautiful, sunny day in June and I had caught two buses from our house in Cannock to get there early, one from Cannock to Walsall Bus Station, the other from there to Fellows Park, the predecessor to the Bescot Stadium. I got to the ground, washed the kit and swept up. Then we went over to the training ground and the first thing we did was a long cross-country run. And I struggled.

More than that, I struggled badly. I hadn't done four to six weeks' preparation. Nobody had told me I had to. I was lagging behind. I was so far behind everyone else you wouldn't believe it, and from thereon in, Ray decided he was going to have me for his bunny. At the end of every session he would allow us all to walk back towards the dressing rooms and then, just when I thought I was free, he would shout: 'Not you, Stan.'

Ray was the ultimate grafter. Even at 40, he still trained like a fucking demon. The only other person who got near him for intensity, in my experience, was Archie Gemmill at Nottingham Forest. Ray couldn't let go. He had to prove he was still a player. Had to prove he was still as fit as all of us. So for him to see a lazy, black, eminently talented player come on and score a couple of goals for the youth team as a late substitute used to infuriate him.

The bloke was five foot nothing. He had played for Carlisle for five years between 1971 and 1976, a defensive midfielder who was the cornerstone of the success they enjoyed in that period, which even took them into the top flight. He was popular with the fans because of the effort he put in, but people told me the senior pros used to laugh at him because he was this little fucking sergeant major type figure. He was never racist. He didn't even shout, really. That was what made him so sinister. He would sidle up to me and whisper what he wanted me to do in my ear. I hated him, but most of all he terrified me. He made my life a misery. He always made a point of leaving that little gap between letting me walk away at the end of a session and then calling me back for more. It was psychological torture. And it was only me. It was public humiliation in front of the rest of the lads. I have tried to take my rawness into account, but that little man went out of his way, time and time again, to fuck with my mind.

He would get me to come in an hour before the rest of the lads. He seemed to like the ones who were grafters, particularly a group of three or four who had been released by Celtic. They were all hard-working midfielders. But to me, whether you are the laziest fucker on earth or whether you are a grafter, a coach should do all he can to get the best out of you. That was not quite how Ray saw it. He tormented me but he didn't get me any fitter.

His favourite mode of torture was to get me to mop the changing rooms at Fellows Park. He developed this fiendish system where he would hide penny-pieces in obscure places like on the outside of the U-bend behind the toilet or on top of the cistern. If you missed one of these penny-pieces he took it as a sign you hadn't done the job properly and you had to start again. It was pathetic. It was medieval shit. I still feel sad I had to go through it all. I still feel sad that it left its mark on me.

He still haunts me. I think about him and what he did to me most days. I'm still terrified of him. I met him once in New York when I was there with Ulrika. We were in Blooming-dales in the Ralph Lauren section and I caught sight of this little fucking dickhead stretching up, trying to reach some of the T-shirts on the top shelf. It was Ray. He had knitted hair that sprawled over his head like a cardigan. Somehow, he sensed somebody looking at him and turned round. 'All right, big man,' he said. I had to get out of there. I was shaking with anger and fear. There I was, a grown man, still brought low by this guy. Ulrika wondered what the hell was wrong with me.

I never complained about him or objected to any of this treatment to his face. I knew it wouldn't do any good. One day, I thought God had smiled on me because Ray keeled over and had a heart attack on the training pitch. Right there in front of me. It felt like divine retribution. The ambulance came for him and carted him off to hospital, us all standing there in our dirty kits watching. I had never been so happy in my entire fucking life. There was the possibility that he might die, but at the very least we would be rid of him for a few months.

He didn't die. Little fuckers like him never do. But I

thought there was still hope. When he came back, Tommy Coakley, the first-team manager, got the sack and Ray was promoted to caretaker boss. I wished fervently he would be given the post permanently or that the new guy would keep him on as his assistant, but, of course, no one could be that stupid. John Barnwell got the job and booted him back down to the youth team and the torment began all over again.

It was a systematic attempt to break me, and it worked. Instead of leaving me to do the extra work he gave me by myself, he made the other lads stay, too, to watch me. One day, the first team were travelling to an away match and most of the reserve side had gone with them, so the youth team played in the reserve match that night. Except me. I was the only one left out. I had to stay behind and sweep the stands at Fellows Park. By myself.

I wasn't getting much of a run in the team. I was always on the bench. If I got on, I usually scored. But I was getting more and more unhappy. I dreaded waking up in the morning because I was so scared of what the day was going to hold. Often, I wished I would die in the night just so I could avoid Ray the next day. Sometimes, even if I made it to Fellows Park in the morning I'd head for the phone box outside the ground and call my mum in tears.

In the end, I just called it a day. Ray getting the youth-team job back finished me. I went in to see John Barnwell, said it wasn't working out and asked him if I could be released from my contract. He was very good about it. I thought I was free of Ray then, but Ray never left me really. I went on to Wolves as an apprentice and I scored 18 goals in 20 games for the reserves. I was devastated when they let me go after less than a season there, but when Graham Turner (who was the manager then) released me, one of the reasons he gave was my inconsistent appearance record at training.

And it was true. Sometimes I just didn't go in. It wasn't as if I was skiving off so I could do something else. I didn't go out on the piss or smoke fags or go in to Birmingham. I just stayed indoors. I'd developed some mental block at Walsall. Ray had infected me. It was the same at Forest. There were four or five occasions when I didn't go in. Liverpool was exactly the same. It was very unprofessional but I had my reasons.

In training, I loved five-a-sides and I liked to do practical, functional stuff that was relevant to my game. I wanted people putting crosses in for me. I wanted to try to hone my finishing. I wanted to be put in situations where I could take people on. I wasn't like most of the players because most players are low maintenance when it comes to training. They do what they are told. If they are told to lick their own arsehole, they'll lick it. No questions asked. But if I was told to do something mundane like sidefoot volley a ball back to someone who kept on throwing it to you time after time from a few yards away, I lost interest. I could do that standing on my head. The Gareth Southgates of this world did it because it could genuinely enhance their game. But for me, that kind of exercise was like white noise. It was minutiae. Doing stuff like running across the width of the pitch doing sidefoot volleys was a piece of piss so I'd just switch off.

Perhaps I was a victim of the increasing premium on supreme physical fitness. I have never been the fittest. Somebody like Robbie Savage could go six months without training, then go on a long run tomorrow and dash through it like a whippet. But if I do long fitness stuff, I just get bored. And if I was either uninspired or if something had happened in my personal life, sometimes I would decide to skip training.

If you get an intelligent coach like Arsene Wenger, he knows how to manage his players. I look at someone like Thierry Henry and think he must have his days sometimes when he can be temperamental. But some of the sessions at Arsenal only last 45 minutes. When I was at Palace, most of them went on for three hours. If you knew that was coming, the temptation was to sit at home and think 'fuck that'.

My curse is that I've always been blessed with a great touch. I don't need to practise my ball skills. I was born with them. I'm never going to lose them. If someone injected me with a fitness drug and I walked out in the Arsenal team or the Liverpool team tomorrow, no one would ever know that I had not played football for three years. I can guarantee that. But if you took an average player who had been out for the same length of time, you could forget about giving them a ball. You might as well give them a bag of cement to kick around.

The fittest I have ever been was at Nottingham Forest. We had a coach there called Pete Edwards. We used to take the piss out of him because he was a muscle man, but he was superb. He organised very high intensity, short-burst sessions with balls in match environments. Our warm-ups were the equivalent of full sessions for other clubs, but when we finished our matches there was not one Forest player who looked as though he had just played 90 minutes.

It makes me smile now to think of how fit I was then. In my

current state, energy is about as hard to find as rocking-horse shit, but back then I had too much of it. The night before a game against Sunderland, I even felt I had to go to the gym to do an hour on the treadmill just to get rid of some of the excess energy that was coursing through me. I went out the next day against Sunderland and I was still flying around. After Forest, I went to Liverpool, where the regime was not as intense. It was like pulling a thread on my fitness. It all started to unravel.

Maybe I just don't look like I'm trying. Sometimes, it clearly appears as if I don't care. Glenn Hoddle criticised me once in training before England's World Cup qualifying tie in Rome in 1997. The forwards were queueing up for finishing practice and Ian Wright had just lunged for a cross and prodded it in. When it was my turn, the cross came in and it just evaded me. I didn't lunge for it because I wouldn't have got it anyway. 'You see,' Hoddle shouted. 'You see, that's the difference between you and Wrighty. Wrighty lunged for it even in training. You didn't lunge for it.' What a ridiculous thing to say. The problem with Hoddle was that he would get exasperated by people who couldn't do what he had once been able to do. He would still run around the training pitch, tapping the ground as he ran with the point of his boot like a fucking dick. That just lost him the respect of the players.

The press called Hoddle's assistant, John Gorman, 'Coneman'. There's always a fucking Coneman but Gorman acted like a pre-pubescent teenager, just excited to be there. He always called me 'big man', too, and tried to give the impression he knew what was going on. But if I'd asked him anything important, he would have shit himself and hedged around it. He knew halves of bits of stuff that were discussed in the bar late at night. But, really, that amounted to nothing. His role meant not asking Glenn any awkward questions. He was a yes man.

And football's full of them. Full of people scared to be different. Full of people only too happy to let you down and turn you into a fall guy. Something as simple and as harmless as heading home to Cannock after training was enough to put me out there in freak-show territory at a string of clubs. Football doesn't deal very well with anybody who strays from the norm. It's suspicious of anyone who doesn't aspire to the norm. Think of what happened to Graeme Le Saux just because he read the *Guardian* and said he liked going to see art-house movies now and again. Football gave its snap judgement: the guy must be a faggot.

Football's full of contradictions and hypocrisies like that. The players moan about the media, and the tabloids in particular, but they all read *The Sun* and the *Mirror*. If they hate the tabloids so much, why don't they read the *Guardian* or *The Times*? They're too scared to be different. Worried they might get the piss ripped out of them for being a lah-di-dah smart-arse gay boy. Much easier to fit in and toe the party line and do what the others do. Much easier to conform.

It wasn't that I had a problem with authority. I just had a problem with bad management. I couldn't understand why a football club would spend millions and millions of pounds on a new asset and then not try to get the best out of them. Clubs knew what they were getting when they bought me, so why didn't they make plans for me? Why do you break the British transfer record for a player and then try and force him into a style of football that is foreign to him?

From Ray Train at the start to Raddy Antic at the close of my career with Real Oviedo, I feel I have been ill-served by the men who have been in a position of power over me. I know there's a danger of that sounding self-righteous and self-pitying but it was also business suicide on the part of the clubs. There have been honourable exceptions like Colin Murphy and Barry Fry, my two managers at Southend, and Martin O'Neill at Leicester, but for the most part these men who had often paid lavish amounts of money to bring me to their club gave every impression of being disappointed they had signed an individual and not an automaton.

That was one of the things that shortened my life as a footballer. In the end, I'd just had enough of betrayal and bullshit and double-speak and the empty friendships that flourish in football dressing-rooms and die the moment you move on to another club. That kind of friendship is no friendship at all, and by the time I had reached my late twenties I had grown weary of it. By the end, I'd had enough of being treated like a circus curiosity, the sensitive, difficult footballer no one could manage.

Football's full of people who are scared to challenge you. By that, I don't mean it's full of people scared to bollock you. There are plenty of men who think that's enough to establish their authority. But to gain authority over me, you have to interest me, and football's full of people taking the safe option, full of coaches putting on piss-poor training sessions for men who are supposed to be trained athletes every week of the year. There's too much uniformity. Not enough variety.

Too many players with ability are allowed to stagnate. As a player, I felt like I was fighting a losing battle seeking worthwhile stimulation from training.

But maybe the clubs were fighting a losing battle with me, too. I know now that I have been suffering from Borderline Personality Disorder since I was young. It's called Borderline because it was first used to describe people who lived on that edge between psychosis and neurosis. That's where I live. Right on that line. I sit astride it. I exhibit all the symptoms. I'm a textbook study in this particular offshoot of being fucked up.

You'll recognise me, and the way my career has fallen away at times when it should have kicked on, from some of the Borderline sufferer's traits. The chronic disturbance with self, others and society. The ambivalence towards all directions, aims and goals. I didn't have the hunger other players have. Just didn't have it. Not always, but sometimes. Not because I was lazy but because it just didn't feel right to me to behave in certain ways at certain times.

One of the most common characteristics of someone with BPD is the subconscious search for different states of chaos. In my personal life and in my football career, I have gravitated towards situations that are bound to end in schism and conflict. Other people try and avoid discord. My illness propels me towards it. One way or another, we always seem to find each other. We like hanging out together.

People look at me and scoff at this idea that I've got any sort of mental problem, partly because I've got a lot of money, which most people associate with happiness, and partly because they can't see me doing anything extreme like playing paintball in my front room or throwing cats into trees. I wish that made me normal. I really do.

Let me try and give you an idea of how my mind can torture me just as surely as if I was strapped to the rack in one of the seven circles of Hell. Maybe you'll start to see why the longest time I ever spent at one club was two full seasons. Maybe you'll start to see why it often ended in tears. Maybe you'll start to understand why I can't hold down a steady relationship with a woman, why I flit from one to another like a honeybee.

I feel I must be loved by all the important people in my life at all times or else I am worthless. I must be completely competent in all ways if I am to consider myself to be a worthwhile person.

I feel nobody cares about me as much as I care about them, so I always lose everyone I care about, despite the desperate things I do to try to stop them from leaving me.

I have difficulty controlling anger. I have chronic feelings of emptiness and worthlessness. I exhibit recurrent suicidal behaviour. I'm reckless sexually.

When I am alone, I become nobody and nothing. When I am alone, when I have no work to structure my day, I take to my bed. Since I stopped playing football, apart from my work for Five Live, I have slept for three years.

I will only be happy when I find an all-giving, perfect person to love me and take care of me no matter what. But if someone like that loves me, then something must be wrong with them.

My life, like that of most sufferers from Borderline Personality Disorder, has been defined by a pervasive pattern of unstable relationships and a tendency to act on impulse. Since I used to wait by the window at night for my mother to come home from the swimming baths, I have always made frantic efforts to avoid real or imagined abandonment, another BPD classic trait.

One passage from a book by a guy called Jerry Kreisman, called *I Hate You, Don't Leave Me*, seemed unusually relevant to my behaviour and my failure to make anything, from a relationship to a spell at a football club, more than ephemeral. '*The world of someone with Borderline Personality Disorder*, Dr Kreisman writes, '*is split into heroes and villains. A child emotionally, the BP cannot tolerate human inconsistencies and ambiguities. He cannot reconcile good and bad qualities with a constant coherent understanding of another person. At any particular moment, a friend is either good or evil. There is no in-between. No grey area. People are idolised one day, totally devalued and dismissed the next.*

'*When the idealised person finally disappoints, the borderline must drastically restructure his one-dimensional conceptualisation. Either the idol is banished to the dungeon or the borderline banishes himself to preserve the all-good image of the other.*'

I fit these descriptions like a hand fits a glove. I have heroes who can't do any wrong. Martin O'Neill would be one. And there are men who I have come to regard as sworn enemies and devil figures. John Gregory and Ray Train would fit that part of the equation. I recognise it all so clearly that it is unsettling in itself. But it was only earlier this year that I was diagnosed with it. It coexists with the bouts of depression that I have been sinking into for the past six or seven years, but it predates my depression, too. I think it's always been with me.

Let me try to give you an idea of how my thought process contrasts with the way someone deemed to be normal might think. Let's say somebody tells you they love you. A normal reaction would be to process that thought and assimilate the normal, positive benefits that come with it. But somebody like me hears 'I love you' and the reaction sets off on a thousand different routes through my mind. Suddenly, I'm asking myself a billion questions. I have that reaction to every single thought, every single day.

I was talking to someone on the phone recently and they told me they loved me. I got aggressive with them and they became exasperated. They told me to accept it for what it was, a simple statement of affection. 'But that's the whole fucking point,' I said. 'I can't.' I know I should be able to react appropriately but I can't. I'm unable to express myself emotionally. I can't deal with my emotions. My connection between thinking something and reacting to it is all to cock.

Sometimes I get so tired trying to analyse all the thoughts that are racing around inside my mind, that I have to go to bed for a day to sleep it off. It's always like the thermometer in my brain is about to reach boiling point.

A lot of the personality disorder, I'm sure, is rooted in my childhood. The army of Richard Littlejohns out there will say that this personality disorder mumbo-jumbo is just another way of evading personal responsibility for what they like to see as my sick sexual depravity and my failure to knuckle down for a succession of managers. It's almost as if they think I want to be like this. It's as if they think I want my life to feel like one long fucked-up day.

If my neuroses had a radical effect on my career, they also distorted my personal life into a litany of flings that were usually devoid of real feeling and affection. I have been out with people such as Kirsty Gallagher for around a year, and yet I never felt I was in a proper relationship with them. I have maintained several girlfriends at the same time. And through all of it, I have continually feared abandonment and remained obsessed with being loved.

Maybe, at the root of it all, it comes back to the fact that there has been no dominant male figure in my childhood or my youth. That's a classic cause of BPD, often accompanied by the possibility that the mother was depressed in the first year of the child's life. If my mother had had petticoats when I was a kid, I would have been clinging to them. I spent all my formative years in her company and with her female friends. I didn't have any exposure to adult men. Perhaps that was the basis of the gnawing distrust that distanced me from elements of football's aggressively male world.

The inevitable corollary of that was that I craved the affection of women. I had, and I still have, an insatiable desire to be loved and to have women tell me that they love me. In the context of my disorder, when celebrity brought me as many women as I wanted, I made the mistake of thinking

I could use sex as a kind of selection policy. I confused sex and love, not exactly an unusual error, I know. I thought that if I had sex with enough women, sooner or later I would find the solace and the reassurance and the love that I was searching for.

It didn't work, of course. There was a time when I was sleeping with four or five women a day. Terrified of loneliness, I had them coming to my house in Cannock on something approximating a rota system. One would arrive, we would have sex and then she would go. Another one would arrive, we would have sex and then she would go. The ones I wanted to leave would stay. The ones I wanted to stay would go. It was all fucked up.

When that cloying neediness that was the legacy of my disfunctional childhood collided with the pop-star celebrity that Paul Gascoigne's tears and Rupert Murdoch's billions had conferred on Premiership footballers, it turned me into the prototype for a new generation of players where everything, particularly sex and money, came easy. Suddenly, I found myself in a world where fame fed upon fame. If two celebrities started going out with each other, a relationship turned into a media monster.

Some people thrived on that. David Beckham and Victoria Adams seemed to relish the double helpings of attention. They lived their lives at the heart of a media circus of magazine front-covers, newspaper splashes, sarongs and hairstyles and an *OK!* wedding where they sat on matching thrones. Both their careers benefited from the sky-high profile and they took all the attention in their stride.

I felt uneasy with that kind of scrutiny. It exaggerated my

insecurities and shone a light on the agonies that were darting around my mind. I didn't have a solid-enough background to carry it off. At first, I just liked to go out, have a few beers and get a bird at the end of the night on the back of my so-called celebrity. I knew that girls were coming at me for the wrong reason, but when I was a young lad just starting out in football there was a novelty to that. Soon, though, I began to feel uncomfortable with the amount of girls I was having casual relationships with. I didn't stop, I didn't even rein back, but I didn't really like myself.

My mates in Cannock all told me I was living the dream. They got exasperated with me for moaning about how I couldn't meet anyone real, but deep down I knew that because it was so easy for me as a prominent footballer to get girls, it was damaging my ability to form a proper long-term relationship. It's funny, isn't it: I was shagging girls for fun, which is every bloke's idea of the model of machismo, and yet, emotionally, I remained a desperately insecure person who couldn't deal with his feelings.

From time to time, the emptiness of it all would hit me. When I was at Villa, I went to London one weekend and invited a girl I had met the previous week in Birmingham to come down with me. I'd booked a room at the Halkin hotel, just off Hyde Park Corner, which was a favourite haunt of Premiership footballers down in the capital for a weekend on the town. We spent most of the weekend in there shagging. When she fell asleep, I sat on the end of the bed and began writing things down. I'd just finished my treatment for depression at the Priory hospital in southwest London and they encouraged us to put our thoughts down on paper. I scribbled out two or three pages of thoughts. I was berating myself, asking myself what the fuck I was doing.

I was sitting on the end of a bed in a hotel room having just shagged a girl. I had absolutely no interest in her, and, apart from what I did for a living, she had absolutely no interest in me. I didn't feel dirty but I just felt it was all a futile exercise. What I wanted was intimacy, not just sex. I wanted someone I could cook dinner with and have a laugh with, but all I was doing was sending myself further and further away from what I was looking for.

When I look around me now at the way the new generation of young footballers behave, I see so many of them falling into the same trap. I wonder, behind the gory stories of roasting and group sex and scandals in nightclubs and hotels, how many lonely young men there are in the game now, cut off from their own background by their wealth, haunted by hangers-on and armies of false friends who will slither away when the player's fifteen minutes of fame is exhausted.

Perhaps I led the way for this new generation of debauchery, but I think it has got even more difficult now for players to do the right thing, even if they want to. Shagging a Premiership footballer seems to have become an art form now. They are objects of desire for a new breed of groupies whose ambitions do not end at sleeping with them. Now, being a football groupie is seen as a legitimate way of becoming a celebrity, too. If there's a scandal attached, so much the better. Notoriety is good. Notoriety is desirable.

The problems will increase. There will be more allegations of rape and sexual assault and there will be more people in the situation I have found myself in more than once, of wanting to cry out for help but not knowing how to do it. Clubs treat their players like children not fit to take responsibility for anything, so when they let them off the leash, they simply don't know how to make the right decisions.

Show me a young athlete who says his head would not be turned by beautiful women throwing themselves at him and I will show you a liar. All the younger players I know at Premiership clubs are shagging for fun. Availability is unlimited. It's a free bar. Open all hours. Drink until you drop and the well will never run dry. You think it's a dream until you find out that it's actually a nightmare. And you're trapped in it because it's distorted your idea of what is required to hold down a regular relationship.

I should know. I started seeing Estelle, who became my wife and from whom I am now estranged, about seven years ago, and throughout all that time I have seen other people. At first it was because we were only supposed to be friends. However, she was always there for me, always supporting me, and we became lovers. But I never knew whether I loved her in a way that really should have stayed platonic or whether I was in love with her. Until soon before we got married, we never really formalised our relationship. Not in my mind, anyway. And that left its own poisonous legacy.

Estelle was there in the background when I was seeing Ulrika Jonsson and Davina McCall and Kirsty Gallagher. Estelle was constant. She was loyal. She stuck by me. But she knew how promiscuous I was. She knew how many women I was sleeping with. She knew that effectively I was choosing them above her. So, of course, when we eventually settled down, even when we had our daughter, Mia, she could not forget that. She could not rid herself of those images and those memories. She was paranoid about the fact that I would be unfaithful to her. She didn't like the idea of me going to parties without her because she had seen me in action. She is a Cannock girl and she doesn't like the bright lights. And I want to be satisfied with that but I'm never quite sure if I am. Part of me yearns for the serenity of a home environment. Part of me still enjoys elements of the London scene. When I was caught dogging, that confirmed all Estelle's worst fears and she walked out.

Amid the chaos of my promiscuity, it was difficult to determine where some relationships ended and others began. Often, I would have a couple of girlfriends at a time. One relationship would hit a bad patch so I would start another one. Then the old relationship would be rekindled and the line between who I was going out with and who I was seeing on the side would become blurred beyond recognition.

That destroyed relationships that might have come to mean something more often than I would care to recount. It certainly finished my affair with Kirsty Gallagher, which was one of the relationships I managed to keep a secret. After we had been seeing each other for almost a year, she found out that Estelle was living at my house in Cannock, even though we weren't boyfriend and girlfriend at the time, and our affair fizzled out.

I often think now that that the relationship with Kirsty might have come to something, although I suppose I'm kidding myself there because being the way I am, nothing really ever comes to anything. It had started when I went to

Fulham on loan for a few months at the beginning of the 1999–2000 season and got friendly with Stephen Hughes, the former Arsenal midfielder. He told me that Kirsty fancied me and I felt flattered. She was working as a sports presenter for Sky TV then and a lot of players drooled over her. I asked him to get her number but he said he couldn't because she had sworn him to secrecy, and all she'd wanted him to tell me was that she was a Liverpool fan and she thought I'd been great when I was at Anfield.

I used to go to a club called Ten Rooms in Soho every week around that time, and within a couple of weeks of that conversation with Stephen Hughes I saw Kirsty in there with Gabby Yorath and Kenny Logan, the Scotland rugby international that Gabby went on to marry. I went over and started talking to her and asked her for her number. I might have been insecure in many ways but I wasn't shy with women. She was a bit coy at first, but towards the end of the night she gave me that number.

We spent a lot of time together. She was living in a flat in Chiswick, in west London, and I would stay there two or three nights a week. She was very needy, too. She was polite and intelligent and unbelievably attractive and charismatic. In fact, back then she was generally perceived as the epitome of what was desirable in a woman: sultry, dark and very sexy. But sometimes she could seem like a little girl lost. Maybe that made us two of a kind.

We spent a bit of time clubbing but she was a very good golfer, too, not surprising since her dad, Bernard, was a former Ryder Cup player and former captain of the European Ryder Cup team. I remember one particular happy afternoon playing with her at the Belfry. I'm not a golfer but I could just about get round with my pride intact. We talked a lot while we were on the course and it was impossible not to be dazzled by how beautiful she was.

The first night I slept with her, we had been on an evening out with one of my mates and we had all gone back to stay at her mate's flat, which was somewhere on the south bank of the Thames near the London Eye. Sometime during the night, she wandered out of the bedroom in her bra and a thong to make a cup of tea and my mate was lying there on the sofa, wide awake, staring at her with a daft grin on his face. She said it made her feel like Julia Roberts in that scene in *Notting Hill* when Hugh Grant's housemate walks in on her as she's lying in the bath.

She was an incredibly sexy and sexual woman. That first night, she did a few things with some Chocolate Fingers that have stopped me looking at them in quite the same way since. And even though she seemed shy in some ways, she wasn't averse to experimenting with different things in the bedroom. One night we went out with a friend of hers, and we had all had a bit too much to drink by the time we got back to her mate's flat. The friend fancied me and one thing led to another and the three of us ended up in bed together. It was a wild, wild night.

I felt very strongly for Kirsty but I never really gave her and me a proper chance because, once again, I failed to define what my relationship was with Estelle. In my own mind I wasn't committed to either of them, I suppose. I just drifted into a no-man's-land where the arrangement with Estelle stilted what might have developed with Kirsty. In a curious way, even though we were seeing each other for nearly a year, I never really thought of us as a couple. It was just another case of me letting a shot at a proper relationship slip away in a confusion of affairs.

When Kirsty found out about Estelle, she backed right away. I didn't blame her. She never told me she didn't want to see me any more but our sexual relationship turned into a platonic friendship.

That kind of duplicity was not unusual in my life. It was a mess of confused loyalties and diluted love. It was a theme that ran through my existence. I lost my first long-term girlfriend, Lotta, soon after I joined Forest because she grew tired of my infidelities. I had been going out with her for two years since I joined Crystal Palace. I had lived at her mum's house. Her family had become my family and she had moved up to the Midlands to live with me when I went to Forest. And still I couldn't repay her with loyalty.

One day in the April of 1995, she called me and said she was going home to Croydon for the weekend. She would do that quite regularly so when I got back to Cannock I didn't realise anything was wrong. I had a little sleep and when I got up I opened one of the cupboards and all Lotta's clothes had gone. I looked around a bit more and all her college books had gone, too. I rang her mum and she said that Lotta had just had enough of my womanising. She could hear how upset I was, but she said that if I was so fond of her daughter then why had I been unfaithful to her.

I was 24 and it was the first time I can remember feeling out of control of a situation. I was consumed by pain and hurt. I drove down to Croydon and begged her to come back but she stuck to her guns. Even though I knew she was right, even though I knew I had seen dozens of girls behind her back, I still found it desperately hard to reconcile in my own mind the fact that I had lost her. It might seem unreasonable, but I was distraught.

When I got back from Croydon, I went up and sat in my bedroom, and after a couple of minutes' staring into space I picked a vase up off a chest of drawers and hurled it at a window. It smashed and sent shards of glass and pottery into the next-door garden. I looked out and there was a bloke digging his lawn. He just looked up at me and said 'all right, Stan', as if nothing had happened.

When Lotta left, that just gave me even more free time for shagging. I'd pick up girls' numbers at nightclubs or even when they were wandering down the street or browsing in shops. Then I'd phone them and get them to come round to my house. I'd organise my time so that I would never be alone. I had girls in on shifts, and in the mornings I would be waking up with strangers.

I even started to grow a conscience. The volume of girls just got ridiculous. It was horrible. It was grotesque. I have slept with a huge number of women and it still hasn't given me what I wanted. Part of it was that I began to worry about hurting these girls' feelings, but sometimes they knew I was seeing other people and they didn't care. Where the guilt really came in wasn't about hurting people: it was about spreading the emptiness of my life to so many others and seeing it reflected back in them.

Gradually, I have stopped sleeping with women in quite

such a prolific way, but I didn't really learn my lesson in terms of simplifying my relationships. In some ways, the anarchy of my various liaisons continued to grow until it reached some sort of dubious celebrity zenith when I was seeing Ulrika Jonsson and Davina McCall at the same time and still having sex with Estelle and a Villa groupie called Linsey, just to make things a little bit more complicated.

I seemed to have a particular talent for pulling television presenters. There was this weird crossover between our worlds. One world would feed the ego of the other in the service of the great god Television. Back in the mid-Nineties, when I was at the peak of my ability, football had suddenly become mainstream mass entertainment, as popular and glamorous as pop and the movies. Television presenters wanted to talk to footballers and, if they were female, I wanted to talk to them.

I became an integral part of the lads and ladettes thing, that people like Ulrika and Chris Evans popularised. I knew Robbie Williams. I was mates with Jay Kay of Jamiroquai. He came to watch me at Liverpool. I got backstage passes at his concerts. I even had a fling with Sara Cox, Zoe Ball's best mate, who used to present a Channel Four programme called *The Girlie Show*. It was usually her and a couple of other girls slagging off blokes as much as they could. Somebody had told me that she fancied me, so when she invited me on the show while I was playing for Forest, I accepted.

We swapped numbers after the show and I went out with her a few times in London. She stopped off in Cannock once when she was on her way up to see her parents in Bolton. I only slept with her twice, but the next week there was a lot of gossiping in our incestuous little world that we might be seeing each other. The following Friday, John Barnes was a guest on *TFI Friday* and Chris Evans asked him if it was true I had a big willy. Digger played dumb but Chris Evans wouldn't let it go. 'Sara Cox calls him "Stan the Can",' he said, 'because his dick is as wide as a can of Coca-Cola.' I went into training the next day and I was a legend with the rest of the lads. Nothing was secret in that world. Nothing was private. Everybody knew the details of what you were doing and who you were doing it with.

There were other celebrity flings, too. I had an affair with Jenni Falconer, the GMTV presenter, after I chatted her up at an airport arrivals gate. She said she was waiting for her boyfriend, but when I asked her if I could have her number she gave it to me without hesitating. I had a brief liaison with the model Sophie Dahl, too, after we met at the Brit awards when I was there presenting a prize. That was after yet another falling out with Ulrika.

But my relationship with Davina McCall was an altogether more serious affair. It was my great lost opportunity, a chance of real happiness that I threw away. As usual, I only realised that when it was too late and I had plenty of time to dwell on the fact that I had turned my back on something very special.

I first met Davina in April 1998, when my relationship with Ulrika felt again as though it was unravelling and we were having a period where we weren't talking. Strictly speaking, we were together, but it was a sham. Events in Paris were just around the corner and I probably should have seen them coming. When I think now that I went back to Ulrika instead of staying with Davina, I know that I made a terrible, terrible mistake. Drawn back to chaos again. My curse. If Ulrika hadn't been around, messing with my head, Davina and I would have got married. I have got no doubt about that.

I spotted her at *An Audience with Julian Clary* where we were both among the invited guests. We clocked each other in that way you do and I asked her out. Davina was different. She was sorted. She didn't play silly games. If she said something, you trusted her. She had been a heroin addict and a coke addict – you name it – and she had been saved by counselling. She had faced her demons and moved beyond them. She had been clean for ten years. She knew what she wanted out of life and she was always straightforward and honest with me. Even when I left her to go back with Ulrika, she was incredibly generous with her advice to me. In the minutes after I hit Ulrika, when I was panicking with the shame of it all, she was the first person I called.

Even now she's still helping me. When she heard about the dogging scandal, she phoned me and told me about the counsellor who carried her through her own troubles. She said this man had saved her life, which was about as good a recommendation as you can get. She gave me his number and I started having therapy with him. A little later, Davina told me how great she felt because she had started working out. That struck a chord with me, too. I started getting myself fit and that seemed to alleviate my mood. It gave me an aim in my life.

When we met, Davina was on the brink of the presenting stardom she has achieved subsequently with shows like *Big Brother*. She was doing stuff for MTV but she still had her feet on the ground. She made me feel comfortable and secure.

She was pretty but she wasn't overtly glamorous and, unlike Ulrika, she didn't have to be the centre of attention whenever she walked into a room. She was a self-contained, confident person. She was homely, she was kind, she was warm.

I took her out a couple of times and it was such a refreshing change to be seeing someone who was honest. She was honest. I wasn't. I went to New York with Estelle, and even though she was technically a friend we were sleeping together as well. When I got back I went to Davina's place and a reporter from the *Mirror* turned up and told her he had pictures of me and Estelle together in New York. Davina was cool about it because she thought Estelle was just my mate. She was absolutely golden but I told her soon after that that I didn't want to see her any more because I was missing Ulrika. I don't know why I was missing her. I suppose it was just what I was used to. I was addicted to a fucked-up relationship where it wouldn't be a normal day unless Ulrika and I had had a row before training every morning. Davina took it really well and I consoled myself with that, but a few years later she told me it had devastated her. She was convinced that if I could have just got over Ulrika, she and I would have been married.

Instead of that, I got back with Ulrika. That relationship lurched on from one crisis to another until Paris and beyond. In fact, in the days after Paris, when I was public enemy number one and I was practically in hiding, Davina invited me out to Nice with her family, who had rented a house somewhere on the outskirts of the city for a few weeks. When I was at such a low ebb, that house and its grounds were like a haven for me. I ran up a £1,000 mobile-phone bill ringing

Ulrika from out there, desperately trying to repair some of the damage and pleading with her to forgive me. She was in St Etienne for the England v Argentina game where David Beckham was sent off for kicking out at Diego Simeone. In a bizarre way, that gave me a respite from the attention. Suddenly, everybody wanted to hang Beckham, not me. They called the dogs off and set them chasing him around America.

I started sleeping with Davina again while we were in Nice, but even then I hadn't got Ulrika out of my system and Davina and I never got back together properly. I still regret that. I regret it bitterly. I walked away from a relationship with Davina that was solid and steady and positive for something that drove me to the brink of insanity.

I was still caught up in football's maelstrom then; still chasing the adrenaline buzz of scoring goals; still chasing famous, beautiful women. I was a member of the glitterati. I was a symbol of that age when suddenly everyone and everything seemed within a footballer's reach. I know now that that was just a grand illusion.

CHAPTER THREE

CRYSTAL PALACE: THE ISSUE OF RACE CARD

My father's legacy to me was not just womanising, nor was it only fear and loathing and the sense of being haunted by domestic violence. I have never been proud of him, but I am as proud of my black heritage as I am of coming from the ferociously caucasian working-class area of South Staffordshire. You couldn't get much more mixed-race than me: part Barbados, but also part Cannock, where the closest you get to soul food is battered cod and mushy peas at the local chippie.

Sometimes I feel thankful I've got both sides to draw upon. Sometimes I feel torn apart and isolated, as though I am neither one thing nor the other. Show me two rooms, one with black footballers in it, one with white footballers, and I would pick a room on my own. Sometimes I wonder which culture other mixed-race players like Rio Ferdinand lean towards. I wonder if they share the inner conflict that grips me.

Ambrose Mendy, who used to be Paul Ince's agent, met me once to try to persuade me to let him act for me. He met me off a plane at Gatwick when I was about to join Nottingham Forest, and the first thing I saw was him surrounded by this entourage of gangsta black dudes looking mean and moody. They thought the black thing was going to work with me but the way they talked and acted was totally alien to me. I was still a boy who had been brought up on an all-white estate in Cannock.

Often, I think I'm lucky. I get immense pride, for instance, from reading about the heroic deeds of the South Staffordshire Regiment at Arnhem during the Second World War. Earlier this year, I drove down through France to visit the beaches where the Allied forces came ashore during the Normandy landings. I wandered around the cemeteries, too, and when I saw how many of the young men killed were from the South Staffs Regiment, it made me well up with pride for their heroism and sacrifice.

I drove inland for a few miles while I was there. Every so often I'd come across the grave of a kid from the South Staffs. Killed on 8 June. A little bit further inland and it might be 9 June. These lads from the Black Country were lasting only a few days as they pushed the Germans back and were then being cut down. It made me think that every child in this country, once they're old enough to understand the gravity of what happened, should be made to go out and visit those beaches and those cemeteries.

I feel black pride, too. I feel moved when I read about the deeds of Marcus Garvey and his Universal Negro Improvement Association and the liberation of the realisation that black is beautiful. I am drawn to the speeches of Malcolm X and Martin Luther King and sometimes I even find myself inspired by the radicalism of the Black Panthers and the lyrics of bands like Public Enemy. I want to fight the power. Sometimes, I feel black resentment and oppression very keenly.

There is very little recognition, for instance, of the part that black soldiers from the Caribbean played in the Second World War. They joined up in their droves from the West Indies, and the high command decreed that they weren't allowed to fight against white European Germans because they thought it wasn't right. Then they come here in the 1950s to fill all the shitty, menial jobs and their reward is that they get spat on and people cross the road to avoid them. Meanwhile, my mate's grandad, who was a German prisoner of war, stayed on, married a local Staffordshire girl and never got any bother at all. I'm not advocating the idea that he should have got any bother. I'm just trying to point out how unjust that double standard is. I'm just saying how unjust and sad that kind of racism is. My mate's grandfather had been part of an army that had killed millions of English soldiers and he was accepted. People from the West Indies had fought for Queen and Country and yet they were persecuted. It sickens me to think of it.

So I'm a real mix. I am proud of both sides but I know they contradict each other. If you took your average factory worker in Wolverhampton and an average member of the Nation of Islam, they would have nothing in common. They would hate each other's guts. But they are part of me. And I think that is a problem that a lot of mixed-race kids have. You don't have an identity. There is no National Mixed Race Forum. I wouldn't feel 100 per cent confident going to a Black Nationalist meeting and I certainly wouldn't feel confident going to a BNP meeting.

I'm not for political correctness. I'm not for positive discrimination. I'm not for having set quotas of black people filling jobs. I'm not for dressing in African gear just because you are black. I don't want the politically correct telling me off for celebrating St George's Day. I am proud to be English and I think it's ludicrous if someone tells me I shouldn't feel that way. I'd hate to be a white bigot out of fear. I'd hate to see the white man as the enemy. I am fascinated by the strength of character on both sides.

I'm happy the bullying I got when I was a kid hasn't really left any racial grievances. I'm happy that the victimisation of my mum and me on our little Close faded away. I'm happy that I've been able to see attitudes in Cannock and around soften as the years have passed and people have grown used to minorities living with them side by side. Most of the time, I don't feel any anger or resentment towards the white man. Much of the time, I almost think of myself as a white man. I grew up among them, after all.

But when I see persecution and inequality, it enrages me all the more. When, out of a clear blue sky, Ron Atkinson spits out his poisonous words about Marcel Desailly, it makes me despair. It makes me realise that for all the progress we have made, it's still there. Still there more than we thought. Still festering in underground minds, still a joke between friends, still okay as long as you don't get caught, as long as you say it around the dinner table with no politically correct snoops around. Think it, mate, just never say it.

It's not a surprise to me that Ron Atkinson said what he said about Desailly after the Monaco versus Chelsea Champions League semi-final. I've heard plenty of stories about him before. Some of the press boys told me about being on an England trip to Poland with him once. England were playing in Katowice and some of the press lads made the short journey to Auschwitz to see the concentration camp there. When they arrived back at the hotel, most of them, for obvious reasons, were a little subdued. Big Ron was in the foyer. He was boisterous as usual. He wanted to know what was the matter with them all that they were all looking so fucking miserable. One of them told him where they'd been. 'I suppose you went there by fucking train an' all,' he said. Nice one. Subtle as a fucking brick. I know ITV and the *Guardian* sacked him, yet the knee-jerk reaction over his comments about Desailly seems to excuse him in some ways, to say that it was a one-off and he was just being careless.

Careless is right. Ignorant, stupid, boorish and racist are all right, too. He called one of the most decorated players in the game, a player who has won the World Cup, the European Cup and the European Championships, 'a thick, fat, lazy nigger'. It shouldn't happen. No excuses. Particularly not the bullshit about him not realising his microphone was switched on. What difference does that make? If the microphone is switched off, does that mean he didn't say it? Or didn't think it?

The flawed logic of some of the arguments that the Big Ron apologists spouted astonished me in their naivety. I'm just surprised so many people were surprised that he said it. Then, to make matters a lot worse, he came out and said that all these people in the game had rung him up to sympathise. And so what are we supposed to think about how those conversations went, because if Ron's boasting about it, we have to assume they weren't ringing him up to tell him what a dreadful thing he had done. I can imagine it would go something like this: 'We've all said it, we've all done it. Just you got caught, Big Ron, you daft sod. You'll be all right in a couple of months, mate. Just keep your head down, pal. It'll all blow over. You'll be back in no time.' Do you think one of those managers would have rung him up and said: 'You fucking twat, Ron, you were bang out of order.'

They fucking should have done. Otherwise, that kind of behind-closed-doors racism is only going to be flushed out of football when the old school of management is out of the game. When they die off. Because so many of them come from that old school. And no one bats an eyelid that, according to Big Ron, the glitterati of football management are voicing their support for him in private.

Lo and behold, a couple of weeks later, another sports broadcaster, Jimmy Hill, came out and said calling someone a nigger was no worse than calling him 'Chinny'. Thanks for that, Jim. And yet his employers, Sky TV, let him off after he apologised. They think he's still fit to broadcast and yet the BBC take me off the air because I went to a few car parks to watch people having sex. Forgive me if I sound unforgiving about Big Ron and Jimmy the Chin. Why do I expect clemency for my dogging and yet I don't offer them any for their racism? Well, that's because I don't think the two things are in the same league in terms of their offensiveness.

I do feel bitter about what Big Ron said. I felt so despondent and upset that every black player who had ever played for him came out and said 'Ron's no racist'. They dragged out Brendan Batson and Cyrille Regis because he had played the two of them at West Brom. That is what really narked me. All these people coming out and saying 'yes, he said these things, but he's not a racist'. I'm desperately disappointed in people like Carlton Palmer and Viv Anderson. If they are friends of his, that's fine. If he has been good to them, that's fine, too. But don't use that to try to excuse what he said.

These were people that I grew up admiring and for them to align themselves with someone who has said what Big Ron said is just not good enough. Brendan Batson is at the FA. It makes you wonder about the work Kick Racism Out of Football has been doing. They have made some important strides but there is still an awful lot to be done, not least in trying to eradicate this natural deference that some former black players still seem to feel towards a racist like Ron Atkinson.

The only two people who summed up the outrage most black people felt were Robbie Earle and Ian Wright. Robbie Earle, who worked with Big Ron regularly on ITV, said that he had always valued their professional relationship but that he could not excuse or forgive what he had said. Wrighty mentioned that Atkinson's words had carried a 'plantation vibe' and he was spot on there. When I heard what Big Ron had said, it made me think of a redneck sitting on a verandah in his rocking chair with a piece of straw coming out of his mouth.

And yet, in the newspapers a lot of the columnists and the feature writers didn't touch the Big Ron stuff after the initial story. They joked about it a bit but it was almost as if a lot of them felt uncomfortable with it, as though they were going to be hypocritical if they slaughtered him too much, as if they were going to be attacking one of their own. Every feature that I read held out the prospect of him being welcomed back with open arms in a few months when all the fuss has died down. And believe me, he will get chance after chance after chance.

Let's not forget it wasn't so long ago when Alf Garnett was on our television screens talking about 'yer blacks' and 'yer darkies'. It wasn't so long ago when racists were posting abusive notes through my mum's letterbox at our house in Cannock. Then, when a public figure comes out and uses language like that, you wonder if it has really gone away; if we ever really had become a more tolerant society, or if that kind of attitude is just lurking beneath the surface like the pus in a boil.

I don't want to brand Big Ron an evil man. But let's not be embarrassed to say we were deeply offended by what he said. Let's move on. It's 2004. Make yourself realise that black people have got two arms, two legs, a nose and a mouth and they are no more of a threat than the man from the moon. And most of all, let's not dress Atkinson up as some pioneer for racial integration who made one uncharacteristic slip. Don't forget, he branded Batson, Regis and the late Laurie Cunningham 'The Three Degrees' after the famous black pop-group. They were favourites of Prince Charles. The singers, I mean, not the football players. Anyway, not exactly the actions of an enlightened manager. In fact, about as patronising and pathetic as you can get.

Okay, so he played them in his team. So what? I read a few articles in the press after Atkinson had called Desailly 'a thick, fat, lazy nigger' that said he had changed the world just by putting Batson, Regis and Cunningham in the side. I couldn't believe that. I couldn't believe that someone could seriously think that; that someone could be that stupid. Changed the world? Come on, please. We're not talking about Jackie Robinson or Muhammad Ali here.

Think about the premise of those newspaper articles. The black players break through but it's the white man who's changed the world. That's the worst kind of lazy, limited, institutionalised, traditional racist thinking. Give the credit to the white boss, not to the black kids who have had to fight their way through the system to even get to that point. Trying to give the credit to Atkinson for that is like giving a white promoter credit for Ali or a white baseball coach credit for Jackie Robinson. It's bollocks.

Ron Atkinson, a pioneer. Excuse me while I retch. We're not talking about Tommie Smith and John Carlos and the Black Power salute at the Mexico City Olympic Games. These were men with real balls, not some champagne-swilling, perma-tanned prick. We're not talking about a blow for freedom and equality. We're not talking anything even remotely in that league. To suggest otherwise is offensive in itself. Atkinson didn't even sign two of West Brom's famous three. It's not as if he went out on a limb. It's not as if he put himself on the line to pick them. There wasn't an outcry, but there certainly would have been if he hadn't picked them. That's the point. English football in the late Seventies may not have been particularly tolerant but it wasn't exactly the segregationalist Deep South. What Big Ron did wasn't even in the same ball-park as Graeme Souness signing Mo Johnston, a Catholic, to play for Rangers. That was courage. That was balls.

Big Ron just did what was best for him professionally. He did what served his interests and his career. And he obviously didn't feel totally comfortable with it because he had to make a joke out of it by calling them 'The Three Degrees'. Those three players were so far ahead of anything else they had at West Brom that it was blatantly obvious to anyone on the terraces that they would improve that side beyond all recognition. It was a business decision. The idea that it was a social experiment is utterly flawed. So let's not have racist apologists dressing it up as a decision that changed the world.

I was lucky that in my time in football I was only the victim of serious, foul racial abuse once in my career. But when I joined Crystal Palace from Stafford Rangers for £100,000 in November 1990, a few months after they had lost the FA Cup final to Manchester United in a replay, I found myself at a club that was only just emerging from a period of deep racial tension, and one that was still split down the middle, white on one side, black on the other.

Four or five years before that, when Ian Wright first joined the club, there was a group of English rednecks there, led by people like Micky Droy, the former Chelsea centre half, who was a giant of a man, and Jim Cannon. Black players who were there at the time said there were a lot of obstacles to overcome, but because they were from the street the white guys couldn't break them. That was how bad things were not so long ago.

Andy Gray, the black Andy Gray who played for Palace and Spurs, was there in those days and still there when I arrived. He remembered Cannon and Droy rubbing Wrighty's face in the mud during training as a matter of routine. They were always calling the black lads 'nigger' and 'black bastard'. They seemed to think they could treat them how they wanted.

One day, after the abuse had been particularly bad, Palace played a match at Brighton's Goldstone Ground, and Andy Gray, who reminds me of someone out of Public Enemy because he's a radical Black Power man, urged the other black lads to walk off in protest, to boycott the game. That would have made a statement, but not one of them, not Wrighty or Mark Bright, turned round and said a thing.

In the phalanx of black lads at Palace there was Wrighty, Brighty, John Salako, Eric Young, Andy Gray and a kid called Bobby Bowry. They were all Londoners. They all used a kind of Brixton patois that was alien to me. I'd never been exposed to black culture before and suddenly here were all these guys kissing their teeth and chilling out. For a while, to try and imitate them, I asked my girlfriend, Lotta, if she'd cook me rice and peas for my meal when I got home. I got boiled rice and green peas, which wasn't quite the way the other boys ate it.

On the other side there was Gareth Southgate and his mate, the Del Boy of a reserve goalkeeper, Andy Woodman. There was Andy Thorn and Alan Pardew, who was fiercely ambitious even then, and Geoff Thomas, who I never liked because he fancied himself so much. And there was Nigel Martyn, who used to get the piss ripped out of him by Wrighty, who must have enjoyed turning the tables on a white country boy. 'You thick Cornish cunt,' was Wrighty's favourite way of greeting Nigel.

The last of the white boys was a bloke called John Humphrey, a defender whose nickname was Tasty. He was coming to the end of his career. I remember taking a video of the *101 Greatest Goals* on to the team coach once for an away trip. All the young lads sat down the front. The more experienced you were, the further back you sat. I stuck the video on and from the back this voice yelled out. It was Tasty. 'Get that fucking shit off,' he shouted. I asked him what his problem was. 'Tasty, we're footballers aren't we,' I said. 'Can't you enjoy Marco Van Basten scoring an overhead kick?' He just said: 'Stan, put the ball away. I have been doing this for 20 years. I have had enough of football. It's bad enough playing it, let alone watching it as well.' Fair enough, I suppose. Tasty always used to run himself down. He said if he was a car, he would be a Fiesta. Always dependable but nothing special.

When they went out on the pitch, black and white worked well together. So well that we finished third there in my first season, the equivalent of a Champions League place today, and Palace's most successful season ever. But off the pitch it was two teams, not one. Me? I was 19. From my physical appearance I should have been in the black camp. But I didn't talk like them. I didn't have the same eating habits. I didn't have the same experiences or the same background.

But to Alan Pardew and the rest of the white lads, I was a black Brummy. So I never felt I belonged. And I think having those two polar opposites at my first professional club had an impact on me. Neither side accepted me and perhaps that contributed to the reputation I gained at Nottingham Forest later in my career for being a loner. My only real mate at Palace was another reserve striker, Jamie Moralee. We hit it off immediately.

It was a real windfall for Stafford when they got six figures for my transfer fee to Palace. The Stafford chairman, Dave Bundy, was so happy he drove me down to south London in his Bentley to sign the contract. I had been down to Palace on trial for a week, staying in digs with a family in Biggin Hill. I hated it, but when Steve Coppell offered me the chance to sign I knew I had to take the opportunity. On the way back, the chairman pulled his Bentley in at Rothersthorpe services on the M1 and me, him and the manager, a brilliant bloke called Chris Wright who had rescued my career after I was released by Wolves, had a celebratory dinner at a Little Chef.

When the time came for me to leave Cannock properly, my mum and my girlfriend, Sharon, drove me to the station to put me on the train. I had one suitcase with all my stuff in it. That was it. They came up onto the platform to wave me off and I swear that with every retelling of the story that battered old InterCity train changes into a steam locomotive in my mind and Sharon's dressed like Celia Johnson in *Brief Encounter*.

I got to London and hopped on the Tube, a cornflake in my throat the whole way because I was so homesick already. Someone picked me up from Morden station, at the southern end of the Northern Line, and took me to my digs. I stayed with Bryn and Leslie Jones in a little annexe at the back of their flat in South Croydon. All I remember about that first day was going up into my room and *Byker Grove* blaring out from the television.

I hadn't gone down there with any expectation of playing in the first team initially. Steve Coppell had told me I had the raw materials and that they would try and develop them. He said they would teach me my trade. And he was right about that. From Steve Harrison in particular, the first-team coach, Jamie Moralee and I learned everything we needed to know about how to make our runs, how to time them, how to bend them, and which runs tended to yield the most goals.

The two things that were obvious when I met Steve Coppell were how small he was and how unnaturally deep his voice was. Particularly for a bloke who was so small. If you were called into his office at the training ground at Mitcham, it was going to be something fairly serious. For such a little bloke, he commanded a lot of respect, especially from somebody like me who was wide-eyed and nervous about everything.

My first game in the reserves at Tooting & Mitcham was against Ipswich. I came on as a substitute and I scored. I scored ten or fifteen goals between then and the end of the season. I was on £300 a week with a £10,000 signing-on fee. I felt like I had won the lottery with that signing-on fee but a lot of it went on buying a Vauxhall Belmont that Andy Woodman managed to flog me.

I got the piss taken out of me the whole time I was at Palace for that car. It was like an Astra with a boot on the back of it, hardly a pulling machine, but it drove well, and anyway I didn't even have a full driving licence then. Too impatient even to get a licence. But Andy Woodman didn't care about that. He would have sold his granny if he could. I never understood why him and Gareth got on so well because they were like chalk and cheese, but they were inseparable.

Wrighty and Brighty ruled the roost. No question. They were the top men. They both drove a Mercedes. Everyone else had a Vauxhall Calibra or something of that ilk. When Wrighty and Brighty were together, you had no chance. You couldn't shout them down. You couldn't outwit them. They would always come out with some funny line to put you down. Wrighty was the off-the-wall guy, a bit of genius in him. Brighty was the archetypal solid pro who would cycle into pre-season training every day. He was having pasta on the team coach when everybody else was still eating fish and chips and sucking back the beers.

Wrighty was a goal machine. He was instinctive. Brighty was a bit more calculating. I learned a lot from both of them. Wrighty was a one-off and Brighty knew he was never going to be Wrighty so he worked the percentages. I had a bit of both of them in me. I could be a cocky fucker like Wrighty even though I wasn't an extrovert like him, and I could be a target man like Brighty. I didn't like being in their shadow at the time but my time observing them improved my striker's education.

Then there was Salako. He was Wrighty and Brighty's gimp. He was their fucking slave. He would put the crosses in, they would score and then they would reward him. Wrighty would say: 'Salako, listen to me, right, if you put three good crosses in for me, I'll buy you a nice pair of shoes.' And Brighty would say he'd buy him a jacket. They'd compete with each other over who could feed the gimp the most treats.

Salako knew he was talented. He was stuck in the team fairly early and he was on fire. He was getting in the England squad but Wrighty and Brighty treated him like they had him at the end of their leash. 'Salako,' Wrighty would say, 'you put those crosses on my head this afternoon, otherwise I am going to fucking kill you.' On Monday, one of them would come in with a pair of Oliver Sweeney shoes or an Oswald Boateng shirt for him. That was his reward.

I roomed with Salako a few times. He was a nice-enough lad. He was a born-again Christian. I would go and have a walk around the hotel, and when I came back, almost invariably, he'd be lying on his bed, banging one out. Having a wank with *Penthouse* in front of him. I'd say, 'I thought you were supposed to be fucking born again.' And he'd be all sheepish and say, 'I am, but we all succumb to our desires now and again.'

Fashion seemed to be everything with the black lads at Palace. A former player called Tony Finnigan used to come in every Tuesday with loads of John Smedley shirts for the boys to buy. It started to feel like you were in a chapter of *American Psycho* down there sometimes, everyone analysing what everyone else was wearing. It was label and logo heaven.

I always felt Wrighty thought I was a bit of a threat. I don't know why, really, because I was never given anything like a run in the first team. But unless you agreed with him 100 per cent, he could be quite brusque with you. He was usually all right with me but he was scoring shed-loads of goals and it was obvious he was going to move on to bigger and better things. Both Wrighty and Brighty knew they were kings of the castle and Steve Coppell indulged them in that thinking. They were his babies.

We played in a pre-season tournament one year in Gijon, against Sporting Gijon and some Bulgarian team. We were at the Gijon training ground and there was me, Wrighty and Brighty doing some shooting practice. There was some minor disagreement and words were said between me and Wrighty. I told him to fuck off and he said, 'You know what, I don't even think you've got what it takes to fucking do it. I don't think you're even going to fucking make it.' There was real disdain and scorn in his voice. That stayed with me. It gave me special pleasure when I was with Liverpool and we beat Arsenal, when Wrighty was in the side. We beat them at Highbury and at Anfield. Of course, when I saw him socially he was always dripping with sentimentality. 'I've got so much love for you, baby,' he says. All that kind of false shit. I always knew with him. I always remembered what he said that day in Gijon. When I was nothing, he tried to push me further down. When I was someone, he wanted to be my friend.

So when I scored a decisive goal for Liverpool at Highbury in my second season on Merseyside, it was nice to look over at him and know that I had made it in my own right, despite what he had said. I've got no problem with him, really. I never really wanted to prove him wrong because I'd always rather prove myself right. Maybe it was just the way he said he didn't think I'd make it. The spite of it. I don't know, but it stuck with me long enough to make a bit of a difference. It's people in the football industry who can wind you up the most, not the press.

*   *   *

Wrighty had gone to Arsenal at the start of my second season at Palace. I already knew I wasn't going to get bumped up to the first team in his place. Coppell signed Marco Gabbiadini from Sunderland in October 1991 for £1.8 million. He was on big money and I remember being in the canteen with him and listening to him reading out his Mastercard statement and telling everyone how much he'd just spent at Harvey Nichols. That went down like a lead balloon, as you can imagine.

Gabbiadini didn't do well at Palace. In fact, he had a fucking disaster. The crowd didn't like him. He wasn't Ian Wright. Wasn't like Ian Wright in any way. They played him and played him and played him. And it affected Brighty badly as well. I thought I must get a chance. But then Coppell bought Chris Armstrong from Wrexham. And he did well. And when he was injured, the gaffer stuck Chris Coleman in rather than me, even though Cookie was a centre half. He tried Jamie Moralee but he never gave me a run of games. I had 20 appearances for Palace and only four of them were starts. The rest, I was coming off the bench.

I broke into the first team in January 1991 against QPR at Selhurst Park. I was playing as a winger because that's how Alan Smith, the reserve-team manager, who went on to be the first-team boss later, saw me producing my best football. My first goal was against QPR in the league at the beginning of the next season. I ended my first season by playing 30 minutes at Anfield in the same match that Gareth Southgate made his league debut.

Gareth had been there since he was an apprentice but we were both the same age, both trying to make our way in the game. I know he comes across as a sweet-tempered, affable, wonderful middle-class guy but I never really felt comfortable with him. He was very adept at saying one thing to one person and another to somebody else. Alan Smith sucked up to him, and he had a good ally in Andy Woodman who was a chirpy chappie that everyone liked.

Gareth and I were just like oil and water. I never felt he was sincere. He can sit in front of a camera and he comes across as a nice bloke. That is not the impression I had of him. I played with him for two seasons at Palace and two at Villa. That is just the vibe I got from him. Smile in your face and then once you have left the room he would be saying 'what a fucking prick' behind your back. I knew he worked his bollocks off with the limited ability he had and he saw me coasting through training sessions and he resented it.

There was definitely something festering there about me in his mind. When he was playing for Villa and I was in the Liverpool side, we met in the 1996 FA Cup semi-final. He tried to do me and I tried to do him. All through the game. I told him I was going to break his fucking jaw. I swept the ball past him at one point and he just went for me with one of those tackles that made it obvious he had no intention of getting the ball. He was just going for me. And I was glad. I was glad all that seething enmity we felt for each other was out in the open at last. I just wanted to get it on. It was the best place to do it.

Even though Gareth and I never got our dislike for each other out into the open at Palace, I did have a few proper rucks with people while I was there. It wasn't the sort of club where people hid their light under a bushel. It was in your face. It was put up or shut up. Most of the players and the coaches there didn't take any shit from anybody. Most of them had worked bloody hard to get to this level from the lower leagues and they weren't about to let anyone push them aside without a fight.

Someone like Geoff Thomas, though, was an accident waiting to happen. The better he did, the cockier he got, and when I was at Palace he was being picked for the England squad. So he was at the high end of his cockiness. I helped by serving myself up on a plate. The club went on an end-of-season trip to Gibraltar. I was just a kid and I'd bought an England shell suit to take on the trip. I got on the plane wearing it.

As soon as they saw me, Geoff and Wrighty started laughing at me. They were pretending to wince at the sight of the shell suit. Geoff said: 'Fucking hell, we've got a real one of those.' I felt really embarrassed. I was just proud to be English but in their mind you only wore an England tracksuit if you played for England. That stayed with me, too. One day at training, Geoff was moaning about something so I got up and chinned him. Same with Brighty. There were always loads of rumours about his sexuality, so one day we had an argument about something on the training pitch and I called him a faggot. He came over and clocked me.

And then there was Wally Downes, nicknamed 'Wals', one of the founder members of the Crazy Gang at Wimbledon, who had been brought in as the reserve-team coach under Alan Smith. If he could pick on you, he would. He got to me after a game at Swindon. I'd played a back pass from the halfway line right into the path of their centre forward who had taken it round our goalkeeper and scored. Wals had a bit of a go at me in the dressing room afterwards. I thought he went over the top so I got up and smacked him.

There was never any question about disciplinary action being taken about any of these incidents. The culture was different then. Physical retribution was seen as part of normal interaction. After I chinned Wals he said he was actually glad that I had reared up and smacked him. He had been worried I was too quiet. Because my middle name was Victor, for some reason he would call me Verne. He'd always be saying 'all right Verne' in this really mocking manner. But he knew a player. The ones that weren't talented, he didn't give a fuck about.

Alan Smith was all right, I suppose. He was always very dapper. Immaculately dressed. All-year-round tan. He would come in at half-time of a reserve-team game and say, 'You lot are a fucking disgrace. See my fucking Rolex. See my fucking Jag outside. See my fucking Savile Row suit. Do you think my Jag drove itself into the car park here on its own? No, I had to fucking work for it.' He had his favourites, mainly Gareth and Jamie Moralee.

But the best coach at Palace and probably the best coach I ever worked with in terms of technical input and knowledge was Steve Harrison. He was beginning his rehabilitation. He had been sacked by the FA when he was a coach under Graham Taylor for sitting on a banister and shitting into a cup ten feet below. It was his party piece, but on one particular occasion it had been witnessed by the wife of an FA committee member. She was not quite as impressed with the trick as most footballers appeared to be, and that was the end of Harry's England experience.

He was a funny guy. His dad had been a comedian, a vaudeville act in Blackpool, and Harry was never short of a routine or two. At Mitcham there was always a lot of surface water on the pitches, and for no reason and fully clothed he would just run and throw himself headlong into these puddles. Another time, we were on our way to a reserve-team game at Crawley Town. He pulled up at some traffic lights. The lights were on red and he just got out and walked off. He came back about ten minutes later, got back in and drove off as if nothing had happened.

I linked up with him again at Villa but the relationship didn't feel quite the same there. Nothing to do with Harry, really, just that he was part of the John Gregory regime that soon became anathema to me and which seemed hell-bent on destroying me. But I didn't blame Harry for that. The last time I saw him, I walked into my mate's porno shop in Birmingham and he was standing there lost in the pages of *Escort*. He seemed a bit startled when he saw me. 'All right big fella,' he stammered. And then he scarpered.

I look back on those days at Palace now and I think they were happy days. So many new things coming at me, so many possibilities opening up for me. There was Lotta, the first woman I was in love with. I was living away from home for the first time. I was playing in England's top league. I was scoring goals in my own right in the reserves. I was playing at the shrines of English football, places like Anfield. I was sampling London nightlife for the first time.

Some of it scared me a bit because I felt I didn't come off

well against certain personalities. Some of my fears and self-doubts were exacerbated by some of the people there. They were strong characters. They could play with you and try to mess with your mind. These were guys who had cut their teeth in the lower leagues. No cunt was going to knock them off their perch, certainly not a naïve, raw Brummy. When I left in February 1992, sold to Southend for £80,000, I felt a little bitter because I thought I should have been given more of an opportunity at Palace. But my time there was two good years of learning behind some of the best in the business and some of the most hard-nosed players in the business.

I learned my lessons well. Off the pitch, too. I bought a Golf GTI off Jamie Moralee in my second season and Andy Gray's brother, Ollie, financed it for me. He said he would lend me the money. I was supposed to pay it back over two months. He kept saying he was doing me a favour and I should never forget it. I was a bit late paying him back and then I wrote the car off. Ollie used to ring up Lotta's house every day. It all got a bit sinister then. 'Stan, I can't lose, brother,' he would say in his Cockney accent. 'I can't lose. Listen to me, hear me out. Unless I get my money, you're going to get it, bruv.' You come across people that are harsh fuckers.

Curiously, though, the one thing Palace didn't prepare me for was being the target of racist abuse. I say 'curiously' because there were so many racial undertones there and the racial split seemed so obvious and so defined. But the days of Micky Droy had long gone, and despite the banter between, say, Wrighty and Nigel Martyn, despite the fact that the black guys hung out with each other and the white guys hung out with each other and there was little social mixing, there was still respect between the two groups. Racial abuse was never an issue. It was never a possibility. It just wouldn't have happened. Anybody who indulged in it would not have had a prayer at that club. It would have made things unworkable. The only time I was ever confronted with rampant racism in my playing career was long after I had left Palace. It caught up with me when I was playing for Villa, and the culprit, funnily enough, came from among my former team-mates at Anfield.

When the Liverpool game came around on the last day of February 1998, I was in the middle of a goal drought at Villa. I hadn't scored for seven games. It was also John Gregory's first match in charge after Brian Little had been sacked. Because of that, and because it was Liverpool, I was wound up for the match. I played well. In fact, the Liverpool central defenders, Jamie Carragher and Steve Harkness, couldn't get near me. And then, early in the second half, it started. It was the kind of abuse I had never suffered before and would never suffer again.

Harkness was the culprit. The ball was up at the other end and he stood right next to me. 'You fucking coon,' he said. 'Fucking nigger.' I was taken aback more than anything to begin with. Then he stepped it up a bit. 'At least my mum never slept with a fucking coon,' he said. Nice bloke, Steve Harkness. Fucking neanderthal from Carlisle with a very, very small brain. Then, it was all the time: 'coon' this, 'nigger' that.

When we were at Liverpool I had organised a collection

for Children in Need one year. A lot of the players were very generous. Some of them put a grand in. I wanted us to make a really big donation. Harkness sneered. 'I ain't giving anything,' he said. 'Charity begins at home.' I never got on with the cunt. I always thought he was the most mealy-mouthed bloke you could meet. He was a nasty, horrible, mean, racist little prick.

He managed to keep it up right until the final whistle. I'd scored two goals but I was shaken and incensed by what he had been saying. I told the referee during the game but he did nothing. I wasn't hurt by what he said because he was just a moron, but I felt degraded.

When the game was over, I was ready to kill him. I ran straight down the tunnel and waited by the Liverpool dressing-room door. Two of their coaches, Sammy Lee and Joe Corrigan, were first in and I told Sammy he needed to have a word with Harkness, that that kind of behaviour and language just weren't acceptable. 'Why don't you fucking say something to him,' Sammy said. So I thought I would.

As soon as Harkness came down the tunnel, I went for him. I threw a punch at him and then it all kicked off. It was a screaming, yelling, flailing melee. Everyone seemed to be involved. Stewards, players, coaches. Eventually they got me out of there and bundled me into the Villa dressing room and I was still shaking with the anger of it all. I was so enraged I had to go and sit down away from everyone else by the baths in a corner of the dressing room. John Gregory came over and told me to concentrate on the fact I'd scored two goals. I just told him I wanted to make an official complaint.

I made sure no one forgot about it and that the issue was

not allowed to fade away. I reiterated in the press what Harkness had said and he responded by denying everything and threatening to sue me unless I stopped calling him a racist. What a joke that was. He trotted out the usual shit that racists always come out with about how a black man was one of his best friends. In the case of Harkness, it was Paul Ince apparently. The two of them used to share lifts in from Southport together. Something like that.

I wonder when people will start to realise that just because you might smile at a black man occasionally, even shake his hand, that doesn't guarantee you immunity from being a racist. We never seem to learn. Okay, so somebody claims a black guy is his friend. Or somebody says he can't be a racist because he let black players play in his football team. Does that mean that if the same man goes back home, puts on a white hood with holes cut out for the eyes and mouth and starts burning crosses and singing racist songs, he is still not a racist?

That is the kind of logic that people like Steve Harkness and Ron Atkinson seem to apply to their actions. They haven't even got the guts to admit what they are. They try to hide it away. They try to conceal it. They try to keep it indoors among friends, among like-minded people. That is what makes them dangerous. And, usually, society lets them get away with it; lets their sickness fade away and then beckons them back into the warmth.

Well, I didn't want to let it fade away. So the PFA got involved and Harkness and I were summoned to Manchester for a meeting. Harkness turned up with his lawyer. He insisted he couldn't remember what he had said to me on the pitch but he denied again he was a racist. Gordon Taylor, the PFA Chief Executive, tried to get us to sign a joint apology to the fans for bringing it all out into the open. I was absolutely flabbergasted. I mean, the PFA brings out all these glossy brochures about kicking racism out of football, and when they've got a real live incident out there begging to be dealt with, they bottle it. They wanted me to apologise for being called a coon and a nigger. They wanted me to apologise because Harkness had taunted me about my mother sleeping with a black man. I couldn't believe it. It had all been swept under the carpet. A cosy little cover-up to keep all the boys and girls happy about the Premiership. It left me feeling disgusted and disillusioned with football's ability to police itself on race.

The next time we played Liverpool, I knew what I was going to do. The first time Harkness got the ball I was on him in a flash. I took him out. He was carried off. I found it fairly gratifying at the time, especially as I only got a booking for it. With hindsight and some time to heal the wounds, I regret it. Whatever he had done to me, there is no excuse for trying to injure a fellow professional.

So I'm glad he didn't break anything. I got my come-uppance later in the game anyway. I had a tussle with Michael Owen, grabbed him by the throat and got sent off. I did my Harry Enfield 'calm down, calm down' impression to the Liverpool fans as I was walking back to the tunnel but at least I felt I had achieved some form of retribution for what Harkness had done to me.

And that was it. The only time I've been overtly racially

abused as a player. What else lies beneath at football grounds and in football minds, I don't really care to imagine. Once, playing for Villa at Tottenham after I had been admitted to the Priory, the Spurs fans had a field day with me. 'You're mad and you know you are,' they were singing. Well, substitute the word 'mad' for 'coon' and that probably gives you a more accurate idea of what they were really thinking. Gazza never got any of that after his problems, did he? Nor Paul Merson. Nobody ever called them mad. Tortured, maybe. Or recovering. But, I'm sorry, when it's a black man, it's different. Frank Bruno has some problems and suddenly the front page of *The Sun* is 'Bonkers Bruno Locked Up'. Even they realised they'd gone a bit far with that one. They had to pull it after the first edition. A few days later, they set up a charity for the mentally ill. You couldn't make it up. The hypocrisy of it is unbelievable.

Funny that they didn't decide Big Ron was mad for calling one of the best black footballers there has ever been a 'thick, lazy nigger'. Funny how they set their standards and choose their targets for White Van Man. Papers like the *Sun* think they know what White Van Man wants so they give it to him. If they're right and White Van Man wants thinly veiled racism, that tells us what we already knew: that promoting racial tolerance is still in its infancy in this country.

We'll have to wait and see what happens with Big Ron. Perhaps forgiveness will find him quickly. Perhaps the public will want to forget what he said. Perhaps his influential friends in the game will smooth his path back to the limelight and public acceptance. My guess is he'll be back broadcasting before we know it. He'll be back before me, I guarantee it. What does that tell you about English football and society? It tells you it's better to be a racist than a dogger.

CHAPTER FOUR

SOUTHEND AND FOREST: OPPORTUNITY KNOCKS

By the end of 1992, I knew I had to get out of Palace, even though it meant leaving the Premiership. I was nervous about going to Southend because they were struggling right at the foot of Division One. I knew I was going to be thrown in at the deep end and that if I didn't swim, I would sink. I knew that it was possible their eccentric manager, Colin Murphy, who had managed a succession of lower league clubs, might get the bullet, and, if he did, the new manager might not fancy me. I knew I might find I had swapped a place in Palace reserves for one in Southend reserves.

But I was 21, and somehow I realised it was time to try and make my move. I knew I had the ability to do it, I just didn't know about all the other things. I didn't know if I could last 90 minutes. I didn't know if I could sustain an amicable relationship with a manager. I didn't know how the fans would react to me. By then I had played at Anfield and I had scored in the top flight, but in other ways I was still a novice. My apprenticeship at Palace had been valuable but they still saw me as a wide player, and I was desperate to return to being a central striker.

If you're a striker, you're a striker. It's in your blood. It doesn't matter how many times someone tells you you're great at whipping crosses in. Johan Cruyff tried to do the same thing to Gary Lineker at Barcelona. Stuck him out wide on the right and tried to make the best predatory goalscorer that the England team has had believe he was a right winger. It did Lineker's head in, just like it would have done with any striker. So when Colin Murphy told me I would be playing up front week in and week out, that was the most important thing for me.

Murph paid £80,000 for me. I was on £300 a week at Palace; that rose to £500 a week at Southend. I signed on a Friday and drove down to Roots Hall the next day for my first game. There's a nice feel about Roots Hall. It's not too far from the seafront, in a nice little area called Prittlewell, near where the tennis player John Lloyd grew up. Very middle class. But the club was floundering in Division One. It was trying to mix it with teams like Kevin Keegan's Newcastle and another northeast giant, Sunderland, and in that kind of company it was struggling to punch its weight.

I met the lads and got changed. There was no fuss or hoopla. It was good not to have too much time to think about the move I'd made. I had a wander round on the pitch. Nice and flat. There were only about 3,000 fans there that day. Most of them were demonstrating against the chairman, Vic Jobson, because they were so unhappy with the way the season was going. They had begun to see relegation as a certainty, and I suppose the recruitment of some bloke from Palace reserves hadn't done that much to fire their imagination or revive their enthusiasm.

Half an hour or so before the game, Murph's assistant, Bobby Houghton, pulled me aside. He'd been a top line-manager abroad, a bit of a wanderer like Murph, and he knew players. He asked me if I was nervous and I said I was. 'You shouldn't be,' he said. 'You have got absolutely fuck all to worry about. I've seen some players but you can top the lot. You've got everything.' Bobby went back to Sweden a couple of months later, where he had been most successful, but he made sure that when I went out at Roots Hall that day against Notts County I felt as though Southend had just signed Gary Lineker.

I scored after six minutes. A lad called Andy Ansah crossed the ball in from the right, and I kneed it up once and then volleyed it over the keeper. That goal set me up for everything that was to come in my career. It sounds ridiculous to invest so much importance in one strike at Roots Hall against Notts County, but it put me on a roll that didn't end until my second season at Anfield. I never looked back after that. There was no agonising wait for my first goal at the club, no chance for the pressure to build on me and for me to start doubting what I had done. That goal was my passport to a new world.

I scored again against Notts County, too. Hit the post as well. I was an instant hero and my confidence was suddenly elevated to a new level. That game told me I could last 90 minutes, that I could cut it as a player at that level and that I could score at that level. I scored 15 goals in 30 games at Southend. I felt like I couldn't stop. I felt like I was going to score every time I went out on the pitch and the fans felt the same. They still sing my name even now apparently, and I still look back on my days there and think that in many ways they were the happiest of my career.

Murph was a bit mad but he was great. You knew he was mad as soon as you read his programme notes. They were rambling, confused tomes, often about nothing in particular, but you noticed they were not quite the same as the usual groin strains and excuses formula that most other managers seemed to go for. Most braindead footballers would read that and think, 'What the fucking hell's he talking about?'

There was no denying the fact that his methods could be strange. I remember an entire training session once that was devoted to catching practice. Catching practice with all the players standing around him in a circle while he held a cricket bat and smacked a ball at us. If you dropped it, you did ten press-ups. On all my travels in football, I never came across that particular routine again. I doubt it's in Jose Mourinho's book of drills. But Murph knew what he wanted. He knew players. He knew how to hold their attention. He knew how to keep them interested, even if they were a bit puzzled sometimes.

We didn't have a bad side, either. My strike partner was Brett Angell, who went on to play for Stockport County, Everton and West Ham, among others. He was great in the air. He could hold the ball up and lay it off. He was a good, honest lad. Chris Powell was the left back. He was a good player, too, but I never thought he'd have the kind of career he went on to enjoy. Simon Royce was in goal and Andy Ansah was in midfield. He's a producer on *Dream Team* now. And then there were a lot of journeymen pros, most of whom seemed to have played for Leyton Orient, and who were

Me and Mum in our back garden. It looks peaceful, but it wasn't.

Despite everything, I remember most of my childhood with affection. I was a happy kid.

School play at Broomhill Junior School in Cannock. I was a page boy.

Right: It's easy to spot me in team photos: there weren't any other black kids in Cannock.

Below: Me and some of the trophies I collected for Longford Boys in 1982. I loved that team.

Top right: Me at 17, just before I joined Walsall. I didn't know what was lying in wait for me.

Middle right: Proud to be at Palace. Steve Coppell gave me my introduction to the big time.

Right: Scoring for Forest. I hit the ground running at the City Ground and never looked back.

Broomhill Junior School team. We weren't bad. All the other lads were a year older than me.

This page, top to bottom: Me and Stafford Rangers boss Chris Wright: he saved my career when nobody else seemed to have any faith in me.

Happy days at Southend. I had a great relationship with the public at Roots Hall.

Sitting and chilling in the English Garden in Munich in 1991. It wasn't the beer festival that took me there. It was a woman.

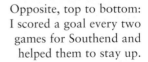

Opposite, top to bottom: I scored a goal every two games for Southend and helped them to stay up.

Putting my point of view: I didn't have a bad disciplinary record but I wasn't afraid of having my say.

Celebrating Forest's return to the Premiership in May 1994 with Stuart Pearce auditioning for Mr Muscle at the local fair.

Above: Centre of attention: a paparazzi shot of me strolling on the beach at Aya Napa in Cyprus after signing for Liverpool.

Below: I didn't see much of Tom before he was five but this was a rare outing to the Sea Life Centre in Birmingham.

Above: Mia riding on a donkey at Deauville in France. She's a beautiful child.

Below: My mum is the most accepting and generous person I know. She's always stood by me.

My hopes for the future. I'm going to guide Tom and Mia past the traps that snared me.

typified by a bandy-legged centre half called Dave Martin, a Romford cockney. He would tackle anything that moved and he played his heart out every week. To supplement his income, he used to try to flog black-market porn videos to the rest of us at training. He was your archetypal barrow-boy. Playing with those boys and the spirit we had, it was like being part of the Dirty Dozen. Most of the lads had played in the lower leagues all their lives or had been released and pottered around. I loved them to bits because they were real people. Just normal lads. When I thought I was going to be offered the chance to be Southend manager last season, I was going to take Dave with me as one of my assistants.

Murph was fired in the spring. Towards the end, results weren't coming, even though I was scoring. There was a lot of speculation about Barry Fry coming. Everybody was talking about his wheeler-dealer reputation and his turbulent relationship with Stan Flashman, the famous ticket tout, at Barnet. When he arrived, his first match in charge was Sunderland away. There were no formal introductions at training or anything like that. Baz met us at a service station on the A1. He got out of a Mercedes. I think the numberplate was BAZ 1.

When we got to the hotel we had a meeting, and Baz made a speech. Some of the lads were a bit distracted because Gazza's mate Jimmy Five Bellies was bouncing about outside one of the windows in the room where we were sitting. He knew one of the Southend lads, apparently. Anyway, Baz said his philosophy of football was that he didn't mind if we conceded four as long as we scored five. That was what we wanted to hear because we knew we had goals in us. And we began to make a run at survival, however unlikely it appeared. I scored early at Sunderland and gave a thumbs-up to Murph, who was sitting in the stand. I knew I owed him a debt.

By then, the goals I was scoring were starting to attract attention from Premiership clubs. Brian Clough, who was in what was to be his last year as Nottingham Forest manager, made a £1 million bid for me but Southend rejected it. And then it got messy. There was talk that Cloughie retracted the bid. Then there were rumours that the deal had broken down because the financial arrangements were not to Cloughie's liking. I don't know what the truth of it was and I wasn't even that bothered. I was playing with a swagger at Southend and loving it. I was taking the piss out of opponents just like I had when I was a kid on the school playing-fields. I knew a move was coming but I was in no hurry to get away.

Baz kept talking up my price. He was like a street trader. It got to the point where every goal I scored seemed to add half a million to my fee. We played Millwall in an FA Cup game that was live on telly in the south and I scored two crackers. We played Keegan's Newcastle and drew 1–1. We got to the fifth round of the Cup against Sheffield Wednesday at Hillsborough and I came out on top against a Premiership defence. That got noticed. That was another step up for me. I was starting to realise I could cut it at the highest level.

Baz was almost beside himself with glee. There was no attempt to try to pretend I wasn't for sale. No bullshit like that. Baz went the other way. 'Another goal,' he'd say, 'he must be worth at least £2 million now.' Sometimes he milked it a bit too much. 'You know what,' he told reporters after I'd scored again in that relegation run-in, 'I'm starting to think Stan's moving beyond the reach of the Premiership. I think it's going to be Juventus or Real Madrid for him. I think he's going to be too expensive for any English club. They won't be able to afford him.'

I only worked with Baz for about eight weeks but he was brilliant for me. He loved the game and he loved being around the lads. He was a lot less intense than Martin O'Neill (who would later manage me at Leicester City) and more jovial, but he still knew how to make everyone tick. He just said he enjoyed seeing me play and maybe if there had been one or two other managers during my career who had recognised, like he did, that I loved my football, too, they could have diverted me from the off-the-field stuff that cursed me. Even since we moved in different directions, Baz has always been a great defender of mine. I have never asked anyone to defend me because I can defend myself, but he is somebody I will always respect.

He got Southend to the stage where we needed a draw against Luton Town at Roots Hall on the last day of the season to be sure of avoiding relegation. By then, the ground that had been dotted with 3,000 people when I made my debut six months earlier was crammed full of 10,000 fans. The atmosphere was brilliant. We won 2–1. In the end, because of the way the other results went, we could have lost and still stayed up. For once, I didn't score. I went close with a free kick. But I don't remember much about the game anyway. What I remember is its aftermath.

*　　*　　*

STAN COLLYMORE: TACKLING MY DEMONS

There were two occasions in my career that made everything I have gone through worth it. Two occasions that I will never forget. Two *Boy's Own* occasions that encapsulated why I wanted to play football in the first place. One was the Liverpool v Newcastle game in 1996 when I scored the winner in the 4–3 win that was judged the match of the decade. At the end I saw incredulity on the faces of fans who thought they had seen it all. That night, the 22 players on that pitch at Anfield gave the supporters something special, and just to have been involved in it was a privilege. The other game I still cherish having been a part of was Southend v Luton Town on the final day of the 1992–93 season. Two games at opposite ends of the football scale, but two games that are wedded together in my mind.

When I look back at those occasions, it takes away any regret I might have that I haven't got any winner's medals to show for my years in football. Medals are for putting in a cupboard. They're for gathering dust. They're for your family to flog off at auction a generation down the line when they've pissed all the money you earned up the fucking wall. Memories are what count. I might not have anything finite that I can stare at but I have got memories that will never leave me and the recollection of the happiness that I brought people.

I wouldn't swap that day at Southend for winning the FA Cup or the championship. Really. There was a purity and an undiluted joy about that day at Roots Hall that really got to me. Being carried off shoulder-high at the end, all these fucking sweaty bodies taking my shirt and my shinpads off for souvenirs. I threw my boots into the crowd myself. I was in my pants by the end of it. And seeing a thousand faces beaming back at me, so fucking happy and lost in their happiness. The faces of people who had never had that kind of success before suddenly filled with celebration. A lot of people will have had very successful careers but will never have understood what it is like for the fans at lower-league level. Who gives a fuck about Southend in the bigger scheme of things. But I understand.

That was why I played football in the first place, to see that kind of joy on people's faces. In those moments at the end of the Luton game, I thought back to the times when I was a kid and I'd skip past four or five challenges and I'd be aware of parents on the touchline turning to each other and whispering 'fucking hell, he's a good player'. It was about proving you could do something other players couldn't do. It was achieving something that people thought wasn't possible. What price can you put on a day like that day in Southend. What price can you put on a day that has left me feeling that the middle of May is still my favourite time of year because it reminds me of that day at Roots Hall.

They sold me to Forest for £2 million in the end. Cloughie had gone by then after Forest were relegated from the Premiership, so it was Frank Clark who signed me. It was big money for a club like Southend. With various add-ons (£250,000 payable on my first England cap, an extra £250,000 payable when I scored 25 goals and a final extra £250,000 if Forest got promoted), it rose to £2.75 million. In some ways I wanted to stay because I had had such a brilliant time, but I knew the move to Forest was the right one for me and the Southend fans didn't begrudge me it. That was the way a move should go. Me happy, the club happy, the fans happy. They were grateful I'd kept them up. They felt I was part of them and I felt that, too. Southend even took a coach of supporters to Wembley to see me make my England debut a couple of years later, and it wasn't unusual for Southend fans to come up and watch me play for Forest if Southend didn't have a game. I know even now that I could go down there any time and get a great reception. Which means a lot to me. They have got a Stan Collymore Suite down at Roots Hall. I was a bit disappointed I didn't get the new stand named after me, seeing as my transfer to Forest funded it. But the suite will do for now.

And that was bye-bye little league and hello big time. That was me heading for the stratosphere, whooshing like a comet and ready to burn out like one, too. I did a reprise of my Southend Midas Touch for Forest in that first season there, although I missed the first few games with a virus that gave me an ulcerated mouth. I was eating through a fucking straw and there were stories that I was missing the games because I'd been involved in a scrap of some sort. That was the first time I was the victim of false rumours. First of many. I shed about two stone in weight with that virus. I was like a fucking skeleton when I came back, and Forest were struggling badly. They had only won twice in their first nine games and the shadow of Cloughie seemed to be lingering over the club's fortunes.

When I recovered, I hit the ground running, just like I had at Southend. I scored six goals in my first eight games, including a hat-trick at Wrexham in the Coca-Cola Cup. We were still sixteenth in the First Division going into November and there were more and more mutterings about whether Forest had made the right choice in Frank Clark. The turning point came when we played Birmingham at St Andrews early that month. Lars Bohinen made his debut in that game and he made a massive difference. I scored, we won, and Forest were on their way.

I was always proud of the way we played our football at Forest. We passed and moved. We used clever angles. We ran well and hard off the ball to make space for others. I scored a lot of individualistic goals, too. We weren't scared of mixing it up and playing it long. Sometimes the boys would punt a ball up to me and I would turn and run at someone and score. I'm not being arrogant. Watch a video of that season. That's the way it was. That's why I started to attract so much attention from top clubs. I scored some fucking belting goals. Jinks, dribbles, runs, shots into the top corner. The lot. I was right at the top of my game. I was flying.

Mostly we played a five-man midfield with me on my own up front. Sometimes we varied it and I played with Jason Lee or Robert Rosario. I thought Rosario was a bit flash. He liked himself too much for an average player. He was always very cocky around the dressing room. But the only way you can ever have a swagger is if you have got the ability to do it. If Thierry Henry walked in all confident, you would think he had earned it. Robert Rosario wasn't quite in that league. I had a bit of an argument with him on the pre-season tour to Italy. I didn't want to room with him because I thought he was a twat and he took exception to that. He always used to say that all he wanted to do was save enough money to buy a hotel in America at the end of his career and then earn an income from that. I thought that was a bit of a boring ambition for a flash prick like him.

So I ended up rooming with Jason Lee instead. Frank Clark had bought him when I got a hamstring injury midway through the season and he came in and did well for us. He scored some crucial goals but he had that strange hairstyle that Baddiel and Skinner picked out on *Fantasy Football*. It started that chant about him having a pineapple on his head. He got merciless stick for that, to the point where it began to affect him quite badly and he got his hair cut short. His haircut wasn't even the half of it, though. Rooming with him was a bizarre experience.

Jason had a cleaning fetish. He used to bring a sort of fold-down cleaning kit with him on every away trip. He'd unravel it when we got to the room and in all the pockets he would have containers of Harpic and Ajax and Jif. He had scourers, cleaners, wire wool. He had the kind of gear a bog cleaner would die for. And even though the hotel bathroom was always spotlessly clean when we checked in, he would make straight for it and clean the fucker out again. 'I ain't going in no fucking bath that no fucking dirty bastard's been in,' he would say. And then he would start scrubbing.

If I was fit, Jason was usually on the bench. And we kept climbing the table. I was particularly pumped up for the game against Wolves at Molineux because Graham Turner, the man who had let me go when I was banging in goals for their reserves, was still in charge. I scored a great goal that day, threading the ball between their last two defenders, taking it one-on-one with their keeper and slotting it past him. I went over to Turner in an angry celebration just to let him know what I thought of his decision to offload me. My form continued and I scored two more beauties at West Brom and two more against Sunderland in a 3–2 win. We won eight games in nine matches and started to close in on promotion.

It was a credit to Frank Clark that he held his nerve after the start we had had. I liked playing for him. He was quite fatherly. He always had a smile, always called me 'son'. You could imagine him as your dad, sitting at a family dinner. He never said anything contentious, he was just an all-round decent bloke. A bit dour, but with a good-enough sense of humour. He was trying to guide us as much as anything. It was him that first suggested I had an agent. It was him that listened to what I was saying about how we could modify the team to get some more success.

After the wildly successful years of the Clough era, he was the ideal bloke to come in and steady the ship. Imagine walking into that club after Brian Clough, but despite that tricky start he did it seamlessly. Forest pulled a master-stroke with that. They'd had rock and roll, and they chose to follow it with a bit of smooth jazz. Something different, but still something good. And it worked perfectly. Never once did I hear anyone saying 'Brian would have done it this way'. Cloughie left his legacy but Frank Clark was not intimidated by that. Maybe it was because he had played under Cloughie himself.

Clark wasn't the greatest tactician or the greatest motivator but he wasn't the worst either. With the quality of players we had, we knew we should go up, but if some firebrand had come in trying to make a name for himself, who knows how badly he could have upset the applecart. That club could have gone into freefall a lot earlier than it did. In the season after Cloughie quit, Frank Clark added a defender in Colin Cooper, a creative midfielder in Lars Bohinen and a 20-goal-a-season striker. Which was me. And it was a winning formula.

I overlapped with Roy Keane for a couple of weeks but I don't think we ever swapped a word. Keane trained pre-season but he trained with the kids because it was obvious he was on his way to Old Trafford. I was a bit wary of him because his reputation was that he was a fucking loon. There were these stories of legendary rucks he had had in Nottingham clubs. I thought the last thing I needed was to be seen out on the town with him, which seems funny now that he is the model professional.

He and I have at least got one thing in common. We both had bitter arguments with Alf Inge Haaland. Keano tried to cripple him; I just fucking flattened him. We were playing a five-a-side in training and he was all over me like a rash. I said, 'Fucking hell, Alf, if you don't fuck off I'm going to chin you.' He said, 'You fucking chin me, then.' So I clumped him and he went down. He looked more surprised than anything.

The Norwegian lads are all very serious. Around the dressing room they have all got their white socks and their flip-flops on. They read on the coach on away trips. They are low maintenance; a manager's dream. But sometimes they can be a bit fucking stiff. After I'd smacked Alf, the gaffer sent me off the training ground. He said: 'Get yourself in, you're a bloody disgrace, you are.' I had to walk down the towpath by the side of the Trent. When the lads came back in they were pissing themselves laughing and singing the theme tune to *Rocky*. They were calling me the undisputed champion.

The team spirit was very good at Forest. It was helped by the fact we had a captain we all respected in Stuart Pearce. Pearce was a brilliant captain. He was fair to me. I don't know if he liked me but he was always fair to me. The lads he got on with were Steve Chettle and guys who had been there a long time. If you see him doing an interview he can come across as a bit miserable, but he was like that with everybody. If he didn't like you, he didn't give you the impression he didn't like you. If he did like you, he behaved just the same. You could have a bit of banter with him but I looked up to him big time. He maintained a certain distance between himself and the rest of the players. I looked to him for guidance and leadership and he had both in bundles. He wasn't snide. He didn't need to be. If he wanted to come up to you and say 'I think you're a fucking twat' he would say it to your face. He never minced his words. I remember a little kid coming up to him and asking for his autograph while he was eating. He just looked up, stared at him and said: 'I'm having my dinner.' Another time, we were walking down the towpath and a kid came up to him. 'Can I have your autograph, Psycho?' he said. Pearcey fixed him with the same stare. 'My name's Stuart,' he said. That's what he was like. What you see is what you get with him.

Steve Stone broke into the team that season I signed, too. They used to call him 'the Magpie', because if you left your toiletries bag open in the dressing room, Stoney would be straight in there. He wouldn't bring any of his own gear with him, no shampoo, no deodorant, no nothing. If he couldn't ponce anybody's shampoo, he'd go into the shower room and there'd be a crusty old cobalt there and he would wash his hair with that. No wonder he's bald, using that crap for so long. If any of the sponsors sent any samples through, they'd go straight in Stoney's bag. It was always, 'Got any shower gel, got any smellies?'

By the spring we were favourites for promotion. The media had built up excitement over my return from the hamstring injury to fever pitch. A few thousand turned up to watch a practice match we had at training because it had been billed as my return to competitive action. Finally, I made it back to the bench for a home game against Bolton. I came on, scored the winner and then got sent off for elbowing Phil Brown. In the middle of April I scored my twenty-second goal in 27 games, at Millwall, and a couple of games later I hit a left-foot-cross shot into the roof of the net at Peterborough. That sealed our promotion to the Premiership and sparked a pitch invasion of joyful Forest fans.

Part of me was still thinking about Southend. I had scored 24 goals by then, even though I'd missed more than eight weeks of the season with injury and illness, and Southend were due another £250,000 bonus if I made it to 25. Naturally, Frank Clark and the Forest board didn't want me to play in the penultimate game of the season against Grimsby, but I insisted. I then managed to play in the final game against Sunderland and scored the second goal after I latched on to a through ball from Steve Stone. I was pleased for Southend. Good luck to them for structuring the deal the way they did. I wanted them to have that money.

Everything was working smoothly. In many ways the whole set-up at Forest seemed wonderfully simple. In many ways I had settled in more easily than I could ever have dared hope. But as that first season wore on and I struggled to recover from my hamstring injury, the sniping started. It was the first time I had really encountered what it was like to be the target of a whispering campaign. I hadn't had that kind of problem at Palace or at Southend. But it seemed that with the higher profile and with the success I was having, jealousy and factionalism was creeping in.

I thought I got on well with the rest of the lads. I drove back to my house in Cannock most days. I didn't go out much in Nottingham, but most of us had a good laugh in the dressing room. Then all this bollocks began about me being a loner. A loner? If only everyone had known how much I needed company at all hours of the day. There was no way I could be alone. I hated my own company. It shows you how intolerant English football is, that it remains inherently suspicious of someone who isn't a lairy twat and doesn't go out and get pissed with the rest of the boys every night.

I couldn't win. If I had lived in Nottingham and gone out with the lads on the piss every night, people would have said I was a nightclubber who wasn't committed enough to the cause. Just because I didn't hang out with people I didn't particularly want to hang out with on a social basis didn't mean I was in any way less passionate about how the team did. It just meant I had friends in Cannock that I trusted and that I felt safe with, and I preferred to socialise with them. I didn't feel then, and I don't feel now, that there is anything wrong with that.

Some of the resentment a couple of the players obviously felt was brought to a head when Jimmy Greaves said something on television about Forest being a one-man team.

Nobody said anything to my face but it was apparent from articles that began appearing in the *Nottingham Evening Post* that Greavesie's comment had gone down like a sack of shit with some of the lads. I could understand that. If I had been in a team where one person was getting all the attention, I wouldn't have liked it either.

I contributed to some of the problems myself. I admit that. We went on a pre-season tour to Sweden in the summer of 1994 to prepare for our first season back in the Premiership and the club organised a team outing to go trotting (sitting in buggies and being pulled along by a horse). It's a Swedish thing. Anyway, the rest of the lads dutifully went trotting, but I couldn't be arsed. That was why I didn't want to go. But I made up an excuse about refusing to go on principle because I objected to the horses being whipped. It was a load of bollocks. I was completely up my own arse on that trip. Frank Clark said he would fine me two weeks' wages for not going trotting so I took the hit. Not going trotting cost me £8,000. It probably cost me a few more bar-room suggestions that I was getting far too big for my boots, too.

I just didn't see the point of doing things I didn't want to do. I didn't see the point of being part of the group just for the sake of it. I wasn't into artificial bonding. Later in that second season at Forest, our game against Aston Villa was called off because of a frozen pitch so the lads decided they'd go to a Madness concert that night instead. They went down to the Bullring in Birmingham and bought 20 pairs of Dr Martens boots to wear. I didn't go. I wasn't going to make myself look a fucking knob by jumping around pogo-style with dubious BNP geezers at a Madness concert.

But there wasn't an actively hostile vibe towards me in the dressing room. There was nothing like that. I was quiet, I suppose, but I would always sit in my usual place next to Scott Gemmill and have a chat with him. Of course, there were players I didn't get on with. Ian Woan was one. He didn't like me; I didn't like him. But that happens. Rob Rosario was another. Some of them probably thought I wasn't very approachable. Maybe I got away with things that other players wouldn't have got away with because I was doing so well. I was treated like a Messiah in Nottingham. I turned the Christmas lights on one year.

Before that second season was over, when I was constantly being linked with moves to Manchester United or Liverpool, some newspapers even started to report that none of the other lads were talking to me. That was a load of bollocks, too. People pointed to an incident at the City Ground when I scored against Everton and none of the other lads celebrated the goal with me to try to illustrate how unpopular I had become with my team-mates. Blanking a guy who has just scored was supposed to be the ultimate insult.

What actually happened was that, a week earlier, I had had an argument with Frank Clark. I'd bleached my hair blond before a game with Tottenham and I had played fairly poorly. Bryan Roy, who had been bought as my strike partner at the start of the season, had had a poor game, too, and the gaffer criticised us both heavily afterwards. It was the first time all season that my performance had dipped, but Frank Clark said neither of us worked hard enough for the team. He said I should spend more time on the training pitch and less in the hair salon.

So when I scored with a header against Everton the following week, I just turned and jogged away without celebrating. I thought I was fucked if I was going to celebrate in front of that bloke. That was a direct protest to Frank Clark. And the rest of the lads just jogged back as well. I never felt that was a deliberate protest against me. I just felt they could sense my sullen mood and they didn't want to celebrate either. The *Nottingham Evening Post* then reported that the players had refused to celebrate with me. That started the 'loner' stuff off again. It all added to the patchwork of a story that I was only interested in scoring goals.

Well, that part was right. In terms of commitment to the team, my idea is that the ultimate way of showing that is on the pitch, not by going out and getting pissed the night before a game. I have always been fucked off with players that don't pass to each other because of petty feuds that may be going on between them. That does go on, and to me that is the ultimate lack of professionalism, not whether you go out and have ten pints with a bunch of your team-mates.

If the situation with the players had been that bad, I wouldn't have been able to perform. If there had been major headaches in the dressing room and I felt unloved and unwanted, I would have struggled big-time, because I wasn't that thick-skinned at the time. But I had started my career with Forest in the Premiership like a dream. I missed the first game away at Ipswich Town with an ankle injury and Bryan Roy scored two crackers on his debut in a 2–1 victory, which started me panicking about not getting back into the side. But I played in the next game against Manchester United the following Sunday. It was live on Sky: they were the champions and I was being touted as the new kid on the block. Inevitably, I scored. I always scored against United. Almost always. I picked the ball up midway inside their half and touched it past Incey who was tempted to go through me but rather uncharacteristically backed off. I think they must have changed the rules about the tackle from behind that season and he was still wary. I took it on and shot from about 25 yards and it beat Schmeichel at his near post. Andrei Kanchelskis equalised and it finished 1–1. We came off the pitch at the end and I knew questions had been answered straight away. I thought that if I had scored against the champions I could score against anybody. I scored more than 20 league goals that season and Forest were only behind Blackburn and United in the table.

But as the campaign wore on, it became increasingly dominated by all the bullshit about my popularity, or lack of it, in the dressing room, and speculation about me moving to Manchester United. I had an agent by then, Paul Stretford, and he kept telling me that Fergie was interested and that it was only a matter of time. The *Nottingham Evening Post* was running stories nearly every day saying that the move was about to be finalised. I scored one and made one in a 2–1 victory against United in the return fixture at Old Trafford in March and I felt pretty confident that that must have sealed the move.

I had got involved with Stretford, whose most high-profile client these days is Wayne Rooney, after my game against United earlier in the season. I was plastered across all the back pages for the first time after I scored in that match.

People like Incey were being quoted as saying that I had the world at my feet, and Forest were being deluged with offers for me to do personal appearances and photo shoots and promotional stuff. Frank Clark called me in and said he thought I needed representation of some sort because the club couldn't really cope. He recommended Stretford but I decided I'd shop around a bit.

I went to see Jon Holmes, who made his name acting for David Gower, Will Carling and Gary Lineker. I sat in his office in Nottingham and listened while he told me how clever he was for getting Lineker the Walkers Crisps contract. He said he wasn't sure whether I'd fit in with the clean-cut image of the players he had on his books. Really? No shit, Sherlock. He was very condescending and very, very pleased with himself.

There was another guy who came round to my house in Cannock and pulled up outside in a red Ferrari. Can't remember his name but he pulled out this big piece of paper that had a picture of a Coke can stuck on it. He started talking about how he was going to brand me, how he was going to lever my brand, how he was going to build me into a global icon. I felt a bit intimidated by it all. It seemed like overkill.

There were a couple of others. The former Arsenal captain, Frank McClintock, tried to get me to go with him. He took me out for a sandwich at a coffee bar somewhere in London, which I thought was a bit cheap. I knocked him back. When he got his job with Sky, sitting round with all those twats on a Saturday afternoon watching the monitors in the studio, he took every opportunity he could to dig at me. Another sad, embittered, ex-player prick. I mustn't forget Ambrose Mendy, either, and the black brothers who met me at the airport that time.

And then there was Stretford. He came round to the house in a nice suit. He was very polite. He was younger than the rest. He told me a bit about himself first. He had a bit of literature and some newspaper cuttings. He said he had got his break because his wife, Margaret, knew Frank Stapleton's wife, and he had got himself into a position where he handled Stapleton's return from French football near the end of his career. He talked about the lessons he had learned from studying the way the NBA handled its players in the States. Colin Hendry was one of his main clients. The other was Andy Cole, who was busy tearing up trees with Keegan's Newcastle.

Stretford's pitch was based around the ethos that he would be totally devoted to me. He didn't have many clients so that allowed him to work like a slave for his chosen few. His attitude was very much that it didn't matter what time of the day or night it was, he would always be available if I had a problem and I needed to call him. If I allowed him to represent me, he said, all I would have to worry about was my football. He would take care of the rest. He was hungry and ambitious and I liked that. So I went for it. I signed with him.

He came to watch me regularly that season. He was always there for me. He would call two or three times a day. He was always saying he had been approached by *Shoot* or the *Daily Mail* or whoever, asking if they could do an interview with me. He was constantly telling me about deals that I was being offered. Everything was cool, apart from the fact that the speculation about United was reaching fever pitch. Stretford told me he had it all in hand and that I just needed to sit tight and be patient. It goes without saying that I would have loved to have gone to Old Trafford.

Unbeknown to me, Fergie followed his interest up by ringing Frank Clark to try to open the negotiations about the transfer. Frank was desperate to hold on to me, so when his secretary rang through to tell him Fergie was on the line, he told her to stall him. He told her to say that he had flu and wasn't well enough to talk. A couple of days later, Kevin Keegan rang Fergie to ask about Keith Gillespie. Fergie asked about Andy Cole, never thinking there was any chance of signing him, and Cole duly signed for Manchester United amid great secrecy.

I couldn't believe it when I heard. Ian Edwards, the journalist from the *Nottingham Evening Post* who wrote most of the stories about me, rang to tell me. I was absolutely gutted. It was made worse by the fact that Andy Cole was Stretford's client, too. I knew how close the two of them were. I knew Andy had stayed at Stretford's house when he was having his own home renovated, but I just felt very let down by Stretford. He had kept assuring me that the move to Old Trafford would happen if he just kept plugging away at Fergie, and now it had collapsed. Now it was ruined.

I tried four or five times to phone Stretford on his mobile and he was very curt with me. He kept telling me he couldn't talk. That went on for four or five days although it seemed like an eternity. At that stage I was in denial about it. I didn't want to believe the Andy Cole move was happening. Stretford never rang me back and I was livid with him. I didn't blame Fergie. That's just business. But the fact was that Stretford had shoehorned his other client into Manchester United at my expense. There was nothing I could do about Fergie's opinion, but the fact that my own agent didn't even have the bollocks to call me was infuriating.

Eventually, he returned one of my calls. He was embarrassed. He blamed Frank Clark. He said it had been taken out of his hands. And then he guaranteed me that he would get me a move to an equally big club. He asked me how I felt about Liverpool. He said they were interested. He said they were on the dawn of great things. He even got Fergie to call me. He told him that he needed him to do that or else I was going to fuck him off as my agent. The phone rang when I was driving past Derbyshire County Cricket ground on my way back from training. He said he was sorry my move had not come off. 'I think Eric's going soon so maybe I'll come back in for you then,' he said. The next season Eric Cantona helped United to the Double.

All that placated me. Perhaps I shouldn't have been so easily mollified, but I was. Stretford was running my life by then. I was being wined and dined by Diadora in Venice because they were offering me a massive boot deal, and he was at the hub of it all. After the move to Liverpool, they wanted to do a campaign based around a logo of a pound sign because I had been sold for a British record fee, but Stretford flatly refused. He said we wanted to do it in a different way, and I was impressed by the way he was protecting my interests. I didn't have a dominant male figure in my life, never had had, really. So to have somebody like that who was a big brother and a dad rolled into one meant a lot to me. He fought my corner well. My friends liked him. He dealt with all the stuff surrounding my ex-girlfriend Michelle and the arrangements for my son, Tom. He would come down to see me two or three times a week and I would go up to see him at his offices in Wilmslow, just south of Manchester. We had a very close working relationship and, despite what had happened over the move to United, he soon regained my trust.

As the end of my second season with Forest grew nearer, it became apparent that both Liverpool and Everton had made an identical £8.5 million offer for me. Forest were offering me £12,000 a week to stay, which, at the time, would probably have put me second only to Alan Shearer among the best-paid players in the Premiership, and Frank Clark was hassling me to sign it. But I had set my heart on a move, so Roy Evans, the Liverpool manager, flew back from his holiday in St Lucia to meet me at Gatwick for an hour and then got on the plane to go back and rejoin his wife. Joe Royle, the Everton manager, came back from a holiday on the Algarve to meet me at a Cheshire hotel called Mottram Hall.

I liked both of them. Joe Royle nearly swayed me towards Everton. He was a charming bloke. Straight as a die. He explained all his plans for the club, and I liked them, but the romance and the history of Liverpool made my mind up for me. Stretford told me I ought to ring him first to let him know my decision and he was very understanding about it. Then Stretford rang Roy Evans at his hotel in St Lucia and left a voice-mail message for him. 'The man from Del Monte says yes,' he said into the receiver, and that was it. I was on my way to Anfield. My wages had gone up to £10,000 a week.

Paul was my mentor then. He sheltered me from everything. When there was a fuss over an article I did with *FourFourTwo* magazine early on in my time at Anfield, he drove me up to a meeting with Roy Evans that I had been summoned to. In the car on the M6, I told him I was so fed up with all the controversy I was going to quit. He just told me not to be so stupid. He smoothed it all out. He just seemed to make problems go away. Chairmen always said he was a hard man to deal with and I liked that. He was like a super-agent. I told him once that I felt he could make anything happen and he beamed and beamed about that. He referred to it a few times down the years.

I told him I liked Jamiroquai. He got me backstage passes. I told him I wanted to go to a London club. He got me on the VIP list. When my mum wanted to go on holiday he sorted the tickets and the hotel. When Estelle came back from somewhere abroad he made sure she was picked up at the airport. When I wanted to buy a Mercedes, all I had to do was go to the dealership and pick the car up. For all of this, he got a percentage of my contracts if I moved clubs and 20 per cent of all my off-the-field deals for endorsements and things like that.

But things didn't stay that way. As he became more and more successful, he changed. Or his attitude to me changed. He didn't care as much any more. He couldn't afford to care as much any more. He didn't have the time. Suddenly, I would be trying to call him at his office and his secretary would be saying he was in Amsterdam or Bangkok. Suddenly, particularly after I left Liverpool and went to Villa and my career started going down the tubes, I was chasing him rather than him chasing me.

* * *

When John Gregory arrived as manager of Villa, that was the beginning of the end of my relationship with Stretford. I didn't know it – and Stretford never told me – but Gregory was his client, too. So when Gregory and I came into conflict over my illness with depression, Stretford effectively had to choose between us. He still didn't tell me that Gregory was his client, too. But he chose him. Not me. There is no question in my mind about that.

I had been a little taken aback when, six months after I completed the move to Villa, Stretford rang me begging for money. At the time of the move, in the summer of 1997, Stretford had told me I wouldn't have to pay him anything because Villa were paying him. But his business was expanding rapidly and one day he rang and he had calculated it all and I owed him £80,000. I sought some legal advice and the guy said I owed Stretford fuck all. A couple of days later, Stretford rang again. This time he was near-enough in tears. He said: 'You do love me, don't you, Stan?' I said: 'Of course I do.' That was the kind of hold he had over me. He said he needed that cheque or else his business would go under. So I wrote a cheque for £80,000 and sent it to him. All my friends said I must be mad.

He still didn't tell me about Gregory. In my second season at Villa, when the shit hit the fan, Stretford was nowhere to be seen. He was starting to cut me loose now that I'd made him all his money. He only got involved again when it became clear Gregory was desperate to get rid of me. So he started pimping me round to a variety of clubs linked by one common thread – they were all managed by people who were his clients or who had shares in his business. First it was Celtic, where Kenny Dalglish, who was a big contact of his, was in overall charge. Later, at the start of the 1999–2000 season, I even went on loan to Fulham, where Paul Bracewell, another of his clients, was the manager. I enjoyed the loan at Craven Cottage, up to a point. At the end of it, Bracewell wanted to sign me on a permanent deal and surprise, surprise, Stretford was very enthusiastic, even though they were offering me vastly reduced wages. I was on £20,000 a week at Villa and Fulham were only offering me £12,000 a week.

We had a meeting at the Fulham training ground at Motspur Park, just off the A3 in southwest London. Stretford made a rare journey down. He thought he was just coming to tie up the loose ends because he had got used to me doing everything he told me to do. It became apparent they were only offering me an 18-month deal, and as the meeting progressed Stretford got more and more agitated about me accepting it. Somehow, it just didn't ring true. Of course, knowing now that Bracewell was his client, too, it all makes sense. I had obviously been promised to him like some piece of cut-price sirloin.

When the money was mentioned, Stretford said he thought it was a great deal. That wasn't the Paul Stretford I had come to know. That wasn't the tough negotiator. That wasn't the guy who always stood my corner. The contract was sitting right there on the table in front of us and they wanted me to sign it. Stretford said one more time that he thought the move was a great idea. 'Why do you think it's a fucking great idea, Paul, dropping down a division and getting half the money I'm earning now?' I asked. He said he was going to ask me one last time to sign it. I just said, 'No.'

Stretford snapped his briefcase shut and stood up. He was so angry he started running up and down on the spot, right there in that small office. Running up and down on the spot and shouting like a two-year-old having a fucking tantrum, just because he couldn't get his way. Because I had made him look stupid in front of his mate. He had probably told Bracewell he had me eating out of his hand and suddenly the dumb animal had made him look like a cunt. I had always been a doormat where Stretford was concerned. I had always done whatever he said. I said yes to all sorts of things, often without looking at them. I had trusted him but that trust had diminished to all but nothing. He asked Bracewell to get him a car to take him to Heathrow. I said I'd give him a lift. He said he didn't want a lift, and I thought it was all getting a little bit childish.

Gregory was surprised to see me back at Villa. He had obviously been told I would be leaving, too. He made me train with the kids. It was about that time that Gregory signed Steve Stone, Steve Watson and Alan Thompson. Guess what linked all those players? Yep, you've got it in one: they were all clients of Stretford. I'm not saying it's unusual. Look at most Premiership clubs these days and one agent will handle the majority of the transfers. The potential for abuse and financial impropriety is there for everyone to see. But football's like a casa nostra. No one ever squeals. If they do, they're ostracised.

Stretford's success had gone to his head by then. He had changed dramatically. He's an ugly little twat but suddenly he thought he was a fucking fashion model and a bon viveur. In January 1998, while I was at Villa, I had invited him to Estelle's twenty-first birthday party at a restaurant in Birmingham. I told everybody the food and the wine was all paid for but if they were going to buy bottles of Dom Perignon, they could buy it themselves. Stretford turned up in a long Gucci coat and sunglasses. This is a guy who is not a clotheshorse. The whole night, he ordered £300 bottles of champagne and then lumped me with the bill. More significantly, he blanked some of my friends that he had once pretended to be pally with. I started to realise I was outliving my usefulness to him.

Just before the move to Fulham was mooted, he had phoned me to say Panathinaikos were interested in signing me. I fancied that. It felt as though it would be a fresh start. Stretford and I flew out to Athens to hear what they had to say. There were 5,000 fans at the airport and we were driven into the city in a bulletproof Mercedes with police outriders. That night, we were going to meet the club president, who was an oil tycoon. I waited for Stretford in the lobby of the hotel. I saw him coming. It was pretty hard to fucking miss him. He was wearing these fucking stupid Dame Edna Gucci sunglasses, a Hawaiian shirt, shorts and Gucci flip-flops. By that stage my mates were calling him Toad because he looked like Toad of Toad Hall.

He had gone from a thorough, professional, understated guy to this horrible parody of an agent. I looked at him and thought 'Big Time Charlie'. I liked the Panathinaikos set-up. The training ground was great. The facilities were brilliant. I asked them how close to the beach I could live and the flunky was saying 10 or 15 metres. They offered me £25,000 a week, net, and I was very keen. But when we got back to

England, Stretford suddenly started talking about the possibility of going to Fulham on loan with a view to a permanent move. I asked him what had happened to the interest from Panathinaikos and he just brushed it aside and said they had dropped out. Two days earlier they had been gagging for it. I think he had promised me to Paul Bracewell so he gave Panathinaikos the flick.

When Fulham didn't work out he tried to get me to go back to Forest. David Platt was the manager then and he had spunked a whole load of money down the drain, and the club I had helped to take up to the Premiership was now struggling in the bottom half of the First Division. I met Platty at the Hilton near East Midlands Airport but I wasn't impressed. I didn't want to go back to somewhere where I had previously had so much success. I told Stretford I wasn't interested.

A couple of days after that, I got on the team coach taking Villa reserves to an away game somewhere and picked up a paper. My eyes shot straight to a headline. 'Agent Blasts Colly', it said. Stretford was quoted in it, saying that I was foolish to have turned down Forest. That was the first time he had ever crossed that line because one of his golden rules was that he would never criticise his clients in public. For me, it was the last straw. I released a statement to the Press Association thanking Paul Stretford and his wife Margaret for everything they had done for me and confirming that our partnership was now at an end.

That was it. I just binned him. It was blatantly obvious to me that he was manipulating his contacts to try and get me out of Villa, even if it was going to cost me a lot of money. He wasn't happy. He rang. 'What the fuck's going on?' he said. I just told him the shit had been going on long enough. I still didn't know about him and Gregory. I found out eventually from some small item on the Sky Sports ticker that mentioned Stretford was Gregory's agent. I thought I was seeing things. It was a clear conflict of interest but he had kept it a secret. It was his guilty secret and I felt betrayed by this man I had trusted completely.

It was my fault. I had allowed the line between him being my surrogate father and my agent to become blurred. And he played on that big time. He abused it. My relationship with him was unhealthily dependent and he milked it for all it was worth. He started off as a very nice, friendly, proper, professional guy and he turned into a guy bouncing from deal to deal, consumed by greed. I've never fronted him up about it. Not to this day. I suppose it's out of embarrassment more than anything else. It would make me feel small to ask someone why they had treated me like that. I let Stretford get away scot-free with the way he had abused my trust.

I hope he treats Wayne Rooney better now that he's at Man United. I hope Rooney knows what kind of animal Stretford is. I hope he doesn't fall for all the emotional shit. I'm not saying all agents are like him. It's too easy just to blame them for all football's ills. It's too easy to say they're the person in the shadows who strolls in at the last minute and walks away with pot-loads of money. But I guarantee you they earn more money from clubs now than they do from players. Agents themselves are often not corrupt. But they are sometimes asked to facilitate corruption on behalf of chairmen. They're corruption's middle-man.

I wonder if Stretford still keeps in touch with Gregory now that Gregory's career is fucked, too, tainted by his transfer dealings at Villa. Some time after I had retired, I was working for Five Live at a Derby v Spurs game. Gregory was Derby manager by then, and he came over. 'How are ya, Stan?' he said, bright as a button. No fucking shame. 'Strets is in the office,' he said, pointing down the tunnel, 'do you want to come down and see him.' I looked at him for a second. 'No thanks,' I said.

CHAPTER FIVE

LIVERPOOL: LIVING THE DREAM

Back in the summer of 1995, a few years before my problems with Villa and Stretford, I signed for Liverpool and thereby started the journey that led me to Ulrika and the parasitical, inward-looking world she inhabited. I thought I had reached the top rung of the ladder when I arrived at Anfield, but when I peered over into what I imagined would be my promised land I found a club fatally undermined by a manager who was not strong enough, and a powerful player hierarchy that twisted team selection out of shape.

Discipline was slack at Liverpool when I joined. The club was clinging to its links with past glories through players like Ian Rush and John 'Digger' Barnes as if it couldn't bear to let them go. The truth was they weren't worth their place in the team any more, but Rushie and Digger were untouchable. No one at the club had the guts or the will to thank them for what they had done and send them on their way. And so it felt like you were stuck at the end of an era, not reaching out for the start of a new one.

You could hear the death knell of the Boot Room when I was there. I probably hastened its demise. Perhaps I, as much as anybody, exposed the lack of authority and discipline at the club. Perhaps I exposed the fact that the players were overindulged and the succession that had run through Bill Shankly to Bob Paisley to Joe Fagan to Kenny Dalglish to Graeme Souness had finally broken down and new blood needed to be injected.

At Melwood, their training ground, they even still had four wooden boards that players used to use for passing practice during the Shankly days. I remember seeing footage of Jimmy Case banging shots against them one week when he was the only player left there after all the rest had gone away on international duty. By the time I arrived they were practically rotting away. But no one wanted to take them down. They were monuments to a time when Liverpool ruled Europe. Perhaps they should have turned them into a heritage site, organised coach tours so people could stare at them because that's all they were good for. But for people at the club, they brought back happy memories – for those who had memories that stretched back that far. Only after I had left and Gerard Houllier, an outsider, had arrived did a thorough modernisation of Melwood go ahead.

The same reverence for links with the past meant that the senior players, in general, could pretty much do what they wanted, and even the younger ones took the piss. Some of them would wander out onto the training pitch at Melwood still munching on a piece of toast from the canteen. Others, myself included, would be late almost as a matter of routine. One of the old Boot Room coaches, Ronnie Moran, took to calling me 'Fog in the Tunnel' because he thought I should have added some unlikely hold-up in the Mersey Tunnel to my repertoire of reasons for panting in 15 minutes after everybody else. 'What's the excuse today, Stan?' he'd say. 'Fog in the tunnel?'

Once, early on in my time there, I saw Rushie take aim at Ronnie Moran as he wandered over to one of the training pitches. He pinged the ball about 40 yards with his right foot and it hit Bugsy flush on the back of his balding head. He wheeled round in a rage, ready to give someone the bollocking of their life. 'Who the fuck did that?' he said. Rushie just put his hand up. 'I did,' he said. Bugsy started laughing and said something about Rushie being a joker and that was it.

When Robbie Fowler did the same thing to Phil Thompson a few years ago, soon after I had left, the culture had changed at Liverpool and it wasn't tolerated. Fowler aimed a shot at Thommo which hit him, and Thommo went berserk. They had a blazing row and it turned into a huge confrontation. Houllier backed Thompson, and, even though Robbie eventually apologised, the incident turned into an issue that hastened his exit from the club he loved to Leeds United.

As for John Barnes, he was more than just the captain. If Roy Evans, the manager, had put a particular training session on and Digger didn't like it, he'd just walk back to the changing rooms. 'I ain't fucking doing this,' he would say. 'It's crap.' Don't forget that Roy had been the reserve-team coach when people like Digger were the superstars of the first team, and they still looked upon him as an underling. They patronised him. Digger had more of a say in our tactics than Roy Evans ever did. Roy was a lovely bloke but he wasn't strong enough to challenge the old guard.

That's why Digger and Michael Thomas, who was his big

mate, played in the centre of midfield. And centre of midfield was where our biggest weakness was. They were at the heart of everything when it was clear to everybody that they should not have been in the team. The two of them just weren't up to it. Digger had been a sublime player in his day but he wasn't a central midfielder. I think he was holding on, trying to manoeuvre himself into prime position to become the next manager when the time came for Roy to get the boot.

Rushie wasn't as forceful as Digger but he didn't take any shit. Mostly he just sat in his corner, getting on with his own business. He would give his all on the pitch but in the dressing room he gave the impression of not giving a fuck what was going on because he knew he was coming to the end of his career.

On another occasion we were all wandering out to training one morning when Roy made some quip to Robbie Fowler and they started joking about. Robbie got the gaffer's head in an armlock and started rubbing his other hand across his head, frizzing up his hair. I caught myself imagining what would have happened if Gary Neville ever tried that with Alex Ferguson. Somehow, I couldn't see it.

That was just one of the things that summed up the difference between Liverpool and Manchester United. We thought we were winners, but they *were* winners. We had all the trappings of winners but they had all the trophies. We acted like the big shots but they were the best team. We led the superstar lifestyle but they got the superstar results. We didn't even win a pot to piss in during my first year there. United won the Double. Life at Anfield in my time there, just as it is now, was spent labouring in United's shadow. Maybe we used our flash lifestyles to try to convince ourselves we were better than them. But it never quite worked.

I remember reading once that the young Formula One driver Jenson Button had bought a yacht in Monaco during his first year in Formula One. People were saying he was having the party before he actually had anything to party about. And that is what it was like at Liverpool. We seemed pretty pleased with ourselves a lot of the time but we didn't actually have anything to show for it. We weren't far away but we weren't close enough.

Things happened that shouldn't have been allowed to happen. They were small things but they were still things that, however subtly, undermined the idea that this was an outfit that was utterly dedicated to its profession. Robbie Williams, the pop superstar who was a mate of our goalkeeper, David 'Jamo' James, was allowed to travel on the team coach to the last match of the season once. And the group of us known collectively as the Spice Boys – Jamo, Jamie Redknapp, Phil Babb, Robbie Fowler, Steve McManaman, Jason McAteer and me at the margins – were allowed to develop the kind of celebrity lifestyle that was eventually to send me spinning towards Ulrika.

Robbie and Macca would do most of their socialising on Merseyside, but for the rest of us, as soon as a game at Anfield finished on a Saturday afternoon, we would get changed as quickly as we could. Then we'd jump in a taxi we had waiting for us so that it could rush us over to Manchester Airport to allow us to catch the shuttle down to Heathrow. Sometimes we would drop our stuff off at the Halkin Hotel and then jump in another cab to take us the short ride to Soho. Most

Saturdays we would be trawling our golden triangle of night-clubs in the West End – China Whites, the Emporium and Ten Rooms – by 9 p.m. A few hours after the final whistle we were embarking on another big night out.

I had a lot of respect for Roy Evans and Ronnie Moran because they were real football men, but we just got away with too much as a group. Although we nearly got there, the way we were behaving off the pitch and the insubordination to the manager affected our final push to clinch a championship. The devil is always in the detail. Things like mobile phones going off when we were walking around the pitch before a game. That just infected things. It clouded things.

Of course, I was complicit in all these occurrences. I was an offender, too. I took liberties as much as the next player. And I'm not saying we weren't professional. I'm just saying we weren't professional enough. I still feel that that Liverpool side, when you look at its best 11 players, was more than a match for United in terms of talent, but there was no structure and no authority to keep all the strong personalities in check.

Neil Ruddock fitted into that category, too. He was a strong character and a big man. Very popular in the dressing room. Razor was one of those people that you see described as larger than life. Always the soul of the party. Always joking. Not the miserable bloke I saw on *I'm a Celebrity, Get Me Out of Here*. I can only assume the lack of food in the jungle made him grumpy, because that wasn't the Razor I knew.

Razor was another player who was past his sell-by date when I arrived at Anfield. He was at the stage of his career when he was taking short cuts. If he could get away with something, he would do. And he would glory in it. I think some of the younger lads thought he was streetwise and smart and some of the stuff he did made me laugh. But again, it sent out a message that this was a group of players who didn't take their football seriously enough.

Razor seemed to pick up quite a lot of injuries, and once, he and I and a couple of the other lads were in the little gym at Melwood doing some recuperative work while most of the players were outside on the training pitches. Mark Leather, the physio – we called him Judas because he came from Burnley but supported Liverpool – came in and told Razor he wanted him to do half an hour's running on the treadmill while he went out and supervised a couple of the lads who were just returning to full training. He told me he wanted me to do a weights circuit and then he walked out and wandered down to one of the pitches furthest away from where we were. As soon as he was a fair distance away, Razor, who weighed about 18 stone by then, hopped off the treadmill but left it running. He reached down into his bag and pulled out a foil container which had a bacon and egg sandwich in it. He sat down, whipped out a copy of *The Sun* and started reading through it, munching on his sandwich, as if he was a bloke settling down for the afternoon in his armchair.

I was keeping a lookout for him and eventually I saw Judas start to make his way back towards the gym. Razor had a bag of ice that was supposed to be for him to strap on to his injured foot. Some of it had melted so he rooted around in it and splashed the water over his hair and face and a bit on his T-shirt for good measure. And then he jumped back on the treadmill. Judas came back in, saw a guy who seemed to be sweating like a pig, and was full of admiration. 'Razor, fucking great professional,' he said, looking at everyone in the room as if we should all be using Razor as our model.

If you could get away with it at Liverpool, you did get away with it. If you could wind somebody up, you wound them up. If there was a practical joke to be played, you played it. Razor seemed to be at the heart of a lot of it. The Aeroflot flight back from a UEFA Cup tie at Spartak Vladikavkaz in September 1995, led by a pilot who looked so knackered we were all joking he must have been working for three weeks solid, was a particularly good example of the anarchy that often took over. The players were throwing paper balls back and forth, people were flicking my ears, everybody was shouting at each other. Razor and Robbie Fowler were involved in some particularly raucous banter and then Razor cut the end of Robbie's tie off. So Robbie cut the tongue off one of Razor's expensive shoes. When we arrived back in Liverpool, the joking obviously went a stage too far. As I was walking into the arrivals hall I noticed this trail of blood on the white floor. Razor had lost his temper with Robbie and chinned him.

The banter never stopped. There were two players in the side that we called Trigger because they were so stupid. Rob Jones, the right back, was always getting the piss ripped out of him because he was so dumb. He'd walk into it every time. We'd be pulling up outside Old Trafford and one of the guys would say 'the stadium must be around here somewhere'. Rob Jones would never get it. 'It is, it is,' he would say. 'It's right here.' Mind you, Jason McAteer made Rob Jones look like Stephen Hawking.

We were like a bunch of kids, really. A bunch of talented

kids who got away with murder. We desperately needed someone to take a look at what we were doing and say 'hold on
a second here'. If Martin O'Neill, for instance, had been in
charge in the two seasons I was at Anfield, we would have
walked away with the league. He would have embraced some
of the good things we had, especially the camaraderie, but
he would have drawn the line at going down to London after
games. That would have been forbidden.

I was still living in Cannock, over an hour and a half's drive
away. If Martin had taken over, he would have told me to
move to Merseyside the next day or watch him put me
on the transfer list. I think people like Steve McManaman
and Robbie Fowler would have respected him for that. People
usually conform to the ruling mood at a club. Martin, or
someone like him, would have utilised the talent we had a
lot better. He would have motivated us. He would not have
allowed us to let ourselves down in smaller games against
clubs we should have been hammering.

Roy Evans never harnessed our talent. He never really convinced me he was a man who had real footballing principles
other than 'pass it and move, pass it and move'. That was the
Liverpool mantra but you needed something more than that.
There was no one to provide it. Doug Livermore, the assistant
manager, was the same kind of character as Roy.

I had been given a vivid introduction to the hedonistic lifestyle I could expect at Liverpool before I had even officially
signed. I had got quite friendly with a few of the Spice Boys
at England get-togethers, so on the day after I played my last
game for Nottingham Forest against Manchester City I drove

down to London to hook up with them and have a night out in the haunts that were to become so familiar to me the following season.

This was a brave new world for me. It was a culture shock. Small time to big time. Footballer to celebrity. Jamo was modelling for Armani. Jamie Redknapp was going out with Louise Nurding, who was regularly voted the sexiest woman in the country as well as being a famous pop star. Jason McAteer, who signed at the same time as me, was going out with Donna Air. I tagged along with them at just about the time football was exploding again in popularity. Suddenly the game was cool and hip again and footballers were people everybody wanted to be seen with, particularly women.

Being a footballer was like being your own personal aphrodisiac. You didn't need to feed a girl oysters or whatever else it is that is supposed to give you a helping hand. You just had to turn up. You didn't even have to say anything. They still came running at you like a herd of stampeding cattle. At first I felt like a boy from Cannock who had stumbled into a place he had no right to be, but that didn't last for long. Soon, I was intoxicated by it.

That first Saturday I met up with the team in London, at the beginning of May 1995, Liverpool had lost at Aston Villa that afternoon, but they had still qualified for the UEFA Cup by winning the League Cup at the start of April, so they were in a party mood. I arrived at the hotel they were staying at, which was opposite Lord's Cricket Ground in St John's Wood. I told one of the girls on reception which of the players I had come to meet and she told me what his room number was. I got in the lift and went up.

It was always the custom with footballers in those days that you would leave the door to your room open except when you were sleeping. People used to come and go pretty freely. There wasn't a lot of privacy but there was a feeling of being 'all mates together'. It was all very jocular, very boisterous. So when I got up to the room on this occasion, sure enough the door was ajar. I pushed it open and walked in.

I stopped dead in my tracks as soon as I saw the scene unfolding in front of me. One of the players was sitting propped up on the bed, his hands behind his head, looking like a prince. Further down the bed, two girls were busy sucking him off. Both of them working away at him and him just sitting there watching them go. I stared at it all for a second in disbelief. Welcome to the Premiership, I thought. Then I went back downstairs.

When pre-season began, I stayed with David James and his wife for a while at their home in Heswall on the Wirral. Bad move. Not because of Heswall or the Wirral, but because Jamo was an insomniac. And he was as mad as a hatter. Before I signed for the club, he was so notorious that no one would room with him. The boys told me stories about how he had bad nightmares and he'd be so out of it he'd get his missus in an armlock in his sleep and she would have to scream blue murder just to get him to release his grip. When Muggins arrived, Muggins roomed with him. When Ronnie Moran announced to the rest of the team that I was sharing with him, they all burst out laughing.

The lads said he had a little wood at the back of his house and that he used to go out there when he was in a state about something and start chopping down trees. There were also stories that he'd driven a mini into his swimming pool. I never asked him about that. When I stayed at his house, I was in the spare room, and it was crammed from floor to ceiling with record players, televisions, PlayStations and vinyl. I couldn't work out whether it looked like someone had burgled the place or whether it looked like a burglar actually lived there and had filled it with all his ill-gotten gains. Jamo just didn't seem to understand the concept of trying to repair something if it broke, or sticking with it even if it wasn't in absolutely pristine condition. If he had a car and he pranged it, he would just go and buy a new car. Didn't matter if it was just a little dent. No problem. New car. So there were five cars parked on the drive. If he bought a new pair of shoes and he scuffed them, he wouldn't clean them. He would just chuck them in the spare room and go and buy a new pair. Too much disposable income, I suppose. Too easy just to bin stuff. Too easy to spend money like you're going to be earning that kind of money for the rest of your life.

Rooming with him was worse. The club went to Ireland for its pre-season one year and we stayed in a lovely country-house hotel. The hotel staff were incredibly helpful and friendly and we asked them if they could bring a selection of videos to our room so we could watch a film. A guy came up with 10 or 15 of them and then left. We were sitting on the end of Jamo's bed and he got this pile of videos in his big bear hands and started smashing them against the wall one by one, as hard as he could. It wasn't even worth asking him why he was doing it because he would just start laughing this guffawing laugh like some sort of bloody idiot. This is the England goalkeeper we are talking about here. At times like that he can come across as the thickest, dumbest bloke on the planet, but you only need to listen to him speak in more rational moments to realise that he is a very bright bloke. I think he's calmed down a bit since. I hope he has. For the sake of video collections everywhere.

So I didn't stay in his spare room for long. Lovely bloke. Great lad. Heart of gold. I was drunk once, paralytically drunk, and he just picked me up in his arms like I was a feather and carried me up to my room. But his place was a madhouse. After the second or third day of training, I thought I'd drive home. I told myself it was only an hour's commute. I told myself it was better being around friends and family than stuck on my own in Liverpool. For that first season I had the time of my life, playing well for the team and then going back to my local pub in a working-class town where I could hang out with all my mates.

Nobody asked any questions about me not living in Liverpool that first season because I scored 19 goals and nobody cared. It took Roy Evans and Neil Ruddock 45 minutes to drive in from Southport. What was the problem if it took me 25 minutes longer than them? If you did a survey of current Premiership players, my guess would be that more than 60 per cent of them travel for an hour or more every day to get to the training ground. So me shuttling between Liverpool and Cannock shouldn't really have been an issue. But when I look back now, I think maybe at least it would have showed willing if I had moved to Liverpool. It would have been a bigger commitment in my own mind and in the minds of the fans. I should have dug in and stayed on

Merseyside. As time went on, I did begin to feel a bit isolated because I wasn't going out with the lads in Liverpool, and some players interpreted that as a signal that I wanted to put some distance between me and them and they resented me for it.

Things weren't right in Cannock, either. My world was getting distorted. Some of my close friends started to back off because they thought I was in the big time now, partying in London with people like Jamie Redknapp and Phil Babb. They thought I wouldn't want to know them any more. And in their place came hangers-on. Swarms of them. Kids who had called me every name under the sun in school ten years earlier were now the men coming up to me and telling me how great they thought I was.

And I took up with these people. They became my friends. I fell for it. I took my eye off the ball in my social life and it was the biggest mistake I made. There was one guy in particular, who my mates and I had despised when we were all at school. I hated him and he hated me, and suddenly here he was working for a big sportswear company and acting like he's my best mate. And I indulged him. I encouraged him. I allowed myself to be flattered by him.

I'm not stupid, but if people are nice to you for long enough you start to think they might be okay. So, suddenly, I gained an accessory. A man who couldn't stand me a few years earlier started looking after my house when I was away at weekends. Soon enough I had a whole group of flunkeys surrounding me. I knew it was ridiculous but I did nothing to stop it. I let it ride.

The next stage was the arrival of the tabloid reporters.

They pitched up in Cannock hoping to sniff out stories about me and they discovered that some of my newfound friends were only too willing to feed them a few choice cuts. So when my former girlfriend, Michelle Green, was pregnant with my son, Tom, the reporters knew exactly where to go. They would sit outside her house in their cars for days on end. I'd have to go through back gardens to get into her place without them seeing me.

All these faceless people started coming out of the woodwork doing stories about my private life and it was all stoked up by these new friends. These people who were coming with me on free holidays to Cyprus or New York. These people who were getting tickets to Liverpool games every week and meeting all the players and thinking they were mates of Jamie Redknapp just because they might have been out with him once with me. And they were all getting a few quid on the side for their tips to the newspapers.

I was making a rod for my own back. I look at how I mishandled my situation then, the weekends on the lash in London, the women, the hangers-on, and I wish I had done it all differently. Off the pitch, I wish I had been able to do it the way Alan Shearer and Michael Owen have done it. For as long as their careers last, they are single-minded about their profession. They do their job and they put their socialising on hold. I'm sure they have a beer now and again or a bit of a gamble, but mostly they stick to their family unit and that's enough for them. I know I should have done that, too. I was capable of it. But I didn't do it.

It was down to me, in the end, but with stronger management, I would have done it. If I'd played for Alex Ferguson,

I would have done it. I think he and I would have got along fine. There would not have been any problems, despite my personality disorder. He would have told me what to do and I would have done it. If that's the culture at the club, you fit in with it. I needed that kind of authority. I needed someone who wouldn't give me any room for manoeuvre, someone who wouldn't let me mess about and get my head in a state with extraneous issues that shouldn't have been a problem. But as it was, even though I had a good first season, niggling things started to go wrong right from the start.

I made my Liverpool debut on the opening day of the 1995–96 season, 19 August, against Sheffield Wednesday at Anfield. The Liverpool pre-match routine was for the squad to meet up at Melwood mid-morning, have lunch and then travel by coach to the stadium. There was a lot of expectation about my debut. *Football Focus* was on in the canteen and they were showing a lot of my Forest goals and talking about my price tag. I started to get pretty nervous.

It was a balmy late summer's day, and when I ran out for the warm-up I got a great reception from the crowd and I bowed to the Kop in homage. I felt intoxicated by the history of the club in that moment. I thought about all the things that had happened on that pitch, all the goals that had been scored through those posts, all the triumphs and the great European nights. And I was proud that I was about to become part of the fabric of the club.

For the first hour I hardly touched the ball. Liverpool played a very different style of football to Forest and it was already clear to me that there was no question of them adapting for me. They played a very meticulous game, passing it up from the back, back and forth across midfield, probing for openings, obsessed with trying to keep possession. At Forest we hadn't exactly played direct football, but if they could release me with a long ball, they would.

During that first hour I was determined not to panic, even though I was virtually a spectator. I knew I was bedding in with new players and a new style. I was a bit puzzled that they weren't trying to play to my strengths but I kept working hard, hoping something would come my way. So when I finally got the ball, midway through the second half, I thought I'd have a run because I'd seen so little of it. I think I put it back through my legs and turned. I saw the keeper and I thought 'fuck it, just shoot'.

I saw it fly in and I lost it. I heard the roar of the crowd and I felt the warmth of the sun and the adrenaline rushing through me. In that moment it felt as if the move to Liverpool was already turning into some wonderful dream that was going to propel me right to the very top and force me into the England team. It felt like everything was possible. We won the game 1–0 and I was the match-winner. It was the opening day of the season. A bright new dawn. Perhaps I would be the final piece in the jigsaw after all. Perhaps I would be the difference between Liverpool finishing third and Liverpool winning the title. Everywhere, optimism ran wild. I was up and running.

After the game, I mentioned to the press boys how surprised I was to have seen so little of the ball in the first half.

I suggested that once they had got used to the kind of runs I made, I might get more of it in future. The headline in *The Sun* on Monday morning was 'Do It My Way', which went down well with the rest of the lads. I think I must have made more ricks in terms of saying things that other people just thought than anyone else in the history of the game.

I don't regret anything I said in interviews, though, because I was trying to tell the truth. That's all. I despise the hypocrisy of people who do not speak their minds. I despise the kind of footballer who can be whingeing to me one moment about how much he hates Liverpool and the city and the people and the pubs and the bars and the restaurants and how desperate he is to get away, and then the next moment, when he is asked to do a television interview, he gets up, smiles into the camera and says how much he loves the club and the city and that he wants to sign a new contract. I saw a player do that at Liverpool. That blatantly. That shamelessly. It puzzles me that someone can be that two-faced. If they feel it, why don't they say it? Why doesn't it eat them up inside? Thinking one thing and saying another; that must tie you up in knots. That's not for me. I find other ways to tie the knots.

But saying what you think causes you problems. In my case, I helped to fuck myself at Liverpool with another interview I did, this time for *FourFourTwo* magazine, six games into that first season at Anfield. Nothing had changed from the first game by then. The team was still playing in a way that was totally at odds with how I had played at Forest. My game was getting in behind people, running with the ball, then giving the ball deep and turning and running. What Ronnie Moran was asking me to do was get it, hold it up and give it to Steve McManaman. If they wanted someone to do that, they should have bought some beanpole like Brian Deane. It pissed me off.

I was being told to go wider and come deeper. Basically, I was being told to do everything I had not done at Forest. At Forest I had been such an outstanding success that Liverpool had paid £8.5 million for me. So where was the logic in that? So I said it to the interviewer. I asked in what other industry would you pay £8.5 million for an asset and then not use it properly and neglect to treat it in the way it was used to being treated. Would you buy a dishwasher and then try and do your ironing with it?

The article duly appeared and the furore was amazing. Mike Ellis, the veteran Merseyside reporter for *The Sun*, was particularly apoplectic. He wanted to know where I got off, a young upstart coming into this famous football club with its grand traditions and its great achievements and trying to tell them how to run their affairs on the pitch. I honestly thought I was being constructive. I just wanted them to get the best out of me so I could get more goals for them. But they never really adapted to me. I had to adapt to them.

After the article was published I had to go to Melwood with Stretford to apologise to Roy Evans. I saw John Barnes in the canteen as soon as I walked through the door. He had a big grin on his face. He said he would have said exactly the same but he would not have said it publicly. As far as I was concerned, there wouldn't really have been any point in saying it in that case. I wasn't interested in subterfuge or double-speak. Perhaps I was just too naïve, but I think that sometimes if you make your point in public, things get done.

If you keep your mouth shut, nothing moves forward. The points I made about Liverpool's style of play weren't just made off the cuff for the sake of slagging the manager. They were points that had logic. And when I sat down with Roy he said he knew mistakes had been made on both sides. He never said that in public, either, of course. Inside the dressing room, players said they agreed with me. Outside the dressing room they would never back me up.

Despite the team tactics, I was so determined that things would go well for me that first season at Liverpool that I worked like a fury to make it happen. I was desperate to cement my place in the team so the way I dealt with what they were asking me to do was to break wide, put crosses in and generally try and set Robbie Fowler up with the chances. Sometimes I felt I was coming ridiculously deep in search of the ball, but it seemed to be what they wanted so I adapted to them. I knew that with a predatory striker like Robbie in the team I wasn't going to get 30 goals in a season. I knew he would outscore me because he was the archetypal fox in the box in those days. So I did my utmost to complement him; to turn as much into a provider as a scorer. In that first season, Robbie and I were the highest scoring partnership in Europe with 44 league goals between us. I knew everybody appreciated the role I was playing because sometimes after Robbie had scored, the supporters started singing my name, too.

On the pitch we respected each other. Off the pitch there was nothing. Robbie and I didn't get on. Right from the start. We played a pre-season match against Ajax at the end of July

1995 and we got battered 5–0. We were three goals down in the first half and then we got a chance. He had the opportunity to play me in but he shot instead. 'Fucking hell, Rob, pass it next time,' I said. A routine exchange between forwards, but he just spat 'fuck off' at me. And that was it. We never spoke again in my two years at Liverpool. We would congratulate each other on scoring a goal but that was it. A bit like Teddy Sheringham and Andy Cole at United, perhaps. I could tell by Robbie's body language that he was tense about me joining the club and in a way I didn't blame him. The problem was exacerbated by bad management. Roy Evans didn't have the courage to drop Rushie for the opening game of the season so he left Robbie on the bench. This was a bloke who had scored 35 goals for the club the season before and now he was being left out for a has-been. I would have been upset, too.

Even though we didn't get along, I know without any doubt that he was the best player I have ever played alongside. He was a supreme talent. He was at the peak of his powers then, before injury and problems with his weight deprived him of some of his sharpness. I considered myself a good finisher, but as a goal-poacher Robbie was frightening. I mean, he was unerring. He just didn't miss. If he got a chance, he scored. He was very one-footed but he would make angles for himself that no other player could. It doesn't matter if you can't use your right foot if you score 35 with your left.

They called him 'God' at Liverpool. That was his nickname. I read an interview with Dominic Matteo recently where he said he still has Robbie listed under God on the speed dial of his mobile phone. When he scored his one-hundredth goal for the club, one of four in a 5–1 victory over Middlesbrough in December 1996, he lifted up his shirt to show the cameras a T-shirt with a message on it. 'God's Job's a Good 'Un', it said, and that seemed to sum up the joy and the satisfaction he felt in playing for the team of the city where he was born. He made it to 100 quicker than Ian Rush.

He was a special kind of forward. The best since Jimmy Greaves. Look back at his goals and see how good the kid was. Playing with him – even for someone like me, who fancied himself – was an education. In my first season there, the guy was unstoppable. Four goals against Bolton, two against Manchester United at home, two more against Manchester United away, three against Arsenal. Goal after goal after goal. Never content with one, he was like a batsman who doesn't just want to make a century, he wants to make a big century. Deadly in training and when it really mattered. Better than Gary Lineker. Better than Alan Shearer and Michael Owen, too. Just not as smart or as cute off the pitch. Lineker, Shearer and Owen have all made the most of their careers. Robbie didn't.

Where he was unlucky was that he scored 30 goals a season for Liverpool for three seasons and he should have been able to relax a little bit then, safe in the knowledge that he was absolutely untouchable. But at that point Michael Owen came along, hailed as the next great goalscorer, and Robbie was under pressure when he shouldn't have been. I think his head went down a little bit then. He let all the fuss about Michael get to him.

Back then, I couldn't ever imagine him playing for another club. I felt sad for him and the supporters when he was moved on to Leeds and then to Manchester City. I don't think his heart will ever be in it again quite the way it was when he was at Anfield. I would love to believe that he can re-create his glory days at this stage of his career. I'd love to believe he can become one of the very best again and have an Indian summer in football. But I don't know if he can now, after the injuries and the effect of the years. However, it still makes me happy when I see his name flash up on the list of scorers on a Saturday afternoon.

His running mate at the club was Steve McManaman. They were thick as thieves. At Melwood they were never apart. I'm not sure that Macca was good for Robbie. He was more astute but I don't think he did Robbie any favours some-times. When they went out, it was never Macca who got into trouble. Always Robbie. One thing summed that up for me. They both wore T-shirts under their kit at a UEFA Cup match proclaiming their support for the striking Liverpool dockers and agreed that whichever of them scored first would lift up their top to reveal the message, even though that was against UEFA regulations. It didn't take a rocket scientist to work out that Robbie was more likely to be the scorer than Macca, and so it proved. Robbie duly got his UEFA bollocking. Macca got away scot-free.

Macca didn't like me either. There's a surprise. He was a bit more cute about it than Robbie. He would say hello and smile but he didn't mean it. I knew, once my back was turned, Macca would be having a little stab. I never felt comfortable when he was around. I certainly never wanted to leave a room when he was in there because I knew the barbed comments would start then.

I knew very early on that both of them had taken an instant dislike to me, so I thought I was fucked if I was going to put in any spadework with them either. All the little cliques at that place made me laugh. There was a bitter-and-twisted crew who always sat in the corner of the dressing room moaning. Razor, Jan Molby, Paul Stewart, Mark Walters and Nigel Clough: they all knew they were being shifted out so they'd sit there whingeing. 'This club's fucking gone,' Stewart would say, and they'd all have their little rant about how shit everything was. There was Macca and Robbie, John Barnes and Michael Thomas, Jamo, Phil Babb and Jason McAteer. And then someone like Jamie Redknapp, who got on with everyone, young and old, past-it or up-and-coming. Everybody liked Jamie and he liked them back. I admired that in him. In fact, I envied it. I wished I could have been like that, happy and amiable all the time, everybody's mate. But I just wasn't cut out like that.

Somehow, that fucking diaspora of talents and personalities came together that first season and came close to winning things. Somehow, we also conjured the collective performance of our lives in a league game against Kevin Keegan's Newcastle United team at Anfield at the beginning of April that wins most of the prizes for the game of that decade. It was a special night to be involved in. It was extra-special to score. It was fucking orgasmic to score the winner.

I hadn't scored for a couple of games before that match but Roy Evans had come up to me a few days before the game and told me I would definitely be starting. Newcastle had lost their lead to Manchester United by then because they had lost three of their last five games, but we were third and we knew that to try and get close to them at the top we needed to win. And we absolutely had to avoid defeat.

We met up at Melwood as usual a few hours before the game and had our pre-match meal. When the coach inched through the Shankly Gates an hour or so before the kick-off there was just something in the air that hummed it was going to be a special night. A night game, the glare of the floodlights, the Lowry figures striding purposefully towards the ground, two evenly matched teams, a full house and the special atmosphere of Anfield and all its ghosts.

I set the first goal up for Robbie. The game was only two minutes old. Jamie Redknapp sprayed a long ball out to the left, it was flicked on to me and I jinked past the challenge of Steve Watson and put a really deep cross in. Robbie was waiting on the edge of the six-yard box and nodded it down and in. Les Ferdinand equalised after a sharp turn and a shot he slammed past Jamo. David Ginola put them ahead four minutes later when he sprung our offside trap and slotted it in, but then we started to roll. Both sides had brittle defences. Keegan has never been renowned for the solidity of his sides and we ripped them apart marginally more than they did us.

Our next goal was a classic. Jason McAteer played a great ball out of defence up the line to Steve McManaman. He took the pass, turned and ran at the Newcastle left back, John Beresford, in that swaying, teasing way that was his call-sign. Then he played the ball across the top of the box and Robbie Fowler met it on the run and blasted it past Srnicek, using a little bit of swerve with the outside of his left foot to take it past the goalkeeper. As it nestled in the back of the net, Robbie flung himself after it and headed it for good measure.

That was Robbie's twenty-seventh Premiership goal of the season. He was phenomenal. But Faustino Asprilla, the signing everybody later said cost Newcastle the title that year, put Newcastle back ahead when he ran on to a pass and flicked it past Jamo, who had come haring out of his area when there was no need. Newcastle were desperate to win: three points that night and they would have drawn level with United at the top of the table again with a game in hand.

But then I prodded a centre from Jason McAteer that Steve Howey had failed to clear past Srnicek to make it 3–3. Everyone was flying by then. There were so many brilliant attacking players, all firing. McManaman, Fowler, Asprilla, Ginola, Ferdinand, all running at people, all creating chances. Neither defence knew what the hell had hit it. Ferdinand had another brilliant chance to make it 4–3 but Jamo saved at point-blank range. At the other end, Srnicek kept out a pile-driver from Jamie Redknapp. It was breathless stuff.

Rushie came on then so I moved over towards the left. I had done the same thing a week or two earlier when we had played against Forest at the City Ground and I was in acres of space every time I picked the ball up. I must have created 20 chances in that match. So it made sense for me to do it again. Late in the game, the crowd whistling because they were all emotionally exhausted by then and were scared of throwing it away, I got the ball on the left.

John Barnes and Rushie were playing it to each other on the edge of the box. They were threatening to walk it in. Rushie had his back to me and Digger was the only one who could see me. They were both desperate to pop a shot off but the crowd were yelling that I was in space and Digger passed it to me. I just thought 'get your shot on target'. Like any striker worth his salt, my intention was to shoot across the goal, then if the keeper made the save but palmed it out, either Rushie or Digger would have had the simple task of tapping it in.

I took my first touch and then I hit it with my left foot. It went towards the near post, which was the opposite side to where I had wanted it to go. But I hit it so well that it passed Srnicek before he even saw it. See the replay from behind the goal and it hurtles in like a bullet. The noise was unbelievable. It was like a wall of sound, a great roar that went right through me. I didn't know what to do. I didn't know what celebration to do. So I just kept running all the way around the side towards the Centenary Stand. For the next five or ten minutes I thought my head was going to explode.

What a way to finish a fucking great game. Sky voted it the best sports moment in their first decade on the air. In his commentary, Andy Gray said he was privileged to have been at the game. Roy Evans called it 'kamikaze football'. Keegan just called it 'a classic'. Keegan was right. It was bedlam at the end and we all went over to the Kop. I blew a kiss into one of the television cameras and said, 'That's for you, Mum.'

It was hard to top that throughout the rest of my career. I had been part of a fantastic game, played in the company of some of the best attacking footballers in Europe, and I had scored a late winner. That is about as good as it gets. People will remember that long after a dour 1–0 victory in a European Cup Final. So when people say I've underachieved as a player, I'll point to nights like that. That's what I was given footballing gifts for: to entertain on nights like that. Nights like that gave me my piece of immortality every bit as much as if I had a couple of championship medals to gaze at on cold winter evenings.

Keegan's Newcastle had the reputation of being the best attacking side in the country and we had just beaten them at their own game. Afterwards, Keegan got emotional and said 'we'll carry on playing this way or I go'. The FIFA president, Sepp Blatter, even wrote him a letter after the match congratulating him on his commitment to attacking football. Poor Keegan. United still won the title, and at least we had the memory of triumphing in the game to end them all.

I still think of how people must have walked in their front door on Merseyside that night after the match, still buzzing, still looking at each other and saying 'fucking brilliant'. I have had better games in terms of overall contribution but that didn't matter. Afterwards, we walked back into the dressing-room area and the Newcastle players were disappointed, but we were all looking at each other, too, saying 'what a game'. Some of the newspapers even produced souvenir pull-outs just for that game.

Six or seven weeks after that incredible high, we fought our way through to the FA Cup final at Wembley against, inevitably, the Manchester United of Roy Keane and Eric Cantona. That Cup Final is remembered for two things now. Cantona's winning goal at the end of a dire, scrappy game, and the white suits the Liverpool squad wore. That was our particular contribution to the legends of the Cup Final. In the 1920s, they brought you the White Horse Final. In the 1990s, the Liverpool of the Spice Boys brought you the White Suits Final. It seemed to fit our image down to the ground. It confirmed us in the public mind as flash Harrys. All style, no substance. More concerned with our appearance than our play. You have to be winners to pull off a stunt like that, and, once again, we blew it.

John Barnes and David James were the prime movers behind procuring the suits. Jamo was doing some modelling for Armani and he came into training one day and said they had offered to kit us out for the big day. We were all in on it and we thought we'd go for something different. I think Roy Evans and Ronnie Moran were clever enough to see the shit coming if we lost. They chose more traditional dark blazers.

I felt a bit of a knob in it when we did a pre-match photo-shoot and when we were wandering around on the Wembley pitch in the pre-match walkabout. Andy Cole came over and said, 'What the fuck are you boys wearing?' I've still got mine tucked away in a wardrobe somewhere as a kind of grotesque memento, but I know Razor ripped the arms off his straight after the match. A designer suit with no arms: that was about as close to a symbol of that Liverpool team as you are ever going to get.

We didn't deserve to win. I played like a drain. I was knack-ered, for a start. I couldn't sleep the night before the game. Not a wink. We stayed at Sopwell House, near St Albans, a hotel that's always been popular with visiting football teams, but my mind was whirring with the anticipation of the next day. In desperation, I went downstairs some time in the early hours and there were a couple of Scousers sitting in the hotel bar. I had a tot of brandy with them to try to take the edge off but it didn't work. I just went back to bed and lay awake until dawn.

I don't think I got a chance in the match. It was one of the rare occasions I didn't score against United. Typical, that. The most important game of all and I didn't come through. Sitting in the changing room afterwards, I thought I would get plenty more chances to play in the FA Cup final. I thought I would probably be back the next season. But I looked at some of the older lads like Digger and realised they knew it had been their last chance.

We still had a party afterwards. Of course we had a party. It would have been rude not to. We had hired the Emporium, which, bizarrely, was one of the club sponsors. We even had Emporium written on the side of the club coach as it weaved its way to Wembley that morning. That shows you how fucked up the club had become. We had a nightclub as one of the club sponsors. It was getting out of control.

It was like a Who's Who of showbiz celebrities that night. All of them there to celebrate with the losers. All of them gulping down champagne with the losers. All of them dancing with the losers. It was a party for defeat, but back then, with Jay Kay and Robbie Williams among the boys, it seemed like it was just fine. It seemed like the natural thing to do. You play a final, you have a party. Win or lose, it's all the same. That night I did something that I had been attempting to avoid ever since I arrived at the club almost 12 months earlier: I slept with Roy Evans' daughter.

*　　　*　　　*

I had been aware of Stacey as soon as the season began. She was only about 18 but she was slim and buxom and she was always in the players' lounge at Anfield after the games with the lads and their wives or girlfriends. She was a real flirt and there were rumours that a couple of the players had been with her. I didn't really want to go there. Not because I didn't fancy her, but because Roy and his wife were both lovely people and I didn't want to risk rocking the boat at the club more than I had already done. But, as the months went by, I met her a few times when I was out with some of the other lads at Soho clubs. She seemed to be gravitating towards the nightlife down there, probably because she was aware that me and Jamie and Jamo tended to spend most of our weekends in London. She was often in the same clubs as us. She knew a lot of the same people.

It was inevitable she was going to be there that night at the Emporium, a few hours after the Cup Final. I caught her eye a few times during the evening and we did a bit of flirting. The team and the management were all staying that Saturday night at the same hotel in Knightsbridge so Stacey and I got a cab back together and went to her room. She was a single girl; I was a single bloke. We had sex, reasonably loud sex, actually, and when I got up to go back to my room she seemed a bit nervous, which was unusual for her. She asked me to try and keep the noise down while I was leaving and to shut the door quietly. She said her dad was sleeping in the room next door, which I hadn't known. There was no question of me doing it for a bit of bravado or something to boast about. That piece of information made me rather nervous, too, obviously. So I tiptoed out of there, praying that neither of her parents had heard us and that neither of them was going to be in the corridor as I was wandering out of their teenage daughter's bedroom.

We had to leave early the next morning to go to a pre-arranged parade around Liverpool that had been intended to honour us as winners. That had elements of farce, too. One minute I was standing on the top deck talking to Stig Inge Bjornebye, the next he had been whacked on the head by a branch of a tree that was hanging down over our route and was lying flat-out on the floor. A mate of mine in Cannock, who thought Bjornebye was a crap player, always called that branch 'The Branch of Credit where Credit's Due' after that.

As for Stacey, I feel mixed about the whole thing. For all his shortcomings as a manager, Roy Evans was a lovely bloke, but the reality is we didn't do anything wrong. There was no club rule against sleeping with the boss's daughter. I suppose it's just the kind of thing that doesn't happen that often at football clubs. Good job Sir Alex Ferguson hasn't got a daughter. Having said that, somehow I don't think the players would be queueing up to get off with her. Not if you valued your balls, anyway.

The episode with Stacey is the kind of thing that gives credence to all those people who say that *Footballers' Wives* isn't that far from the real thing. Well, I lived in that world and its truth was stranger than the fiction. Who could make that up? The star striker sleeping with the manager's daughter in the hotel room next to his, only a few hours after the end of the FA Cup Final. That was my life at Liverpool. That was my life, full stop. It was getting weird. It was getting incestuous.

It was starting to close in on me. I didn't like it but it was happening.

My second season at Anfield reflected that. I don't think Roy ever found out about me and Stacey, but the longer the season went on, it felt as though he might as well have done. I still scored 16 goals over the course of the campaign but only 12 of those were in the Premiership and it wasn't a good time. It tasted sour. It felt like things were on the slide. It felt like we weren't moving forward any more. People started asking questions about why I was driving up from Cannock every day. I started to read all the bad things in the papers. I put myself under pressure. All the fucking minutiae started to affect me.

The midfield was ageing and nothing was being done. We needed an injection of some younger blood. John Scales was injured. Rob Jones, the right back, had to retire. Razor was getting old. Midway through the season, Roy Evans stuck Macca up front with Robbie for a spell and that really pissed me off. Even if I wasn't scoring as much, I was still contributing. If I couldn't even get in the team in front of Macca, who wasn't a real forward, then I was obviously in trouble.

The moment that crystallised all my fears and resentments about how I was being treated that season came in an away dressing room before a Cup Winners' Cup match at FC Fion in Switzerland in the middle of September. It was an hour or so before the kickoff and Roy Evans read out the team. I wasn't in it. I looked round that dressing room and some of the other players were looking at me as if they knew it was bollocks that I had been dropped. Even some of the punters came up to me at half time and said I was being turned into a scapegoat.

That was the beginning of the end for me at Liverpool. Because once I feel I have been wronged, I switch off. Maybe that has been my greatest weakness as a player and as a person. Perhaps I'm too precious like that. Perhaps I need to roll with things a bit more and just take the bad with the good. Perhaps it's too easy for me to blame other people and deflect the shit away from myself. If somebody wrongs me, that's my excuse and I'm out of there. In my social life and my professional life, if I am not getting straight answers to straight questions, I turn my back.

I had a series of meetings with Roy Evans. I thought I had been doing well. I had adapted to them in that first season and I had worked hard at that. I had worked hard at being a provider for Robbie and I had scored my share of goals. I didn't see what the problem was. But the meetings just got more and more tense. Roy kept saying he wanted to give Macca a run up-front because he had been doing well. Which was garbage. He started playing Patrik Berger ahead of me sometimes, too. Suddenly there was none of the will there had been the season before about trying to sort it all out. It was stale. Roy Evans seemed to have run out of ideas.

After the game in Finland, he told me I was playing in a reserve-team game at Prenton Park, Tranmere Rovers' ground. I said I wouldn't play, as a point of principle. I told him I was quite willing to come in for extra training but that I would gain nothing from playing in a game like that, which would just be a media circus. Under normal circumstances I wouldn't have had an issue with playing for the reserves, but I had scored a goal in a league win over Southampton a few days before, then I was dropped in Switzerland for no reason. And now this. I just felt I was being thoroughly messed about.

I told Roy on the morning of the game that I would not play. When I didn't turn up at Prenton Park all hell broke loose. There was a feeding frenzy about what a spoiled, irresponsible, overpaid, stupid brat I was. I was fined two weeks' wages. So I switched off. Simple as that. I have got enough of a brain in my head to know that if somebody says something to me that is a complete load of bollocks, I don't have to follow it blindly like some sort of gimp. Football's full of followers. Not enough players who trust their brains to think for themselves. I made some sort of apology but I wouldn't read it out. Roy Evans read it to the press while I was driving away from the training ground in my Mercedes.

Part of my penance for refusing to play in the reserves at Tranmere was being picked to play in another reserve game. How fucking original. By then, I just thought 'fuck it, get it over with'. So I turned up and played up front with a kid called Michael Owen. There were more press there than punters. I scored one brilliant goal. Michael scored one and then he got tripped for a penalty and I buried it. I gestured up to the press box when I got the second, which gave them their pictures and their headlines the next morning.

I didn't really have that much to do with Michael Owen, even though I had always felt his presence during my time at Liverpool. When I made my debut against Sheffield Wednesday there was a big feature in the programme that day about him, with a big picture of Michael standing next to Ian Rush.

It was all about how young Michael Owen was the natural successor to Rushie. It was old generation and young generation. I was somewhere in between. I was the filling in the legend sandwich.

In the first season we all kept hearing stories about this wonderkid scoring hatfuls of goals in the youth team. But he was quite frail physically then and there was really no chance of him being ready for the first team. However, he came away with us to a pre-season tournament in Amsterdam that had matched us with Ajax and AC Milan. We didn't play Milan but Roberto Baggio was named player of the tournament and I asked him if I could have his shirt as a memento. I was standing at the door of their dressing room and I was suddenly aware that Michael had sneaked up behind me while Baggio was giving me this shirt. He was totally awe-struck. He kept saying, 'Stan, Stan, get us Baggio's shirt.' I told him I was having Baggio's shirt. We got back on the team coach and he was still pestering me for it. I told him to fuck off and that was it. He didn't say anything else. A thought ran through my head as I looked at him. It won't be long, son, before players like Baggio are asking to swap shirts with you, so I wouldn't worry on that score.

As my second season progressed, Michael started to train more and more with the first team. As the season wound down there was more and more pressure for him to be promoted into the starting line-up. And it became an issue for me then because I was already in and out of the team anyway. Michael's emergence sealed my fate. The club didn't know Robbie was going to suffer a serious injury the following season. They thought, with Michael coming through, they had an embarrassment of riches up front. They thought I was expendable.

Even I could see he was a breath of fresh air. There was a real sense of excitement about the talent that he had. There was a lot of pressure on the club to secure a European place towards the end of the season and Michael got a few games off the bench. He came on at Wimbledon at the beginning of May, accelerated past a couple of players and slotted one in. I already knew by then that the writing was on the wall for me at Liverpool, but Michael was speeding up the process.

I was feeling low. The season before, I had been the hero of one fantastic 4–3 win over Newcastle. Twelve months on and I found myself sitting on the bench at Anfield watching another 4–3 win over Newcastle, and this time Robbie was the hero. One of the snappers took a picture of me looking gutted when Robbie got the winner as another example of what a prick I was. And the truth is that, yes, I was gutted. A year earlier, that had been me. A year earlier I had been the hero, and now I was being made an outcast. I wanted the kind of adrenaline rush that Robbie was getting and it was being denied me. It was Groundhog Day, except they'd changed the protagonists.

About a month before the end of the season, Paul Stretford pulled me aside after a game and ushered me into the small physio's room opposite the Players' Lounge at Anfield. He said Villa wanted me and that they would pay me £1 million a year in wages. That was double what I was on at Liverpool. And I was fed up with Liverpool by then. I was being treated unjustly. I didn't want to see out the remaining two years of my contract.

Who knows what would have happened if I'd stayed. I'd like to think Gerard Houllier would have seen me as part of his plans, especially as Robbie got a bad knee injury. I could have been part of the Treble-winning side. There are plenty of 'what ifs', and I often think I should have stuck it out longer there. I caved in too easily. I should have dug in and got on with it and maybe things would have turned around.

But it's easy to think like that now with the benefit of a few extra years of maturity. It's easy to think what I should have done. But back then, Villa looked like a club on the up. They were the club I had supported as a kid. Liverpool were fucking me about. I had had enough. I wanted to move on. I looked at Stretford in that little room and said, 'Let's do it.'

CHAPTER SIX

VILLA: GOING NOWHERE

Before the start of every football season I went through the same ritual. Early one morning during the summer holidays I used to drive to my old secondary school in Cannock, park outside and wander up the hill, past the school buildings, to the plateau where the football pitches were. There weren't as many as when I was a kid. Half of them have been sold off. There was a redbrick housing estate sprawled across the area where I had scored a lot of my goals, but I could still see myself playing on those fields in my mind's eye.

I used to stand up there for a while, thinking how simple even my dysfunctional young life suddenly seemed to have been now that it was receding into the past. None of the fame then. None of the scrutiny. I would look down at the little grass bank next to the concrete playground. I scrapped with a kid called Darren Walker on that bank. He had been the cock of Bridgtown Primary School and I had been anointed the hardest kid at Broomhill, so when we arrived at Sherbrook together he wanted to take me on. The fight lasted about 15 seconds.

They didn't let us play with proper footballs on the

playground when I was there in the Eighties. So we played football with tennis balls, which turned out to be brilliant for close control and technique. Now they let them play with leather balls. All the restrictions have gone. Not much else has changed there, though. I went back recently and it doesn't look as if it has been decorated since I left. It looks tired and dilapidated.

I would go up there to those pitches in some desperate attempt not to get carried away with everything that was happening to my career. It was always on the eve of the season when all the bullshit and the circus of the Premiership was reaching its peak as everyone prepared for the big kick-off. I just wanted to remind myself of where I had come from before I went off and got lost again.

I wanted to remind myself why I loved football. I wanted to think back to the times when I played for the sheer joy of it. When it was the first way I found of expressing myself properly. When it was the first way I found of impressing girls in the school playground. I would think back to the times when I was 10 or 11 and turned out for a team called Longford Boys in the Walsall League. My first game for them was against a side called Jubilee Colts. The manager of the Colts had kicked me out a week earlier for fighting with one of the other lads. I scored four against them that day and it served them right.

I played for Longford for four or five years. We were all best mates. Still are. The camaraderie was fantastic and I got a lot of the glory. I took all the free kicks, all the throw-ins, all the corners. I just bossed it all. I even took the goal-kicks. And I scored plenty of goals. I was never spotted by a scout from a league club, though. It took a fluke to get me noticed. My best mate's dad was an ambulance service chief inspector and one of his buddies was the physio at Walsall. That was my lucky break. That was the break that delivered me to Ray Train at Fellows Park.

But back then I thought football would always be playing a game with your mates. I never thought the enjoyment of it would wane. I think some remnant of that feeling and its association with my childhood support of Aston Villa brought me to Villa Park in the summer of 1997. I thought it would feel like coming home. I thought it would be the fulfilment of a boyhood dream to play for the club I had supported as a kid. In wilder moments I even wondered whether I might somehow re-create the glory days that Gary Shaw and Peter Withe had brought to the club in the early Eighties when they helped Villa win the league title and the European Cup.

But that was stupid. By the time I got to Villa, I was mentally shot to pieces already. I was having problems even though I hadn't a clue what they were. I was starting to feel tired and utterly worn out, even after routine training sessions. My struggle with depression was beginning in earnest. My years with Villa were to turn into the worst of my career.

I was starting to think more deeply about my life by the time I got to Villa. I was 26. I wasn't a kid any more. I wasn't a wide-eyed young boy. By the time I got to my mid-twenties, the realisation was starting to hit me that if going out and scoring a couple of goals in a football match was the only thing that could sustain me psychologically, the only thing that could give me satisfaction, then I was in a fucking mess. What sort of sad life is that when that's all you've got.

Scoring goals wasn't doing it for me any more. I just kept thinking 'get a life'. I scored two goals in my first match against Liverpool since I'd left Anfield and it didn't do anything for me. I scored two goals against a neanderthal who was baiting me with foul racist abuse throughout the game and it didn't move me. I scored two goals for a new manager, John Gregory, and it didn't matter to me. I sat in the dressing room afterwards, shaking with anger about what Steve Harkness had said to me, but I didn't feel any joy about the goals. I just felt flat. In fact, Gregory said afterwards that I looked fucking miserable.

But when you get into the prime of your life and you're still assessing whether your week has been good or bad on the basis of whether you've scored a goal or not, it's fucking sad. I knew I wasn't going to get any better by then. I knew I wasn't going to score more goals than I had been scoring. I knew that I needed to start looking for another solution apart from goals to nourish my life. No one changes that law in football: the older you get, the less goals you score.

I realised early on at Villa that I wasn't going to have the same kind of personal success that I had enjoyed at Forest and at Liverpool. I realised I had taken a step back. I realised, I suppose, that the best was over. And because my foot-ball career was dipping, because Villa are a club that can fall off the radar if they're not doing well, I gravitated towards a relationship that would keep me in the spotlight. And that was Ulrika.

In that first season at Villa, Ulrika was like a surrogate

career. Because things weren't going well at Villa I put a lot of effort into driving backwards and forwards to see her. Until then, I had always sought and received the reassurance I needed in my life from a football crowd or a coach, but when I was at Villa I could sense that the slow death of my football career had begun and that that support network was about to fall away.

Physically, I was still in good shape, but my edge had gone because I didn't feel comfortable being a footballer at that stage of my life. I didn't feel comfortable in my own skin. I felt inadequate. I felt there had to be something more to life than this. I was buzzing off other things all of a sudden, mainly the relationship with Ulrika. That was what sustained me, even though it was fucked up. It was a different kind of addiction to scoring goals. It turned into an addiction to scoring own goals.

What a mess. What a bloody mess Villa turned into. I've always been sad about that. I've always felt sad about the timing. Nothing went right. Everything went wrong. It was so many worlds away from the day when my sister, Lynne, took me to my first game as a belated seventh birthday treat in March 1978. She and her husband came round to our house and said they had a surprise for me. We sat in the lower tier of what is now the Doug Ellis Stand. Villa were playing Derby and I can remember vividly that Andy Gray had a header disallowed for offside. But the game finished 0–0, and in the second half I fell asleep. Perhaps that was an omen about how my two years playing for the club were going to turn out.

I only realised how high the expectations were about my

arrival at Villa when the pre-season build-up began in earnest in the Midlands. Villa had done well the previous season under Brian Little and had qualified for the UEFA Cup by finishing in fifth place, one below the Liverpool team I had played in. There was a strong spine to the team: Mark Bosnich in goal, Gareth Southgate and Ugo Ehiogu at the heart of defence, Andy Townsend in midfield and Dwight Yorke in attack. Once again, just like at Liverpool, my arrival was seen as the final piece of the jigsaw.

All the media coverage seemed to be about my home-coming. There was a romance about my return to my heart-land that seemed to catch everyone's imagination. Villa sold out their allocation of season tickets for the first time in 20 years. The *Wolverhampton Express & Star*, the biggest-selling of the local papers, produced a special pull-out to mark my debut.

I had bad vibes about Villa from the day I signed. Bad, bad vibes. It didn't feel right. It was a disaster from day one. I walked out onto the pitch for all the publicity shots and there was a board saying 'Aston Villa welcomes Stan Collymore' with photographers clustered all around it. But it wasn't the Villa Park I had known when I was a kid. It seemed different. It seemed emasculated. The terraces were gone. I was never going to see one of those eruptions of joy and mayhem from the Holte End that had given me such a buzz when I was a kid. Putting seats where the terraces had once been had changed the whole character of the place, just as it had at other grounds around the country. It didn't feel like coming home, even before things started to go wrong. It didn't feel romantic. Not to me. It just felt like a mistake.

In Liverpool, the supporters had been knowledgeable, optimistic, cheeky and passionate. In the Midlands, it's the Wolves and West Brom fans who are the heart of the Black Country support and Birmingham fans dominate the city itself. But at Villa, one week you can get 20,000 turning up to watch and the next week you can get 48,000. They are very fickle. Most of the new supporters that had jumped on the bandwagon because I was arriving were Range Rover drivers from Worcestershire who brought the kids. They didn't have a clue about football. They were the ancestors of Roy Keane's prawn-sandwich brigades.

I looked around at the Villa playing staff and there was no comparison with Liverpool. I realised they had overachieved the season before. In terms of strength in depth and general quality they were way behind Liverpool. I knew then I was going to have to work a lot harder for a lot less ball and a lot fewer goals. I was already feeling I should have stuck it out at Liverpool because my chances of winning something there would have been a lot better.

Villa went on a pre-season tour of America and I scored on my debut against the Los Angeles Galaxy in the Rose Bowl in Pasadena. But when we got back to England it was clear that something was drastically wrong. Brian Little was determined to play a 4–3–3 system with me, Yorkie and Savo Milosevic up front, but it was clear that the players were confused by it and that it wasn't going to work in the Premiership.

We had a stinking pre-season in Scotland. We played at Motherwell and Partick Thistle with Savo playing just off me and Yorkie and it was crap. We couldn't figure the system out at all. But Little stuck with it. Everyone had deep misgivings but everyone seemed to hope that somehow, magically, it would just come good when the real action started and the Premiership began. Well, it didn't.

I made my debut in our first game away at Leicester City. The match reports from Filbert Street that day say that I was marked out of the game by Steve Walsh. The Leicester fans sang lustily about what a waste of money I was. Ian Marshall, the guy who was to become my mate when I joined the club a couple of years later, grabbed the winner. And that was it: the season had started with a whimper and I knew it wasn't going to get better any time soon.

The first home game was against Blackburn Rovers. It was an evening game and the radio talk-show hosts were still bright and breezy about my Villa Park debut as I listened to them on the drive in to the stadium from Cannock. That soon changed. We lost 0–4. Chris Sutton, another who shared with me the distinction of once having been England's most expensive player, scored a hat-trick. They slaughtered us. Every time either Stuart Ripley or Jason Wilcox got the ball on the flanks, they seemed to be in about 40 yards of space. The 4–3–3 system was turning into a farce.

Next up was Newcastle at St James's Park. We only lost that 0–1. I was booked for having a scuffle with David Batty, and Villa were firmly rooted to the bottom of the table. I scored my first goal for the club in the 3–2 defeat to Tottenham at White Hart Lane a few days later but it wasn't enough to prevent Villa recording their worst start to a season in their proud history. What a way to join a new club. What a difference I had made.

We finally got a win against Leeds at Villa Park in the next match, courtesy of a second-half winner from Dwight Yorke. I missed a couple of sitters. We beat Barnsley as well. Everybody beat Barnsley that season. But there was still discontent in the dressing room with the way things were going, and the tensions came to a head after we had fought out a dull goalless draw with Bordeaux at the Parc Lescure in a UEFA Cup first-round tie.

I didn't have a great game. I was subdued. I didn't get much service and the match reports said I appeared disillusioned and disinterested. They were partly right. I wasn't feeling good. I was at odds with myself. I was feeling drained by my depression. But I didn't stop trying. I stopped to do a television interview on the pitch at the end of the game, and as I was wandering back towards the dressing room one of the lads came out and said the other boys were slagging me off inside. Apparently they were moaning about how I hadn't been pulling my weight, how I was dragging the rest of the team down. They wanted me for their scapegoat. So I went in there and I confronted them with it. 'If anybody has got anything to say,' I told them, 'have the balls to say it to my face. Don't fucking say it with snide little remarks when I'm not here.' Nobody said anything. Everybody looked down at their boots.

My relationship with Yorkie went downhill after that. I think he thought I was pointing the finger at him in particular. Which I wasn't. He and Mark Bosnich were the governors among the players. They were Little's lieutenants. They were his favourites. Generally, after that incident in Bordeaux, the rest of the lads were happy to let me carry the can for the fact that none of them were performing on the pitch under Brian Little. I was accused of disrupting the formula on the pitch and affecting the lads off it because I was going out with Ulrika. God knows how that was supposed to affect them, but anyway, it did, apparently.

There should have been some collective responsibility for the way the results were going but there wasn't. It was all down to me, that was the impression they tried to give. I never forgave some people in that dressing room for hanging me out to dry. All I did from then on was come in, train and go home. I didn't get nasty and shout and rave and argue with them. I didn't say anything but I never forgot it.

The season lurched on in a state of barely disguised crisis. We lost 3–0 on my return to Anfield towards the end of September and the discord within the club was there for all to see. Brian Little substituted Ian Taylor and Tayls just stormed past him down the tunnel. I was roundly booed by the home fans. Obviously. I missed a decent chance with a glancing header and Jamo made a couple of great saves when I might have scored.

It was strange playing against the lads. The team was still similar to when I had been there. The big difference was that Michael Owen was starting now. He won a second-half penalty that Robbie Fowler converted. They'd also brought in Karl-Heinz Riedle, the veteran German striker. He scored Liverpool's third that evening. There was no sign they were missing me. I wasn't really up for the game anyway. I was flat.

A couple of weeks later I was sent off in the last minute of a 1–0 win at Bolton. I swapped a couple of punches with Andy Todd, a talentless prick who was living off his dad's name.

Some sons of former players, like Jamie Redknapp and Frank Lampard, have got talent of their own. They deserve their place in the sport. Others don't. Colin Todd was a player. Andy Todd wasn't. He wasn't good enough to be on the same pitch as me.

Actually, he was one of three players who quite clearly saw it as their mission in life to prove that they were real hard men when they were up against me. The other two were Darren Purse, of Birmingham City, and Andy Morrison, a journey-man squaddie of a centre half who played for Manchester City when they were in the First Division and got fucked off as soon as they made it back into the Premiership.

They had no talent. None. Their only way of stopping me was a bit of verbal, a bit of afters and that was it. Andy Todd just got under my skin a little bit too much that day at Bolton. I felt like saying to him: 'I am so much better than you that I am doing you a real favour playing against you today.'

Those guys should just have been watching me at work. They should have been standing there with their mouths hanging open in awe.They should have been learning. They were so rude. Morrison even stuck his tongue in my mouth when I was out on loan at Fulham and City came to Craven Cottage. As for Purse, I think he got a bit carried away with all the excitement of me coming back to Birmingham for the first time since I had left Villa. Poor little lad got a bit over-excited. I mean, how would you feel if Darren Purse came up to you and told you you were shit. I said: 'Darren, do me a favour, mate. I've knocked out bigger blokes to get into a fight.'

* * *

The season lurched on. Brian Little fell out with Gareth Southgate as well as Sasa Curcic. In October we lost at home to Wimbledon and away to West Ham. The only thing that was redeeming us at all was a UEFA Cup run. We beat Atletico Bilbao to get to the third round and then Steaua Bucharest to get to the fourth. But in the league, it got to December and I still hadn't scored since that solitary strike at Spurs. I still hadn't scored at Villa Park.

I thought I scored once. I ran all the way over to Brian Little to give him a hug after a header went into the net against Everton but I hadn't seen the linesman's flag go up for offside against Savo Milosevic. Eventually I ended the drought against Coventry on 6 December, but that first goal at home was cold comfort. It was 1,223 minutes since that goal at Spurs. Or 14 games. Whichever way you looked at it, it was the longest I had ever gone without scoring a goal.

By January, the fans were restless. They booed us off the park after an FA Cup third-round-replay win over Portsmouth. 'You're not fit to wear our shirts,' they were singing. We responded by losing 5–0 at Blackburn a few days later. When Coventry beat us for the first time ever at Villa Park and knocked us out of the Cup on Valentine's Day, the writing was on the wall for the manager.

You could tell the end was coming for Little. In his last two or three weeks he became really insular. He didn't really speak to us at all. It was as if he was paralysed by the tension. His body language was incredibly negative. He was hunched up. He seemed to want to shrink inside his tracksuit. Training sessions were made up as they went along, and Allan Evans, Little's assistant, came more to the fore.

off and on and feeling more and more hemmed in by criticism and exhaustion. My way out would have been a solid run in the team, but I was in and out of the side, partly through injury, partly through the caprice of Gregory. I started the third game of the season against Sheffield Wednesday and played the last five minutes against Derby at the end of September. But that was the limit of my contribution to Villa's best start to the season since the Second World War. In the UEFA Cup, Gregory gave me my fourth start since he had arrived and I scored a hat-trick against the Norwegian side Strømsgodset.

Paul Merson had arrived from Middlesbrough by then, bought for £6.75 million. He made the kind of start I wish I could have made. Dion Dublin was signed from Coventry, too. He scored seven goals in his first three games. Villa seemed to be unstoppable but I felt I was being marginalised. I started a few games but usually I was either a substitute or I was substituted. Gregory seemed to favour Julian Joachim and Dion as his first-choice starting pair and I felt lower and lower. I did some research that showed that Dion and I were actually the most successful of the partnership combinations in terms of assists and goals scored. I compiled reams and reams of statistics to show Gregory but I never took them in. I knew he wouldn't pay them any attention.

Our unbeaten league record lasted until 21 November when my old pal Harkness came calling with Liverpool. It took me all of eight minutes to try and cripple him. I did a pretty good job, really. He was carried off and I only got a yellow card. One match report said I was 'back to my surly, simmering worst'. Midway through the second half I gave

Owen a shove and got sent off. Cue the Harry Enfield 'Calm Down' impersonation for the benefit of my apoplectic friends in the Liverpool end.

That heralded another run of inconsistent selections from Gregory. Because Dion had a groin injury, I started the FA Cup third-round tie against Hull City and scored two in a 3–0 win. I was left out for the next match, a league match at Middlesbrough, and then brought on at half-time for Dion in the next home game against Everton, which we also won 3–0. It was 16 January. My twenty-eighth birthday was six days away. Estelle wanted me to have a party. I wanted to die.

By then I could hardly climb the stairs at my house in Symphony Court in Birmingham city centre. I was in a constant state of exhaustion. When I tried to lift my head off the pillow in the mornings it felt like it was pinned there by a block of concrete. I had no energy. I was in despair. I felt surrounded. I felt people were looking at me like I was some kind of monster after what had happened in Paris. I felt my dream of being a football hero had gurgled away into the sewers. I felt I would never be worshipped by football fans again. I couldn't get any enjoyment out of anything. I couldn't feel anything. I felt as if my life was ebbing away.

I said no to the party. I couldn't face seeing my friends. So on the evening of my birthday, Estelle and I sat in my three-storey townhouse and I watched telly like a zombie. And as I sat staring at a screen that may as well have been blank, I suddenly realised that I had to do something about the way I was feeling. I realised I couldn't go on like this because my life wasn't worth living. We were due to play at home against Fulham the next day in the FA Cup fourth round. I would probably have started because Dion was cup-tied. But I knew by then I wasn't going to make it.

I rang Jim Walker, the physio, who was a guy I trusted, and told him I was struggling and that I needed help. We met in the car park at Sutton Coldfield station and he told me about a psychiatrist who had done a lot of work with Paul McGrath when he was battling alcoholism and other problems. Jim arranged for me to meet the guy at Wood-bourne Priory in Birmingham early the next morning, the day of the game.

I showed up. I told him I had very low self-esteem. I told him how low I was physically. I felt I couldn't think straight. I was constantly exhausted. His answer wasn't quite what I was expecting. He said: 'Dion's cup-tied, isn't he?' I said 'yeah'. He said: 'It's more than likely you'll start the game then, isn't it.' I just looked at him this time. 'Get yourself a couple of goals and you'll probably be fine,' he said. Marvellous. The miracles of modern fucking medicine. It was just a fucking cop-out. It was the club trying to sweep it under the carpet.

So I went out into the corridor. There was a magazine lying on one of the tables in the waiting room about Roehampton Priory in London. I was vaguely aware of it. I had heard of celebrities like Kate Moss having treatment for addictions or depression there. So I rang Paul Stretford and said I wanted to get checked in. He said it would just be glitzy American bollocks. He said they'd be feeding me grapes and fanning my ego all day. He said they'd just be filling my head full of shit. I didn't know then, of course, that he was representing Gregory as well. I told him to sort it out. I told him I needed help immediately.

I told Jim Walker there and then that I couldn't play that afternoon. I'd been telling him that since the night before. I had reached the end. He said he'd tell Gregory. When he'd spoken to him, he rang me and said there was no problem. I went home and slumped onto the sofa and started letting Sky Sports wash over me. After a while I got ready to drive down to London. They were already reporting that I had been spotted leaving Villa Park in a huff because I had found out I wasn't in the starting line-up for the Fulham game. Of course, I hadn't been anywhere near Villa Park. It was just the beginning of a brutal propaganda war the club played with me.

So the Villa fans thought I was a prima donna. They thought I'd just got the hump. They thought I wasn't proud to pull on the shirt. All that sort of stuff. And Stretford and I compounded it. We dealt with it very badly. He released a statement saying I was suffering from stress. That was bound to make people feel I was being a tart, because who doesn't have stress? He should just have stated the bald truth. I was in the grip of major bouts of clinical depression. I couldn't play. I wasn't mentally fit to play. Somehow I think Stretford thought that sounded too dire. I think he thought footballers would laugh at me for that.

The following Monday, *The Sun* showed their compassion just like they were to do with Frank Bruno several years later. They slaughtered me on their back page with a '*Sun* Says' editorial about how badly I'd let the Villa supporters down. They said the fans should ostracise me and the club should kick me out. Foolishly, I had been expecting at least a little sympathy. But this kind of stuff was beyond my worst nightmares. It felt like I was a bear being baited.

I stopped in to see Doug Ellis before I went to London. He wasn't much better. 'Fucking hell,' he said, 'we're paying your wages and you're off on holiday for a month.' He said the club wouldn't pay my hospital bills. Then his mood brightened. He'd thought of something he figured might persuade me everything would be all right without having treatment. He had some personal insight he wanted to give me. He said his wife had also been upset recently. I nearly said to him 'I'm not fucking surprised,' but I resisted. Doug said: 'I said to her just like I'm saying to you now, "just pull your socks up and get on with it".' I expected that kind of thing from him because he was an older bloke. Still, I couldn't help feeling sorry for his wife. Married to Doug Ellis. It doesn't get much worse than that.

Six days after the Fulham game, Estelle drove me down to the Priory in Roehampton, southwest London. I was apprehensive when she dropped me off. It's a huge, elegant white building, nicely kept on the outside. On the outside it looks a bit like a palace. On the inside there is no doubting what sort of establishment it is. It is a hospital. More than that, it is a hospital for the mentally ill.

There are no frills. My room in the West Wing was spartan. There was a smallish bed; a simple pine wardrobe; a still-life, mass-produced print of some pressed flowers hanging on the wall. A bathroom that was bare and felt cold. It was like a room in a budget hotel. It felt cheerless and soulless and I felt very alone. I think there were bars on my window, too. That's certainly how I remember it. But maybe that was just the way I was feeling.

Depressives like me were kept in the big house. We shared it with women who had weight-loss problems. All the therapy rooms were there, too. In the grounds there was a separate house where the drugs and alcohol people were. There were common rooms, too. Not much in them. An old fridge in the corner. A couple of foul-tasting bottles of some sort of cordial in a whitewashed cupboard. A television playing. People watching aimlessly.

I went back there five years later, after the dogging incident. Just for one night. I remembered how intense and claustrophobic it could be. I wandered into one of the communal rooms that time, too, and found four or five patients in there. One had tattoos all the way up his arm. Another was Arab. There were a couple of women. The television was on, as usual. No one was watching. The air in there was clammy with tension. One man was laughing nervously. A woman rebuked him. She said laughter was a sign of an empty soul.

It was a bit like that the first time in the hours after Estelle had driven away. It was full of sights and sounds that were foreign to me, things that made me feel uncomfortable. There was one woman who cut and burned herself. A few hours after I arrived I saw her giggling madly and doing cartwheels down the corridor. For a long time I wondered why somebody would mutilate themselves like that, but before I left she told me what drove her to do it. 'It's because I can actually feel something,' she said.

On my first full day I went to sit in the smoking area. There was a woman in a trance, walking around. Aware of nothing. Noticing nothing. She was called Pam. I thought she looked like a zombie. I thought she was beyond help. I was full of my own prejudices and preconceived ideas about mental illness, too. I looked around me and I caught myself thinking that I wasn't quite as nutty as this one or that one. I tried to console myself with what I thought was my relative sanity.

I was asked to sit in a discussion group. Just people talking about how they felt and why they thought they felt that way. It was a mixed bag. An American businessman, a girl from the Black Country worn down by devoting herself to a legal practice, a woman with postnatal depression. The Canadian cartwheeler, who was as fit as fuck. There was a tabloid newspaper reporter, a door-stepper whose job had got to her. One of the Liverpool players had rumped her sister. She was always very nervous and sweaty. And there was a columnist from another national newspaper, a man who had been devastated by the recent death of his wife.

The cornerstone of my treatment was Cognitive Behavioural Therapy. In the three weeks I was an in-patient there, we would have a CBT session every morning at about eleven o'clock. The aim was for the therapist to try to challenge all the negative thoughts that were spewing out of us. They wanted to challenge our low self-esteem. They asked how I felt, and when, invariably, I said I felt like shit or I felt like I was scum, I was asked to try to rationalise why I felt like that. Why, at that moment, did I feel so worthless? What had I done to make myself feel so repulsed by what I was? The therapist kept pointing out that all I was doing was sitting in the midst of a group of people who felt similarly damaged. What was so bad about all of us? It was an attempt to try to train your brain into thinking more positive thoughts. It was an attempt to purge some of the negativity from every waking moment.

The day of the depressive in the Priory is less structured than that of the addict. The addict is monitored every minute of every hour. He is kept busy. He is in groups all day long. I had more free time than that. I spent hours sitting in my room, thinking. But I did other things, too. There was drama therapy two or three times a week. There might be a group of ten of us in the room and the therapist would ask us to arrange our chairs in the order in which we perceived our own worthlessness. If someone sat at the back it meant they felt they were the lowest of the low.

On my first day, my initial group-session wasn't scheduled until 3 p.m. so I was sent out on a walk with some of the people from the drugs and alcohol unit. I strolled around Richmond Park listening to a woman telling me her story, about how she had started going out with a guy who was dealing cocaine. She hadn't taken any herself for nearly six months, but when she started she went mad for it. She kept it in the utility room in their flat, disguised in a packet of Persil on top of the washing machine. She was doing a cup of cocaine a day by the time she checked herself into the Priory.

Twice a week I would have a two-hour session with my one-on-one counsellor, a guy called Dr Mark Collins. The rest of the time, we all chatted in the smoking room, sharing our experiences. I got friendly with the newspaper columnist. He said again and again how his life had fallen apart when his wife died, but how the pain his depression caused him was even worse. He was having electro-convulsive therapy that blitzed his memory. So before each session he would write stuff down on a notepad and get me to keep it for him when he came out so he could get some of those memories back. He only wanted the good ones.

I shagged a couple of the birds in there. Both of them were in my CBT group. Funnily enough, they told me they thought I was a sex addict at that point. I didn't disagree with them. There was another bird who wanted to shag me. She was an NHS referral. She was convinced she was the Princess of Egypt. She told me I looked like her son. Then, once, when I was in the smoking room with the rest of the group, she just came up to me and grabbed me. 'Oh, I love your dick,' she said. I just told her to fuck off. There's a first time for everything, I suppose.

Eric Clapton came in to see me once. I was a bit nervous about meeting him but when he arrived he was wearing jeans and a hooded top. He looked like Wayne or Waynetta. I told him I'd shagged a lot of birds. He told me about everything he had done during the 30 years he had been on the road with a rock band. And you name it, he seemed to have done it. First of all, it was women that had done it for him. Then drugs, alcohol, even food. He said he'd done it all. We talked for about an hour. I felt honoured that he'd made that kind of effort for someone he didn't know.

The biggest thing I learned from The Priory is how fragile the mental health of a lot of people can be. It's like a Buckaroo. Stick enough things on it and eventually it's going to kick its legs up and all those things are going to fly off all over the place. That was the overriding lesson for me. Everyone that was in that depression unit was just a normal person once.

It was full of high-functioning graphic designers, television people, PR people, people who had been fried by working to deadlines. They had all tried to think themselves out of trouble rather than just step back.

It taught me that in theory I had to stop storing everything up in a little box at the back of my mind, kidding myself that I would deal with it another day. That way, it builds up into a mountain of trouble. I just tried to deal with stuff as it arose. I started eating healthily, avoiding positions where people could take advantage of me. I felt I could actively avoid making harmful decisions. It was like I was resetting my mind. Rather than driving along thinking to myself, 'you're shit and you'll always be shit, why does anyone bother with you', I tried to latch on to some self-worth.

For a while, it worked. While I was in the Priory I started to feel better. I started to feel like all the shared experiences were beginning to purge me of some of my negativity. Sharing everything, blurting it all out, somehow articulating all these dark secrets that had been hiding in the shadows of my mind, was a release. It bought me a bit of time but I didn't stick it out for nearly long enough. They wanted me to do the sex-addiction course but I couldn't bear to see it through and football began to suck me back in.

I had been an in-patient at the Priory for 17 days when my mobile phone rang while I was doing a bit of grocery shopping in Richmond High Street and I heard Jim Walker's voice at the other end. 'The gaffer really needs you in the squad for the game against Leeds tomorrow night,' he said. 'Are you up for it?' Instinctively, I said I was, but even in that

Ray Train in his playing days with Carlisle. He was a success there but as Walsall youth team coach, he made my life a misery.

Wolves manager Graham Turner broke my heart when he let me go: he blamed my attitude to training.

Steve Coppell was only a small guy but he had real authority when I played for him at Crystal Palace.

Jokerman: Palace coach Steve Harrison in a typically bizarre attempt to get a laugh before his sense of humour got him in trouble.

Palace coup: Palace gave me my first shot at the big time even if it never quite worked out for me there.

Mark Bright, Ian Wright and Andy Gray helped Palace to third place in the old First Division in my first season there.

Wrighty was a terrific character but he felt threatened by me – no wonder, when you look at the state of that moustache.

Making my name: I loved my time at Southend. They gave me some of the happiest times of my career.

Shouting the odds: Barry Fry was never a shrinking violet but he was brilliant to work for.

Scoring again for Southend: what I achieved there gave me a confidence that never left me.

Signing for Forest with manager Frank Clark: he rebuilt the club after the Brian Clough years.

Scoring for Forest in my first season there: my goals helped them back up into the Premier League.

Jason Lee and that pineapple on his head: he became a target for terrace taunts because of his hairstyle.

Bryan Roy and I celebrating a goal: we worked so well together, we took Forest near to the Premiership summit.

Flying after another goal for Forest: celebrating with Alf Inge Haaland who I decked in a training-ground row.

Left: A lot of people regarded Forest as a one-man-band when I was there. It didn't do me any favours.

Above: Me with agent Paul Stretford: once I thought there was nothing that was beyond him but our relationship soured.

Sir Alex Ferguson gets his man: only trouble is, it wasn't me, it was Andy Cole.

The Nottingham *Evening Post* was convinced. So was I. The man who mattered had other ideas.

COLLYMORE 'WILL SIGN FOR UNITED'

Stories about Stan Collymore's future continue to dog Nottingham Forest. So what is likely to happen to the £7m-rated striker? IAN EDWARDS, the Evening Post's City Ground reporter for the past five years, gives an authoritative insight into the Collymore saga.

Story of Stan's season so far . . .

HAVE BOOTS, WILL TRAVEL : Stan Collymore's future at Nottingham remains more in doubt than ever

Above: Scoring one of my frequent goals against Manchester United: Gary Pallister could never get near me.

Left: Signing for Liverpool: Roy Evans was a lovely bloke but he wasn't strong enough to control our Liverpool team.

Dream start: celebrating with Steve McManaman after scoring the winner on my Liverpool debut against Sheffield Wednesday.

Steve McManaman, Robbie Fowler and me after Macca scores against Villa in March 1996.

Fab Four: Macca's John, Rob Jones is Paul McCartney, I'm Ringo and Jason McAteer is George.

Pretty Spice: Jamie Redknapp was a good looking lad who was at the heart of the Spice Boys scene.

instant I was aware that this was a bizarre thing to be trying. It was going to be one of the weirdest experiments in football history.

I drove up to the Midlands in my Range Rover, and I was so stoned on Prozac it was like an out-of-body experience. I was hovering above the car looking at myself driving the Range Rover. I couldn't believe it when I got to Villa Park and they told me Gregory had put me on the bench. I hadn't trained for three weeks. I'd done a few shuttle runs in Richmond Park. That was it. But it got even better. There were 72 minutes gone when Gregory hauled Dion off and told me to have a run.

I felt like the Readybrek Kid. I felt like there was this kind of glow all around me. Between me and reality there was this kind of force-field. It felt so fucking weird. I remember thinking as I crossed the white line that this was going to be the most fucked-up, bizarre experience I had ever had. I mean, I'd been in a mental hospital for two and a half weeks, constructing and deconstructing myself in smoke-filled rooms, pouring out my feelings, listening to harrowing stories of despair and repair, and yet here I was, out of my mind, running out onto a football pitch on a Tuesday night in front of 40,000 screaming, yelling fans.

I played another 14 minutes the following Saturday against Wimbledon, and, gradually, with the approval of the club, I settled into a routine where I would attend the Priory on an out-patient basis, attending sessions at the hospital on Tuesday, Wednesday and Thursday and then attaching myself to the club for the weekend. Mostly, I was made to train with the kids, but I loved that. In a strange kind of way they

looked up to me, and I responded to that. It was a new experience for me. I still count people like Gareth Barry and
Darren Byfield as my friends today.

But the first-team squad weren't quite so accepting. Nor
were Doug Ellis and John Gregory. After that first game back
against Leeds, Gregory told me it would be a good idea if I sat
down with the lads and explained to them what had been
happening because some of them were pissed off with me.
'Pissed off about what?' I said. He just said he thought
it would be a good idea if I apologised to them. 'Apologised
for what?' I said.

It turned out that Gareth Southgate forced the issue on me.
I walked into the dressing room before training that day and
he was staring over at me. 'Where the fuck have you been?'
he said. Nice, friendly, gentlemanly Gareth. I found it hard to
believe no one had read where I was but I explained to
Gareth, in similarly confrontational terms, that I'd been in the
Priory receiving treatment for severe depression.

Mark Bosnich seemed embarrassed. He said no one was
having a go at me, it was just that they were all concerned
about where I'd been. Ironic, that, given what he's been
through himself in the past couple of years. For me, though,
sitting in front of those 20 lads like that and explaining something that made me feel so vulnerable was one of the most
difficult and uncomfortable things I have ever had to do.

Don't think I got any support from anybody like Gareth.
And don't think I got any help from Paul Merson either, even
though he should have been better placed than anyone to give
me some advice. I was expecting a few words from him. I was
expecting a bit of empathy, at least. But I got nothing. He

was never helpful in the slightest. I didn't get a pulse from him at all. I think it was because by then Gregory was openly criticising me and Merse didn't have the balls to align himself with me in any way. He was very much Gregory's man at that stage and we very rarely spoke to each other. In fact, he was right up there with Gareth and the rest of the crew who would say 'fuck Stan off, he's a waste of time'. We never came to loggerheads but he never looked at me and I never looked at him.

The only time I ever heard anything he had to say was when he gave a talk to some of the apprentices about the things he had been through. I was training with the kids by then and I respected what he did because he was giving them the benefit of his advice. Apart from that, I had no time for him. For somebody who had gone through what he had gone through, he showed me no empathy whatsoever. He had no excuse because he should have had an insight into what I was dealing with.

Compared to Gregory, of course, Merse was a saint with a fucking halo round his head. Gregory quickly grew into the persecutor in chief. He dropped any pretence of supporting me as soon as I went into the Priory and he was relentless in his criticism of me and in his utter failure to understand what I was going through. That failure was wilful. At the bottom of it, I think he resented somebody else taking the attention away from him.

He gave one of his round of interviews to the press soon after I had come out of the Priory. 'I have been at this club 12 months,' he said. 'Ten months of that has been spent trying to protect Stan, trying to get the best out of him, concerning myself with non-football-related matters. It's not as if I haven't given the big man every chance. I gather he is suffering from mental depression, but once he gets the full all-clear and comes back to work, he has to do the business. He has run out of chances with everybody. It's not just me he has run out of chances with. It's the entire club: players, directors and supporters.

'I have never believed he needed to have counselling. I'm very anti the whole situation but I've inherited it and I've just got to get on with it the best way possible. We all turn up and run around on the training ground, get a sweat on, and then on a Saturday afternoon we go out and try and kick lumps out of the opposition and try and win games. That's all he is being asked to do. As simple as that. When I hear about his depression I just think about the third-division pro coming to the end of his contract with a wife and kids to support.'

One thing you need to know about John Gregory: he never had the bollocks to say any of these things to me in private. That's because he was gutless. When I went to talk to him about it in his office, he couldn't look me in the eye. He could never look me in the eye. He just kept looking down at his desk, with his flip-flops on and his legs crossed and his fucking Springsteen memorabilia everywhere, saying, 'Well, Stan . . .', 'But you see, Stan . . .', like a fucking dick. In terms of man-management, he was a neanderthal.

In that meeting, I told him what it was like for me. I said climbing up the stairs after training was like pushing the Titanic with a powerboat engine. I told him if nine good things happened to me in one day and one bad thing, I would still concentrate on the solitary negative thing. I told him that maybe if more people realised how many times I came into training when I was running on empty, perhaps people would have had a bit more respect. He regurgitated all that verbatim for the press. He paid a bit of lip service to it because he had got such a coating in elements of the media for the insensitivity he had shown about depression.

The funny thing was, I never had a row with him. He was a chirpy cockney and I wasn't comfortable around him, but he always pretended nothing was wrong. It was always business as usual. It was as if there had never been a problem. It was as if he was living in two parallel worlds, and whenever there was a possibility of confrontation he would retreat into his happy world where nothing was ever bad.

The reality was that his little sound bite about what depression meant to him had struck a chord with the average bloke. 'How can a bloke be depressed if he is sitting on a pile of a cash?' they all said. A joke started doing the rounds at Villa Park. *How does Stan Collymore change a light bulb? He holds it in the air and the world revolves around him.* So I had to do all the chat shows then, defending myself. Am I immune from breaking my leg? No. Am I immune from getting cancer? No. Well then, I am not immune from depression either. I felt shot full of holes and criticism seeped into me like water, dragging me down into the depths.

My season crawled on like slow death. I started my first game since 2 January on 10 March, a 2–1 away defeat to Derby. Villa were in freefall by then, in the midst of a run of eight defeats in nine games that torpedoed our season. I never saw the end of that run, which finally came to a halt with a win against Southampton in the middle of April. I played a full game against Spurs at White Hart Lane, and then, on 21 March, I started the home game against Chelsea. We lost 0–3. It was a fitting epitaph for my Villa career.

There was something poignant about that match and its aftermath. Something must have told me it was the last time I would play for the club I had supported as a boy. I had brought my son, Tom, along. He was three then, and after the match we wandered around on the pitch at Villa Park as darkness fell and the lights in the private boxes were being turned off. I looked up and saw someone in one of the boxes and they waved. Tom asked me if this was the garden that I played on.

Soon after that I was sitting in my room at the Halkin Hotel, where I stayed in London when I was having treatment at the Priory, and I read on Teletext that Gregory had decided I could no longer train part-time with the club. He had tired of that arrangement, presumably because he knew I was responding well to it. I was enjoying training with the youth team. I was starting to feel pin-pricks of enjoyment returning to my football, but the control-freak in Gregory just couldn't accept that. He said I had to return to full-time treatment.

After that he tried everything he could to rid himself of me. He latched on to a newspaper story that claimed I'd been partying with the rest of the inmates at the Priory and doing drugs and going on drinking binges. It was complete bollocks but I had to attend a meeting in a Birmingham hotel with Doug Ellis and Gregory and the FA's compliance officer, Graham Bean. Villa said they wanted my contract terminated because the story proved I had been doing drugs and partying at their expense. I offered to do a drugs test. The club took me up on the offer. It was negative.

Stretford was desperately touting me around by then. At the end of the season, Doug Ellis suggested that I trained all through the summer to give myself a fighting chance of being fit for the start of the next season. I reminded him that it had been his decision to send me back to the Priory full-time and I had been involved in draining therapy day in and day out and I needed a holiday.

I went to New York and I trained in the gym opposite the Michelangelo Hotel just off Broadway. I went to the gym every day and all I ate each day for two weeks was sultanas and fruit. When I went back for pre-season training I was 13 st 5 lb, the thinnest I had ever been. I was fit and pumped and ready to make a real go of it again at Villa. But I got back to England to find that I had not even been given a squad number.

Stretford hawked me around. First it was a trip to Athens to talk to Panathinaikos. Then it was three months on loan at Fulham. I enjoyed that, up to a point. I scored a goal against West Brom in the quarter-final of the League Cup. Had a decent laugh in the dressing room with guys I liked, such as Chris Coleman.

There were two female physios at the club. I was like a dog with two dicks. I spent a lot of time on the treatment table. Apart from massages, I enjoyed the goal at the Hawthorns. I always scored at West Brom, so when I came off the bench I knew I was going to shove one up them. Their supporters were all beside themselves with glee and hate when I came on.

'You fucking woman-beater', all that kind of stuff. 'You Wolves wanker.'

I only got ten minutes at the end. Paul Peschisolido swung over a beautiful cross and I buried it with a bullet header into the top corner. That made me fucking laugh. I went over to the Birmingham Road End where all the West Brom meat-heads grunt out their primitive-man sounds and I started shouting at them. 'I always fucking score against you,' I was yelling. It was sheer bliss. All those arms and fingers pointing at me, all those voices screaming abuse and me screaming back at them. They must really hate me at the Albion.

When the spell at Fulham ended without a permanent move, my attitude was still that unless I had a good place to go to I was going to sit tight, because I had done absolutely fuck-all wrong. It was a case of waiting for the right oppor-tunity. Bradford offered me a good contract, the one they later offered to Beni Carbone, but I turned it down. Then, in November 1999, Martin O'Neill rang and I didn't need any second bidding. I signed for him. I signed for Leicester.

When I look back now, part of me despairs that my time at the club I once loved should have been so wretched. Part of me laughs a bitter laugh at the duplicity of Gregory. I met him one last time before I went. We bumped into each other in one of the corridors at Villa Park. He was the chirpy pain in the arse he always was, acting like he'd always wanted the best for me. 'Good luck, son,' he said. 'Martin's a great bloke. You'll have a real laugh there.' Martin thought Gregory was a cunt, by the way.

Through all the murk there are still one or two consola-tions. I made some good friends. Gary 'Charlo' Charles, who has been brought so low by alcoholism, was a terrific bloke. A genuinely funny guy. I hope he gets his life back one day. I hope he gets his family back. Mark Draper was the same. A man you could trust. Alan Wright was another. In fact, if I could choose eleven footballers to come to my funeral – and I wouldn't want more than that – Villa players would be well represented.

Charlo would be there. And Drapes. And Gareth Barry, Darren Byfield, Lee Hendrie, Michael Oakes and Alan Wright. With them, I'd want Jamie Redknapp, Jamie Moralee, the black Andy Gray and Mark Bright. Eleven good men at my wake. And a place in a purgatory far away at the ends of the earth for John Gregory.

CHAPTER SEVEN

PARIS 1998:
THE ULRIKA AFFAIR

The way it started summed up the whole cursed affair. A shallow attraction between two narcissists, only interested in the other because each was in the public eye. Celebrity eating itself again. Drawn to each other by something as worthless as fame and reputation. And what a sorry advert for football and showbiz we turned out to be.

I had been feeling pretty pleased with myself because I was going out on a date with Ulrika Jonsson, the famous television presenter. I pulled up outside the Hyatt Hotel in Birmingham in my big, flash footballer's Mercedes with its blacked-out windows, pumped up with machismo and confidence, feeling like I was moving up to a different level of woman with this one.

I saw her wander up to the car looking a bit uncertain. She opened the passenger door and peered in. 'Am I meant to be with you?' she said. She didn't even know what I looked like and yet she'd said she would go out for lunch with me. Presumably because she knew I was a footballer. When I think back to that now, it still sends a chill through me. The superficiality of that. The sadness of that.

How easy it seems now to draw a line from that moment to the instant I hit her in the back room of the Auld Alliance. How easy it seems now to predict that this would be the relationship that would finish me as a footballer and destroy my reputation. I had always been a crowd favourite before I hit Ulrika. Suddenly, I was a villain. I was an abuser. I was a target for barracking and abuse. I was the antithesis of what I wanted to be, a squeaky-clean crowd favourite like Michael Owen or Alan Shearer. And that killed me off.

In the tabloids, I was the black monster and she was the white angel. I can understand that. I did something dreadfully wrong, something that I will never be able to come to terms with properly. A relationship conceived in raging egocentricity degenerated into a tormented and protracted argument between two damaged people and wound its way inevitably towards that conflagration in a Sodom and Gomorrah of a cramped little pub full of shit-faced Scottish football fans.

Anyway, if she was drawn to celebrity for celebrity's sake, I wasn't much better. I was feeling unsure of myself. It was the August of 1997, I had just joined Aston Villa from Liverpool and I knew I had taken a step down. Somehow, going out with somebody famous, going out with Ulrika, restored some of my self-belief. It made me feel important when I could sense for the first time that my shelf life as a top-rate footballer was running out fast.

I'd been out with her once before, although she didn't know it. A couple of weeks before that first date, not long after I had joined Villa, my team-mate Ugo Ehiogu had phoned me while I was sitting in my local in Cannock. I'd been to London for the weekend with him and Dwight Yorke but now he was ringing to say there was a *Gladiators* end-of-run party in Birmingham if I wanted to go along. I remember joking with my mates in the pub that Ulrika might be there because they all fancied her. So we drove to the Hyatt in the city centre and wandered in. I saw Ulrika straight away. Five or six of the Gladiators were there, too: Rhino, Hunter – who Ulrika had been going out with – and some of the others. After a while, everybody wandered down Broad Street, past all the pubs and bars, to a church that had been turned into a nightclub.

When I got there, there were only about 20 people inside, scattered round the various chairs and tables. Ulrika was on the dance floor with two other blondes, her stepsister and her stepsister's mate. It also happened to be 16 August, her thirtieth birthday, and she seemed happy and carefree. She looked lovely and I couldn't take my eyes off her.

A bit later, I went over to Rhino and asked him whether she was going out with anybody. He said her relationship with Hunter was over and there wasn't anybody else. I asked for her number but he said he couldn't give it to me. Soon after that, we left because the party was crap. I hadn't spoken to Ulrika. I hadn't even caught her eye. But by then I was hooked and I felt determined to pursue her.

On the short drive back to Cannock, I phoned the Hyatt and told them I would like to leave a message for Ulrika. I gave them my phone number and asked her to call me back. The next day, I was driving home at lunchtime after I'd finished training at Villa's Bodymoor Heath complex when my mobile rang. I answered it and a voice said, 'Ulrika Jonsson here'. I just thought, 'fucking hell, result'. We arranged to meet.

She got into my car outside the Hyatt and we went to a swanky restaurant in Birmingham city centre called Berlioz. We were the only two in there and we talked and talked and talked. She told me her life story. About how her mum up and left when she was seven and left her in Sweden with her dad, who was a boat builder. About how her mum deserted her and went to live in Holland with a new man. About how once when she went back to Sweden after spending the school holidays with her mum, her dad had forgotten to come and pick her up at the airport.

She told me about every boyfriend she had ever had and how she had been wronged by this bloke and that bloke. It made me feel sorry for her. It made me feel protective towards her straight away. And, of course, it made me feel as if we had some sort of connection, that we could each relate to the troubled childhoods we had both lived through, and that in some way we might be able to help each other. How grotesquely flawed and idealistic that seems now.

But for a while, it felt great. She was very captivating. Very bubbly. Very attractive. It was intense, too. Within a week of that first date she sent me a home-made card. There was a picture of her and her son, Cameron, who was a toddler then, on the front. She had written on it. 'Mr Collymore,' it said, 'I present to you your new family.' I showed it to a couple of my close friends and they just started mimicking the music to *Psycho*. They said it was *Fatal Attraction* territory. They said I should steer clear. They employed a phrase we liked using to describe a nutter. They said she was 'a head-the-ball'.

But I just thought how nice it was for her to invite me to be part of her family. I thought it showed a trusting, warm person. It just confirmed to me how wonderful she was. And the first few weeks were idyllic. I went down to her house at Cookham Dean, the same place where she would entertain Sven-Goran Eriksson a few years later, and we went for meals in London, where invariably we would be met by press photographers, who always seemed to know where we were.

And for all their laughing about how odd that card was, my mates thought she was great when they met her. You couldn't help but like her. She was very demure, very effervescent, very user-friendly, and she was also an incorrigible flirt. She was one of those people who saw it as a challenge to win over anyone she felt was not attracted to her. She was needy like that. She needed everyone to like her. It drove her mad if anybody turned away from her.

If somebody didn't like her, she would make them like her. She went to a party with Ellen DeGeneres once after Ellen had come out as a lesbian and had done one of her television shows in England. Ulrika was openly flirting with her, and when I asked her why she was doing it she looked at me as if I was mad, and said: 'Because I can.' I suppose that only increased the madness of the attraction I felt for her. It added a corrosive element of jealousy to everything.

The first night we slept together, we stayed in the Honeymoon Suite at Blake's Hotel in London one Saturday. We woke up some time in mid-morning and I crept outside the door to collect the papers that had been delivered. I looked at the front-page headline. It said: 'Dodi Dead, Diana Seriously Injured'. We turned the television on and the BBC had gone into mourning mode. By then, everyone knew Diana had been killed, too.

And so our relationship was consummated even as the princess of sadness and fucked-up romance, the princess who had taken our celebrity obsession to a new pitch, was dying in a Paris underpass. What kind of an evil cradling was that for our relationship. But I was smitten. I had fallen in love with Ulrika and she with me. That afternoon, as we walked down the King's Road, drunk on our young love in the sunshine, I asked Ulrika to marry me. She was signing an autograph at the time but she looked at me and said yes. We had been going out with each other for two weeks.

It was a short honeymoon period. It lasted until one weekend when we had agreed we would go up to a lodge I used to own on the shores of Loch Lomond. She was working on *It's Ulrika!*, the vehicle Vic Reeves and Bob Mortimer had written for her and which was going down like a sack of shit, but she was going to drive up to Birmingham and the intention was to fly to Glasgow from there. When I hadn't heard from her by late afternoon, I called her. She was pissed. She said she'd join me in Scotland later in the weekend.

I tried to call her back but she had switched her phone off. So I decided to go up on my own. I had a quick dinner with Yorkie and Mark Bosnich and then I caught the flight with a mate of mine. On the Sunday morning, my mate brought the newspapers into my room. He had a sheepish expression on his face and he said I wasn't going to like what I saw. Ulrika was plastered over the tabloids, stumbling out of Chris Evans' house at dawn on Saturday morning.

So I called her and she came out with all the usual shit about how Chris was just a mate and she'd slept on the couch. The same old bollocks. Even in her own autobiography she admitted that she was attracted to him that night and that the only reason they didn't sleep together was because it would have 'complicated' things between them. She also admitted that during the same period she was attracted to some dweeb called Paul Roberts who she met on *Shooting Stars*, but she couldn't make up her mind whether to shag him either.

I may not have been a faithful man but she was certainly not a faithful woman. We were the same. I have spoken to psychiatrists who have told me that she is also a classic example of someone with Borderline Personality Disorder. Our union was passionate and intense but it was also destined to fail in a lingering bout of ugly recriminations. We weren't good for each other. Essentially, we made each other unhappy.

We were both promiscuous people. Where I screwed up was that it got to me. The jealousy got to me. When she stayed the night with Chris Evans, the newspapers had quoted a source saying they'd been snogging each other in the pub earlier in the evening. We had the mother of all rows that day. She likes to paint a picture of me as someone who was always shouting abuse at her, totally unprovoked. It wasn't like that. But our conversations were mutually abusive. I'll admit that. On that occasion she was calling me 'a fucking dick'. I was yelling that she was 'a fucking bitch'. And then, gradually, we calmed down and we both tried to repair it all. I was jealous. I admit that, too. But the way she behaved was hardly condusive to an atmosphere of trust. So yes, I would ring up and routinely start a conversation with 'What the fuck is going on?' We had a very turbulent, argumentative relationship when we weren't physically together. When we were together, it wasn't a problem.

She was happy to mess with my mind. I would have had a lot more respect for her if she had told me straight that she had been sleeping around. Instead, she told me half-truths. She alluded to things without telling the whole truth. She was the one who sent me poetic cards talking about how she had just left me sleeping and how she was keeping that image with her. She wanted it both ways. She wanted the closeness and the intimacy but she wanted to fuck me about, too. And I couldn't handle that.

So that was the kind of dysfunctional pattern we settled into. Puncture it and then get the repair kit out. Smash it; mend it. Break it; put it back together. For a month after the Chris Evans thing we didn't see a lot of each other, but we had a whole series of fucked-up telephone conversations. There was always a subtext of jealousy. It would always get around to 'Where have you been?' or 'Who have you been with?' We would have a row, the phone would be slammed down and then an hour later one or the other of us would call to apologise. It was a fucked-up cycle but it grew into normality. She would be saying I had been pictured coming out of a restaurant with someone and somebody else had told her I was shagging somebody different. And I'd be asking her why she had been photographed coming out of a particular personality's house at some unearthly hour of the morning. I soon began to realise that even though I considered us to be an item, she had other people in the background.

If we were face to face and I confronted her with something, this big grin would always spread across her face. She always smiled when she was just about to lie to me. It was like she wanted to keep me on my toes. She had faced this rejection in her childhood and now she had to have a lot of people in her life. One man was never going to be enough. When you consider both our backgrounds, it was a recipe for disaster.

I tried to stick with it because I did have strong feelings for her. Every time we sat down and talked about her family life and her lack of love from her father and her mother, it would activate all these protective feelings in me. I wasn't doing a great job for Aston Villa and my own life was a bit of a mess, but I thought that maybe I could do something worthwhile by trying to save her. It was a nice sentiment but it soon got washed away by a tide of suspicion and lies. Soon, if she started weeping about her mother and father, I looked at her and all I saw was a bad actress in a bad scene.

It seemed that every day she would be being linked romantically with someone new. And that was humiliating for me. Just like it would be humiliating for any bloke. I would read it in the paper and then walk into a dressing room full of 25 footballers, knowing they had been reading exactly the same articles about who Stan's missus was shagging now. It is natural that that is going to mess with your head. I got very paranoid about it.

But it was addictive, too. Is she lying to me? Is she seeing somebody else behind my back? Is she feeding the press? Is that why there are always photographers outside Quaglino's when we finish our meal? It was all irresistible somehow. There was a strand in both of us, a vulnerable strand that gave us this crazed desire to be liked, that made us almost identical. She was shagging other blokes. I was shagging other birds. It was all part of the ladette image she was cultivating.

She was very charming and very intelligent but she used her intellect to manipulate people for her own benefit. Don't forget, she was a television presenter who was one of the new generation, more famous for being famous than for the worth of any of the television work she had done. And me? I was a professional football player who wasn't exactly setting the world alight at Villa. The last thing I needed was any publicity about extracurricular activities.

Perhaps that's why it's so difficult to mix showbiz and football in romance. Showbiz feeds off publicity. Publicity is its lifeblood. A showbiz career shrivels and dies without exposure in the newspapers. Look at how Victoria Beckham craves it and orchestrates it. But when a footballer gets the same kind of attention, eventually it seems to rebound on him. It's frowned on. It's seen as being a distraction and, actually, it is a distraction. It has to be. David Beckham has managed to keep his head above water, but only just, and even with him it has created tensions and resentments with his team-mates. I know that other players within the England squad think he's a joke and I have heard that his profile has created difficulties for him in the Real Madrid dressing room, too. They think he's a show-pony whose image outstrips his talent. Within football, publicity loses you respect. It doesn't help you.

After the Chris Evans thing, I thought that if Ulrika was going to fuck me about, I ought to try and concentrate a bit more on giving my all to Villa. My football was going badly. Villa were struggling and I was getting the blame. The relationship with Ulrika was very much on and off. We drifted in and out of commitment, separated by her work and my football. From time to time we'd patch things up, and then we'd rip the plaster off again and let it bleed.

A few weeks before Paris we were suddenly madly in love again. We went on a two-week holiday. A week in New York at the Royalton, followed by a week in Jamaica at the Half Moon Club. We had a lot of sex in Jamaica. In fact, we generally had a lot of sex. She was a very sexual person and so was I. She was also perfectly happy to be filmed. She was really into that. She loved playing to the camera. So I filmed her. I filmed us.

Let's just say that the video footage made what Pamela Anderson and Tommy Lee did on their boat on Lake Tahoe look like an episode of the *Tweenies*. It was two young, healthy people enjoying each other and indulging in role play. Ulrika really went for it. She performed for the camera like she was some sort of porn star. She was hot on that trip, so hot that some time later, long after we had broken up, the existence of that video tape created a scandal. The *News of the World* rang Jonathan Crystal, my lawyer, some time towards the end of 2002 and sucked him into some sort of conversation about how much I would be willing to sell the tape for. They made it public and branded me some sort of sicko for trying to sell Ulrika's sex secrets, although the truth was I'd never had any intention of selling it in the first place;, I would never have sold it to a newspaper.

When the *News of the World* broke that story, Ulrika took out an injunction, demanding that the tape be handed over to her solicitors, and the High Court upheld her demands and ordered that the tape be destroyed. By then, there wasn't actually any tape left to hand over. Some time before the story broke, Estelle had demanded I give it to her. She took it into the garage and burned it. I still had to pay Ulrika's legal fees, which amounted to about £35,000. Yet another sad postscript to our failed relationship.

But I had another video from that trip, too. I still keep it and in a way I still treasure it. It consists of footage of both of us peering into the camera and telling each other how much we love one another. There's me, desperately seeking reassurance from her that she loves me and that she wants to have my children. There's her, making a few quips about how she loves me for my money. How she loves me because I've got a good left foot. You can't see me but I'm telling her to stop messing about. I'm saying that I'm serious. And then she gets serious, too, and her eyes get big and round and she talks in that soft voice about how much she loves me.

There's footage of us riding around on buggies in the grounds of the Half Moon Club; footage of us eating breakfast on the private terrace of the room we were sharing. And from the time in New York, there are pictures of us on Fifth Avenue and outside the Rockefeller Center and messing about in Central Park. We look very much a couple in love, and for those two weeks that was exactly what we were.

She says now that that trip was 'truly the worst of my life'. She says she was intimidated and frightened by me. She says I reduced her to tears, that I abandoned her in the street in New York, that I forced her to spend lonely nights on her own in the bar at the Half Moon Club. Well, I'm sorry, but those words are the words of a person with an overactive imagination. It was a happy, harmonious, lovely trip, but it doesn't suit her purposes to remember it that way now.

But when we got home, we lurched back into the bickering and sniping. I don't know why that was. Partly, I suppose, it was that we always seemed to end up going to showbiz parties, where she was perfectly at home and I wasn't. Up to a point, it made me feel good when rock stars or television people came up and said they were big fans of my football, but mainly I felt a bit out of my depth. I was always a little bit on edge and Ulrika was always flirting with other men.

I couldn't handle it. I got jealous and she fed my jealousy. Once, soon after we got back from Jamaica, we were staying at my lodge in Scotland and she rolled over in bed and cuddled up to me and murmured another bloke's name. I said, 'What did you say?', and she started smiling that lying smile again and said she had only been joking. I started packing my stuff because I'd had enough. I wanted to leave and go back to Birmingham.

She went crazy. She flung herself to the floor like a two-year-old, wailing and screaming and begging me not to finish it. She was scratching me like a wild animal, something she'd done before at the Ellen DeGeneres thing, because she got jealous about me talking to Sara Cox. This time, she tried to bite me, too. I'd never seen her that out of control. But I told her it was finished. I walked out, got in my car, drove to the airport and caught the next flight back to Birmingham.

Of course, it wasn't finished. I wish it had been. I wish I could have let go then. I wish I could have put myself out of my misery and just got on with my life. I wish I could have made a clean break and moved on. I wish she had never gone to Paris. I wish I had never begged her to let me go with her.

I wish she had continued to refuse to allow me to come with her. I wish she had never relented. I wish it had never happened. I wish I could turn back time.

At the beginning of June 1998 the World Cup was about to start in France. The first game was to be Brazil v Scotland in the new Stade de France in Paris, and Ulrika had been invited to be a guest on a programme for BBC Scotland that was hosted by Ally McCoist and a comedian called Fred McAulay. It was being filmed on one of the platforms halfway up the Eiffel Tower on 9 June, the evening before the opening game. The other guests were Ewan McGregor, Jimmy Hill and Richard Wilson, the actor who plays Victor Meldrew.

I had finally persuaded Ulrika to let me fly out with her from Heathrow on the basis that we were going to have one last shot at patching everything up and really getting serious. I had booked a table for two at the Buddha Bar, just off the Place de la Concorde, for 10 p.m., which gave us plenty of time after the programme was due to have finished. We dropped our stuff off at the khazi of a hotel the BBC had booked her into and then headed for the Eiffel Tower.

We went up in the lift to the first platform and there was a kind of Green Room that we were ushered into. Ewan McGregor was there with his parents, so, of course, Ulrika started flirting with him. One of the crew wandered over and asked the two of them if they would go down to make-up and there was lots of laughing and joking. When they came back up, Ewan McGregor was dabbing at this stain on his shirt. He said: 'Oh, I've got Ulrika juice all over me.'

I didn't know how to take that. I don't know what he

meant. What would you have thought he meant? I was tense anyway. Ulrika was smiling her smile. Ewan McGregor was giggling. Some fucking dwarf called Paul Jackson, who was the BBC's Controller of Entertainment and was besotted with Ulrika, was sniffing around, too. It was just a bad scene and I was getting increasingly jumpy. I wanted us to be on our own so we could try and sort everything out. I was edgy. I rang Davina and she told me to be calm.

Ulrika did her turn on the programme. It finished, then everybody sat around chatting and Ulrika started downing the pints. It was 9 p.m. by then. I was really edgy. She was a bit pissed. I asked her if we could go. She said she just wanted to chill out. She says now she was the one who wanted to go and I wanted to stay. Yet another case of her rewriting history. Why would I have wanted to stay with a bunch of wankers like that? Somebody asked if anybody wanted food and she said she did. So they brought a pint of prawns, some chips and some mayonnaise and she started getting stuck in.

I put some urgency in my voice then. I said, 'Ully, we have got a table booked for 10 p.m., can we go?' She said she wasn't ready. So I crouched down and grabbed her arm and asked her again. I reminded her we were supposed to be sorting our relationship out, that this wasn't just some casual date, that this was intended to be a significant evening in our lives, a make-or-break evening, and she was acting like she didn't care. She said no again. She says now that I threatened to kill her if she didn't come. That flair for the melodramatic in her again. It just didn't happen.

I told her that if she didn't come, I'd leave. She said I'd have to leave then. So I walked outside, back onto this platform halfway up the Eiffel Tower. I had a couple of passport photos in my wallet of me and her, taken in some station booth, and I took them out, ripped them up and threw them over the edge. I watched them fluttering in the night air down towards the Champs de Mars for a few seconds and then I stormed off.

I was in a foul temper. I was furious with her. I got one of the courtesy cars to take me back to the hotel. I'd told Ulrika I'd wait an hour for her there. I still had to give her one last chance. I still couldn't let go. Why didn't I just give it up then? Why didn't I just realise enough was enough? Why didn't I just accept it wasn't going to work? Why did I have to keep going back to her, like the moth to the flame? Maybe the things that drove me mad about her were the things that drew me to her, too.

I rang Davina again. She told me to leave. She told me not to have another argument. She told me to pack my bags and come back home. She said all the right things. She said all the sensible things. I wish I'd listened to her. But I didn't listen to her. I was still fuming. I was thinking about what a twat Ulrika had made me look in front of everybody on that fucking platform halfway up the Eiffel Tower. I was upset that she didn't appear to give a toss about saving our relationship. I kept telling myself that this had been our one chance to sort everything out once and for all. I was probably kidding myself. You can't sort something like that out over dinner. Trying to fix me and Ulrika was like playing catch with a bar of wet soap. It wasn't a good game. But I was blinded to that then. So I sat up in my hotel room, which overlooked the street, waiting and watching and still hoping that a car would pull up and she would get out.

An hour came and went and there was no sign of her. The courtesy cars were shuttling to and fro. Occasionally they dropped off passengers but it was never her. My heart was still beating fast. I really wanted her to come back. I kept torturing myself with the idea of the relief and the new hope I'd feel if she got out of one of those cars. Eventually, Richard Wilson rolled up and I asked him if he'd seen Ulrika. He said she'd gone on to a Scottish pub called the Auld Alliance with the rest of the gang.

Well, thanks for disrespecting me. Not only had she not bothered coming back, she'd fucked off to a Scottish pub to get pissed and carry on flirting. I jumped in Richard Wilson's taxi and told the driver to take me to the Auld Alliance. It was a short-enough journey. The pub was part of a small row of bars and restaurants in the rowdy Les Halles area, close to the Pompidou Centre. I pushed one of the doors ajar just enough to see the place was crammed full of about 500 pissed-up Jocks, busy preparing to celebrate yet another World Cup defeat.

There didn't seem as if there was any room to move, so I looked around a bit and found a side door. I pushed it and it opened onto a back room behind the bar. The first person I saw was Ally McCoist with his kilt on. I asked him if he'd seen Ulrika. He said she was in the bar. I looked in the direction he was nodding and all I could see was a couple of barmaids and, beyond them, this sea of shitfaced Jocks, screaming for drink and practically climbing over each other as they tried to get to the bar to get another pint in. Some of them were on each other's shoulders, hunched down because the ceilings were so low. It all felt cramped and claustrophobic. Everybody was shouting and yelling, the din was so loud I could hardly think. Gradually, as I took everything in, I became aware that one of the barmaids was a blonde wearing a Scotland shirt. I asked somebody else where Ulrika was and they pointed to the barmaid. It was Ulrika. She was pulling pints.

The Jocks all noticed me at that point, which made their fucking night. They were all shouting 'fuck off, Collymore, you fucking English twat'. In a couple of seconds I got soaked in the beer they were spraying over me. I went up to Ulrika and said, 'Come on, let's go.' That was my madness. I still thought the evening could be salvaged. The Scottish guys started singing 'get your tits out for the lads' at her, so as we moved towards the back room she lifted up her top and gave them a flash of her bra. Cue more roars and more abuse.

I said, 'Can I have a word with you please?' and grabbed her arm. I was angry. The situation was chaotic. I was getting even more beer chucked over me by the Jocks now because I was taking their bit of totty away. Eventually, we made it into the back room where all the people from the BBC Scotland programme were hanging out. It felt like everyone was watching us even at that point, watching this sad twat who'd come back to plead with Ulrika again. I felt she was deliberately trying to embarrass me in front of everybody.

I looked at her and I said, 'What the fucking hell do you think you are doing?' She grinned that fucking grin that she always grinned. 'If you don't like it, you can fuck off,' she said. I hit her. It was a couple of seconds. She went down. On to the floor. I bent down to pick her up. I already knew what

I had done. The horror was rushing over me. She said later I kicked her in the head. First the right side, then the left side, then the right side again, she told everyone. Well, for what it's worth, amid the sordid shame of that night, I never kicked her. I was a professional footballer. If I'd kicked her, I would have taken her head off.

I didn't kick her down any stairs, either. There weren't any stairs. I hit her once. That was bad enough. That was enough to damn me in my own mind and in the minds of all others. That was enough to ruin me. Then I was trying to pick her up. But some blokes came over and grabbed me. One of them grabbed me round the waist and one pinned my arms back and his mate came over and punched me in the face. I could see Ulrika, still on the floor, hysterical, crying uncontrollably, people all around her. That was the image I took with me as they bundled me out onto the street.

I stumbled down the street for a while. I felt like I was in shock. That sounds stupid, doesn't it. I'd just hit a woman and I was the one in shock. But four words were starting to fry my mind. *Just like your dad; just like your dad.* I'd hit a woman, just like my dad had hit my mum. I was no better than him. I was a brute. I was an animal. For those few seconds when I hit Ulrika, I had lost the capacity for rational thought. My dad had done it. Now I had done it.

I didn't know what to do. My mind was whirring. I was reeling. Shame came quickly. And guilt. And self-loathing. I saw Fred McAulay walking the other way, towards the Auld Alliance. I stopped him. I told him something awful had happened. I was panicking. I knew he must have been able to see it in me. I thought he must have been able to sense what I had just done. I felt like a see-through villain. I pleaded with him to get me back into the pub. I still thought I could undo some of the damage.

Despite what I thought, Fred didn't have any idea what had happened. The bouncer on the door wasn't going to let me back in but Fred persuaded him. I walked back in. Ulrika wasn't there. She had been taken round a corner, to a little corridor where some beer barrels had been stacked up. People were shouting to keep me away from her. Chaos again. Another scene from hell.

So she was sitting on one barrel, sobbing quietly, and I was sitting on another, still in a barely controlled state of panic, still scarcely able to believe what I had done. People were hovering around, wondering if I was going to try to hit her again. I tried to apologise to her. I kept saying I was sorry. She was saying she was okay. She was very, very shaken. She wasn't bleeding. I took a scintilla of comfort from that.

Ally McCoist came over and said he thought I should go back to the hotel. My presence was making everybody very uneasy. They said they'd keep Ulrika in the back room for a bit and then bring her back; try and let her recover for a while and come to terms with what had happened. So I went back to the hotel, mind racing, brain scrambled. I had completely gone. I was still gripped by panic that I could have done something so animalistic.

I knew the reaction in England would be massive. I knew I would be crucified. I was already thinking about that. Already gripped by that. I knew I deserved it but that still didn't make the contemplation of the national press slavering for my blood seem any more of a comforting prospect. I didn't know what I was going to do. I felt like a fugitive already. I rang Davina. She was appalled. Why had I gone anywhere near that pub? She'd told me it sounded like trouble. She'd told me to get out of there.

I went up to the room I had been sharing with Ulrika. I paced up and down it. Being still was unthinkable. I felt like I was in the grip of madness. I grabbed Ulrika's bag from somewhere. Hardly seeing it, I tore everything out of it. I ripped up her clothes. I ripped up papers. I flung her toiletries everywhere. I scattered it all over the floor. I didn't know whether it was mine or hers. I felt like I wanted to go berserk with the agony of it all. I forgot I had already gone berserk.

About an hour later, although it seemed like four or five hours to me, a people-carrier came down the road and nine or ten people climbed out of it. I saw Fred McAulay, Ally McCoist and Ewan McGregor's dad among them. They walked slowly along the pavement to a café about 60 yards down the road. I didn't know what to do. Go and try to talk to her again, maybe. Then there was a knock on the door. It was Ally, and Ewan McGregor's dad.

Ally was nice, but he was clearly utterly dismayed and un-comprehending about what I had done. 'There are times when I feel like clocking my missus,' Ally said, 'but I'd never fucking do it.' I tried to tell them about all the tension that had been building up. I was beside myself. I told Ally I wanted to see Ulrika, just to check she was all right. I was desperate and they could see that. One of them went to get her and she came over. She just stood in the doorway with her head resting on her left shoulder. I told her I wasn't going to hurt her and I begged her to come back into the room but she just turned around and went back to the restaurant.

Eventually, I plucked up the courage to go over there myself. I was desperate to see her. Desperate to try and make some of the guilt go away. *Just like your dad; just like your dad.* I had to try and do something to stop the pain that was shooting through me. By then a new dread was starting to creep over me. I was going to have to tell my mum about this. After all my womanising, I'd crossed a new frontier with this. A final frontier. I'd let down the one person I couldn't bear to let down.

Ulrika was sitting at a table with the rest of them. Fred McAulay stared at me like he wanted to kill me. I didn't say anything. I didn't know what to say. She didn't know what to say. I was weeping. I saw that her eyes were puffy from crying. I asked her again to come back over to the room. This time, she came with me. We both just lay on the bed. Spent. Knackered. Not saying anything. I have been told that she wrote in her book that I sat in the room holding a cigarette lighter to my wrist and burning myself as some sort of act of penance. Well, I certainly felt penitent, but, once again, that particular story is a product of her rather over-active imagination. I didn't smoke then, apart from anything else, so I wouldn't have had a lighter. Anyway, we stayed silent and inert for what remained of the night. Eventually, the morning came, and the taxi arrived to take us to Charles de Gaulle airport.

We didn't say anything to each other on the journey back either. I think Ulrika was still in shock. It was more that than outright hostility. More that than fear of this man who had hit her. She was subdued. Mostly, she was silent. When we got back to Heathrow, my mobile started ringing. Stretford called. He was having to field calls from the press. He wanted to know what had happened. I was gripped afresh by fear and panic. The reaction was starting.

I don't know why we came back together to England. I don't know what was still binding us. My desperation to try to make it up somehow, perhaps. Force of habit. Some last vestiges of affection. At Heathrow, Ulrika's driver collected us and took us back to Ulrika's house in Cookham Dean. My car was waiting there. So was Ulrika's agent, Melanie. She asked me to leave. Ulrika asked me if I was going to be all right. I left even though I could see in Ulrika's eyes that she didn't want me to leave. She released a statement saying we would not be seeing each other any more. She said the relationship was over and that she was fine.

I released a statement, too. '*A stupid and silly argument had developed throughout the course of the day between myself and Ulrika, someone who I have realised for some time is very special to me,*' it read. '*My actions were totally reprehensible, something I am not proud of and finding very difficult to come to terms with. In a fit of petulant temper, I struck out at the girl I love and immediately regretted my actions, but by then it was too late. I could hide behind a facade of excuses and no comments, but petulance, jealousy and possibly having too much to drink are the real reasons behind this regrettable and avoidable incident.*'

She had said that when the press came she would tie her hair back and not wear any make-up so they could all see that she wasn't bruised and that she was okay. She didn't have a mark on her. Another tiny consolation for me. Another thing I could use to try to dull the guilt. But the next day, a picture appeared in all the papers of her in the passenger seat of her car which made her look badly bruised. It was actually rain spots on the windscreen projected onto her by the flash of the cameras. But why would anyone want to believe that.

I drove back up to my townhouse in Birmingham. I got close and I could see there were about 50 press boys outside. There were camera crews. There was even an outside-broadcast van. So I drove to a mate's house and hid there. I was Public Enemy Number One. The mood in the country seemed to be 'Find Him'. For a few days I led this clandestine life of slipping in and out of people's houses, smuggled away in the boot of a car or under blankets in a back seat.

The newspapers pulled out all the stops. Lotta, someone I had been out with for a long time, sold her story to the *News of the World*. Except there was a twist. The headline the piece was 'Monster Colly Beat Me For Five Years'. She claimed I had beaten her regularly and that her relationship with me had been dominated by her fear of the next time I was going to hit her. Good story. Only problem was I had never hit her. Ever. I had never hit anyone except Ulrika.

I was in a club in London a couple of years later when one of the doormen came into the VIP section and said there was somebody asking for me outside. I went over. It was Lotta. I told her she had a bloody nerve, trying to talk to me after what she had done, but she pleaded for a bit of time to explain. She was in floods of tears and she said that after we had split up and the way I had behaved with other women, she didn't feel she had any allegiance to me any more. When the furore had grown after Paris, the *News of the World* had approached her to sell her story and offered her £50,000, but they were only interested if it included details of beating women. Lotta obliged. She said it had meant she could put a deposit down on a new flat and start a new life. I suppose that's how the newspapers can corrode your values.

I just asked her if she had any idea of the heartache that article had caused me, if she had had any idea when she did it that it would confirm in the public mind the idea that not only was I a monster for hitting Ulrika, but that I had always been a monster and always would be. I haven't seen her again since then.

I had to tell my mum what I'd done. She burst into tears. Served me right but it nearly killed me. Predictably, someone hung my Villa shirt from a noose in a Birmingham back-street somewhere. They would be doing the same thing to David Beckham's England shirt in south London a few days later. I hid for as long as I could and then I fled to Nice at the invitation of Davina, and tried to kid myself I was returning to some sort of normality.

But Ulrika and I were not finished with each other yet. In a shadowy form, we survived as a couple. Only this time, instead of existing in the spotlight, we saw each other in secret. She appeared on a round of television chat-shows, speaking up for battered wives and saying what a bad man I was; how I had been a controlling and manipulative presence and how I had threatened to kill her. A few minutes after she came off camera she would call me to tell me how much she was missing me.

About a month passed between what happened in Paris and the next time we saw each other. We were phoning regularly by then, but with all the public stuff she was doing on behalf of various women's groups she was petrified about being seen with me. We arranged to drive our cars to a lay-by about a mile off the M40, somewhere near Banbury. We both pulled in and she climbed out of her car and got into mine.

I told her again that I was at a loss to explain my behaviour that night in Paris, and I didn't know how we could move our relationship forward in any way. Soon we were kissing and groping. We couldn't keep our hands off each other. There were too many cars whizzing past the lay-by so we got out and walked into the middle of a cornfield. We collapsed in each other's arms there and had sex, and for those moments I felt like maybe we had a future again.

A few nights later, she went on the *Parkinson* show and was busy telling him and his audience what a monster I was. When she left the set, she rang me and asked me when we could next meet up for a shag. That's what she was like. I know I was the bad guy. No question about that. But she's no angel. She knows how to work the media and she knows how to manipulate, and soon after Paris she began to realise that being smacked in the face by a Premiership footballer was turning into a first-class career opportunity.

Is it right and honest to jump on a bandwagon over something like that? Is it right to join up with Sheryl Gascoigne, who was doing forums for battered women, and present an image of yourself as a wronged and battered woman, when you are secretly seeing the man who hit you? That seems like the worst kind of dishonesty to me. It is misleading a group of vulnerable and wronged people who are suddenly holding you up as some kind of role model and seeing some sort of hope in your stance and in your words. It's publicity-seeking at its worst. She would give interviews in the newspapers saying she had not spoken to me since Paris and that she never wanted to speak to me again. The same day, she would call me and tell me how much she missed me. How much she loved me. I put up with it. I was hardly in a position to claim any moral high-ground. I was still desperate to try and atone for what I'd done. But when her autobiography came out and I saw she had called it *Honest*, it made me laugh out loud.

I suppose that's a celebrity's honesty for you. I'd rather call it denial. Or deception. Or why not just dishonesty. She started talking about how I'd kicked her in the head and how I'd threatened to kill her and how she thought she was going to die that night in Paris. All the stuff that made her fit more neatly into this new pigeonhole she had created for herself, a new lease of life for her fading career. And every day she was phoning this man who she said had threatened to kill her.

It was on *Parkinson* that she said I was manipulative. But if there is one thing I can guarantee you about Ulrika Jonsson, it is that nobody in this world could manipulate her. Any notion that I was controlling her is ridiculous. I was way out of my depth with her. Out of my league. When she goes out of her way to say something, it invariably means the truth lies somewhere in the opposite direction. I had fallen in love with someone who no one should fall in love with.

She has got this incredible ability to wrap you around her

little finger and to orchestrate your affair to be played out in a media environment. I mean, who else could marry a bloke who is part of some reality TV show that she is actually hosting. *Mr Right*? That show should have been called *Mrs Wrong*. I think that at her core is a sociopathic need to be loved because of the lack of affection she received in her childhood. So for her, all the television stuff she does is a very-high-stakes game.

All the publicity she gets, however manufactured it is, however untruthful it is, is designed to maintain this air of interest and intrigue around her. It's a sick game to keep her name in the papers. It's her number-one concern. In her world, it is achieved by any means necessary. But she can't distinguish between her professional and her personal life. She has lost the ability to distinguish. Her priorities are totally fucked. So it annoys me when people trot out that line about how unlucky she's been with men. It's the men who have been unlucky with her.

I don't know where she draws the line. What about at making an allegation of rape, an allegation that coincidentally garnered a huge amount of pre-publicity for *Honest*, and then refusing to name the offender? What about keeping quiet while John Leslie was tried by the media. What about laying that kind of paper trail and then sitting back and watching that man's career and his life destroyed?

I was surprised when I heard about the rape allegation. Because, even though Ulrika talked obsessively about her own life, her serial misfortunes with men and how badly they had mistreated her, she never once mentioned anything about being raped in her youth. It is possible, of course, that she was just too traumatised by it to mention it to a lover. But then why mention it in a book that will open that ordeal up to millions of people? I haven't got the answers. With Ulrika, I never had the answers.

I shagged her again a couple of times after the cornfield. Once was in a car park, actually. A prelude to my dogging days. Once, she came up to my flat in Birmingham, but somebody saw her standing on the balcony and reported it to the papers. She denied it all so it never came out but she took fright after that and we barely saw each other again. She sent me a text towards the end of that year, saying that she was desperate to have more children, and, once, right at the end of my career, when I was in Oviedo, I called her for a chat.

She told the newspapers about that, too. She said I couldn't stop calling her. That I was pestering her every day. A couple of years earlier, she might have been justified in saying that. I rang her a lot. She rang me a lot. But by the time my career was coming to an end, I had seen her for what she was. A few months later, I heard she had met and married some bloke called Markus Kempen. I didn't feel any jealousy towards him. I didn't feel any hatred for him. I just felt sorry for him.

CHAPTER EIGHT

SUMMER 1998: THE AFTERMATH

In the days and weeks that followed the nightmare of hitting Ulrika in Paris, I was still deeply in love with her and was desperately trying to rekindle our relationship. But she was not the only woman in my life by any means. When Estelle heard about what had happened in Paris, she cut short a holiday in Cyprus to come back to England to be with me. Our relationship was sexual but we were not really boyfriend and girlfriend. I was also having an on-off relationship with a blonde Villa groupie called Linsey, who had been introduced to me by my Villa team-mate, Lee Hendrie. I had just finished a relationship with Davina McCall but we were still very close. And on top of all this, I was conducting an occasional relationship with a girl called Nicole.

I began to keep a daily audio diary. At the time, I was living in a townhouse in Symphony Court in the centre of Birmingham, approaching what I knew would be a make-or-break season for me at Aston Villa. Six months later I would check into the Priory, tormented by severe depression. My relationship with Ulrika would be over once and for all and my career with Villa would be in ruins.

5 July, New York

Arrived yesterday on Concorde after a few days with Davina in the south of France and then a few days with Nicole in Munich. Having problems with Ulrika. Things are very difficult. My emotions are up and down. I am missing her very much, but I am trying to convince myself that I am embarking on a change of lifestyle. One that gives me more happiness and fulfilment. Had a really bad night in my room at the Royalton Hotel. Spoke to Ulrika. Felt suicidal. She left three messages for me. Watched the 4 July fireworks display by the East River yesterday. Estelle's coming back from Cyprus. Hopefully I'll sort out my relationship with her in some way. Bought a couple of T-shirts for her. Felt a bit lonely. Wandered into Central Park. Breezed around the shops. Pete Sampras won Wimbledon.

Have embarked on my treatment now. Doing this diary for therapeutic reasons. I have been in close contact with Davina and Estelle and Paul Stretford, my agent, who initiated this whole process. That's why I'm doing this, so I can look back with a bit more pride. I am feeling a numb nothingness today. Read a bit about Ulrika today and how she said she had been kicked in the head in Paris. Went to a porno store and bought some videos and came back and did what you do. Watching *As Good As It Gets*. Poignant because I watched it with Ulrika. Thought about calling her but didn't. Went to Greenwich Village for a meal.

6 July

Had a bad dream about Ulrika. I was sitting with the newscaster Dermot Murnaghan and he was saying that he had walked into a party and had seen Ulrika kissing another guy. More than kissing him, actually. That woke me up. All over the place today. Phone bill is already £400. Keep checking my pigeonhole to see if there are any messages. Deep down, I suppose I'm hoping there will be something from Ulrika. Watched the second half of *As Good As It Gets*. There are lines in it that I think of myself saying to Ulrika. Jack Nicholson's character says at the end that he realises Helen Hunt's character is the greatest woman in the world for him. She's been waiting tables for all these people and none of them could see it. But he saw it. I tried to equate that to me and Ulrika. Ulrika may or may not be honest with me. I'll never know. I know that Estelle is honest with me and I have hurt her badly. If there are any priorities in my life, it should be to help heal the hurt in Estelle. I need to give her the confidence to know that whatever may come of me and her, at least I'm being honest with her. I don't think Ulrika's earned that. I do love her and there is that spark there but Estelle has been there unequivocally. Sitting here now in my room at the Royalton, blinds are shut, clothes are everywhere.

Did some more shopping for Estelle. Went up Madison Avenue and wandered into the Swedish church. Went through the Visitor Book and virtually the first page I opened was signed by someone called Ulrika Janssen. I thought for a moment she had been back without me knowing about it. It was only eight weeks since we were here and I found the page where our names were together. I went up and prayed for my mum, for Estelle and for Ulrika. I lit a candle for the three of them. It is a little oasis. Met a Jamaican pensioner called Vicky who told me to marry within my own race.

I miss Ulrika a lot. I miss her feistiness and her exuberance. I miss Estelle, too. I miss her caring. I miss her being there, knowing that she's there. I miss her eyes and her smile. But I don't miss home. Went to the Metropolitan Museum of Art and it was closed. Walked around Greenwich Village. Got back to the hotel. Felt very anxious. Had a big panic attack. Rang Ulrika. She wasn't there. She must have gone away. Her mobile's switched off. Maybe she's gone away with the Gladiators. Feeling really fucked off. Can't get my head round all of this. Keep trying and trying and trying Ulrika. Perhaps she's at somebody else's house. God only knows. It's driving me mad. Friends keep telling me 'don't call'. I don't know if I'm doing it out of love or out of habit.

Got through to Ulrika on the tenth try. She said she'd been in bed since eight o'clock, which I don't believe because she answered the phone after two rings. I asked if there was anybody there. She said there wasn't. We got into a slanging match. She was calling me immature. She said I didn't respect women, including Davina and Estelle. I told her it wasn't her place to say that. I came off the phone feeling quite strong in myself. I'm beginning to hate her now. I'm beginning to really dislike her. I love her desperately. I will wake up tomorrow and feel bad that we have had an argument. How much more do I have to take before I realise? How much more do I have to take?

7 July

Ulrika called me at 3 a.m. She said she didn't want a fucked-up conversation. I don't know what her motives were. Maybe just to keep the playing surface flat enough so that I don't freak out and threaten this and that and the other. Spoke to Estelle who has got flu. Stretford's organising a car to go down to Heathrow to pick her up when she gets back from Cyprus. Bought a tiny FM stereo with earphones that will be good for jogging. Bought a book called *The Happy Book* for Ulrika. Going to send that to her. Went to an Italian restaurant I had been to before with Ulrika. Collected some photos: pictures of me and Estelle in New York. Some pictures of Davina at her place when I went there after Estelle and I got back, when I told Davina I was still in love with Ulrika. And then some amazing photos of Ulrika in my house. Lots of us in Jamaica. Some really nice photos of her. She is a beautiful woman. She really glows. A couple of the photos really stuck out. She had a green jumper on. She looked stunning.

An Asian guy came up to me on Fifth Avenue and asked if I was Stan Collymore. He had a Puerto Rican girlfriend and they wanted to have their pictures taken with me. That was a little bit of a boost. Bought the soundtrack to *As Good As It Gets*. Bought a book by Ben Watt from Everything but the Girl called *Patient*, about a near-fatal illness he contracted. There are moments when my thoughts run wild. I have been trying to think as little as possible and do things instead. I love this city. It is so fucking alive. This is Day 30 of the new challenge I have put in my life. One twelfth of the year.

Reading a book called *You Can Be Happy No Matter What*. Subtitled, *Five Principles Your Therapist Never Told You*. It's about trying to control negative thoughts. It is almost ridiculously simple but helpful. Spoke to Ulrika. Read her a chapter from the book. She scoffed at it. Saw that Brazil had made it through to the World Cup final. Lots of Brazil cele-brations. Followed some Brazilian birds up to Little Brazil Street. Cute little arses on them bouncing all the way uptown. Thought I might as well go up there, looking a bit like Ronaldo. The street had been blocked off. Bought a little Brazil flag from a vendor and danced around in the road with them all. Drums were banging the salsa beat. Had a nice Brazilian meal. Walked back to Times Square to look for gifts.

8 July, Birmingham

Got back to Heathrow, car waiting for me. Back with Estelle. Great to see her. Starting pre-season training tomorrow. Bit nervous about that, but looking forward to it. Had a bit of a panicky moment on the plane when I read the *Mirror* and there was a piece by Julian Joachim saying he is going to take his chance this season. Good luck to him. But he's going to have to take me on, head on. Not sure whether I'm ready or not yet but time will tell.

9 July

9 a.m. Thinking what I'm going to say to the lads. Just have to walk in and hold your head up high and take whatever comes your way.

10 p.m. Found out the rest of the lads weren't in until the fifteenth. Thought that was a bit of a piss-take at first, but then thought I could use the time to get bedded in. Did a 20 minute run with Steve Harrison. There were a few photog-raphers there. Did the press. There must have been 100 reporters there. Just told them I could only do what I have to

do each day and not look too far ahead. The gaffer rang me and told me to get my head down and everything would turn. Estelle is having a hard time, worrying about every phone call that comes in. Tried Ulrika while I was at my mum's. Not there. Estelle said my phone had rung six times when I got back. Estelle is upset because Linsey rang. I've got this gut-wrenching feeling about wanting to ring Ulrika. I actually phoned her while Estelle was in the car. Didn't speak to her but just listened to her voice. Sounded like she was having a good time wherever she was. Got that awful feeling of dread. Saw a quick flicker of Ulrika's face on the television. Longing to see her. Trying not to succumb to a quick-fix phone call. Have to try and keep the faith in myself that I can overcome this.

Had a big row with Estelle because I had been on the phone to Ulrika while she was there. Doing that was probably out of order.

10 July

Went in to train with Steve Harrison on my own. Estelle and I were very quiet with each other. Went to a tattooist and chose a Celtic design. Very, very nervous. Mozza, a Black Country lad from Tipton, did the tattoo. Estelle kept feeding water to me just in case I was getting dehydrated. There were a couple of girls in there having daisy chains around their belly buttons and scorpions on their tits. Another lad came in and had a smaller Celtic symbol. Then he looked at mine as if to say 'that's a big one'. So I felt quite hard. Did a few autographs for some kids. It was a great atmosphere. No one judged me.

Went to Sainsbury's in Cannock, which was a big deal for me. I knew people would recognise me and the Ulrika thing would be on their minds. Estelle stayed by my side. There were a few people whispering.

Spoke to Ulrika on the phone. Told her I miss her and want to see her. Went to a wedding reception in the evening. There were two on at the same hotel and we walked into the wrong one by mistake. They all started shouting Ulrika-ka-ka-ka and derogatory comments.

12 July

Got up about 1 p.m. Raining and horrible. Got woken up by the boats on the canal. World Cup final today. Called Ulrika. She sounded totally different. She sounded dignified and balanced. Estelle was pissed off I had done that. She went out for a walk.

Watched the World Cup final. Felt sorry for Ronaldo but I know he'll be back. Read a book about Michael Jordan and practise, practise, practise, practise. I didn't practise my trade enough last season. This season I want to practise my shooting and my heading and all the things that will go together to make me the undisputed number-one footballer in the world. I think I will do that. I know I will do that. To get to the top of the mountain, you have to go through a lot of deep valleys. I feel I have had my share of valleys. Now is the time to come good personally and professionally. Everything is in place. Materially, I am very well off. I have got some wonderful people around me. Professionally, I have got the ability. It is just the inner desire. I need to have patience with myself. Not to be scared of anything but to relish opportunities when they come. To get back to being Stan the Man. The road is going to be long, but boy am I going to savour it when I get there.

Estelle is battling with fears and thoughts. The Ulrika thing is very difficult for her. I will never forget Estelle's commitment and loyalty towards me. Never ever.

13 July

Had an endoscopy. They stuck a tiny pipe down my penis to try to figure out the groin problem I have had. Signed a few autographs for the ladies at the hospital. Doctor produced a syringe full of jelly that he stuck down there. Said goodbye to my first challenge of the day.

Got to the training ground. Had an hour on the treadmill. Did a heavy-weights circuit. Met new signing Alan Thompson today and he seemed a really good lad. Had to convince Steve Harrison my tattoo was real.

Switched my phone on. There was a message from Estelle in a voice sounding croaky and upset. She was worried I was going down to Ulrika's. Which I wasn't. I called Ulrika and we had a decent conversation. Got back and Estelle was very tearful. She thought I was going to leave her. The one thing I have learned is to value the people closest to me. Davina left a message on my mobile. Got in the shower. Put on the theme tune to *As Good As It Gets* and lit one of my joss sticks. Feeling quite relaxed and centred today.

Read a bit more of *The Happy Book*. Watched a documentary about chemical warfare. Tried Davina a couple of times. She wasn't around. Hernia scar is painful today.

14 July

Got to training on time. Just. Felt a little bit groggy. Tried Ulrika a couple of times on her mobile on the drive into the training ground. Think she has changed her numbers. Read the paper in the physio's room. Saw a couple of snippets about Ulrika in gossip columns which knocked me a little bit. Did a long run, then a long session in the gym. Drove into Birmingham. Couple of people waved from cars. An Indian couple said they thought I was great. In the bank, I lipread one of the tellers saying 'he's a wife-beater'. Let the other teller know that I had heard what her colleague had said. Drove home. Stopped at a junction and let a lady cross the road in front of me. She had a good look. Bit edgy today. One saving grace was the running. Enjoyed that. It's a not-thinking-day today. Still feel energised instead of completely flat.

Spoke to Ulrika. She gave me her new mobile number. She was very cordial. She said she missed me. I asked if there was any chance of meeting up. She said her mum and stepdad were away for a couple of days so we could talk there in a neutral environment. Spoke to Davina and she's fine. Got back and Estelle was cooking a lovely dinner. Spoke to Linsey, and Estelle got very jealous and delved into the past. Which affected the present. Keep telling her we've just got to live in the moment like *The Happy Book* says. Took the book to Linsey's and gave it to her. Came back and started to watch *As Good As It Gets*. Told Davina about the book. She wanted a copy. I believe I am going in the right direction and that is giving me good vibes.

15 July

The majority of the first-team lads were in for the first time today. Saw Charlo [Gary Charles] and Drapes [Mark Draper] and Bozzie [Mark Bosnich]. Saw all of the lads. Everybody was chatting about holidays and stuff. We all had a run. Ran down to Kingsbury Water Park. People were flying past me but I was pleased with the work that I did. Ran back and passed Ian Taylor, which I was pleased about. Had a bit of banter in the canteen. We were talking about tattoos. Drove Lee Hendrie and Charlo down to the tattoo place. Hendrie was shitting himself. He wanted to have one of an Indian chief's head on his shoulder.

Spoke to Ulrika. She was at lunch with a friend. She is trying to pursue an acting career. She called me back. She said she was going on holiday with her son Cameron, which left me with a little tiny dent but not bad considering. Trying to sort out a time to meet up.

Spoke to my mum and she said she was going to put a new headstone on Andrea's [my sister's] grave. My Uncle Don has got a tumour on his brain and I suggested to my mum that maybe now was the time to speak. They haven't spoken for 25 years. He started blanking her after she married my dad. Her own brother. Anyway, maybe it's time to make up.

16 July

Into training. Jogged up to Kingsbury. Did two laps, which is the equivalent of 25 minutes. It was hard, but it was good work. Stretches, press-ups, sit-ups. Left training. Had a message to call Stretford urgently. Pulled into the lay-by where the bacon-sarnie place is and rang him. He said Diadora had cancelled my contract due to me not fulfilling my contractual obligations. That means being pictured in Nikes, I suppose. It wasn't a bombshell. The next two years would have been £180,000, but there's some relief that I can get back to wearing boots I like. I was having real problems with the boots. I feel disappointed I let them down but I think it has worked out for the best. I could tell Stretford was a bit fed-up.

Called Ulrika and told her about the Diadora thing. Told Oakesy [Michael Oakes] and some of the other lads when I got back to the training ground. Played a bit of keepy-uppy with some of the other lads. Drove home. Estelle got back and she had bought me a couple of candle-holders but I was concentrating on programming my phone. Had a conversation with Ulrika. It's getting to the point now where things have to be sorted out one way or the other. At the moment, the minuses far outweigh the pluses, which is unfortunate because I do have genuine feelings for the girl. Estelle wants to know where she stands, too. We are going to try and be friends without the physicality. It has been a long day but I have coped well.

17 July

Spoke to Davina on the way into training. Said we'd talk later. Did some skill games in training. Harry got everyone 'on the bridle', as he said. Had a game and drew 4–4. Scored a couple of good goals. Felt sharp. Bozzie was moaning about something. He just kept on and on and on. Good initiation for Thommo [Alan Thompson] about what a whinger Bozzie can be. Had a bit of banter with Charlo and Drapes. Got some hate mail from racist groups and all sorts about hitting

Ulrika. Looked at the new shirt. Looks a bit like West Ham's shirt.

The gaffer asked if he could have a word with me. He was all dressed up in his finery. Went into the coaches' room. He said he was impressed with my attitude in training and did I want the number nine shirt? I was proud but I didn't let it affect me to the point of being over-bubbly. Did a bleep test in the afternoon. I got to 11.2. I was a bit disappointed with that. I dropped out when I felt suitably fucked. Pottered around when I got home and did some washing up.

Got a $900 voucher from BA because of the late Concorde flight back from New York. I spoke to Linsey and she said she loved me as a friend. Tried to find out some information about any flats available in my building at Symphony Court for Alan Thompson. Watched *As Good As It Gets*. Programmed my phone with some different numbers.

18 July
Estelle went out and Linsey came over. Watched *As Good As It Gets*. Got a message from Ulrika saying she loved me. She was on her way out to a party. Had a bit of a thought attack about that, but I generally feel centred and calm. Saw Ulrika on a programme called *Blushing Brides*. It was quite comforting to see her face and hear her voice. Moved the fridge to underneath the dressing table. It looks good there.

19 July
Had a fractured night's sleep. Think I was dreaming about Ulrika. It had the aura of a bad day. Thoughts are just thoughts. I tried to get into a higher mood. I was itching to

phone Ulrika. Not really because I'm worried about what she might have done at the party, but to sort out our situation. In a low mood you are going to think low thoughts. I'm thinking the best solution might be not to have a sexual relationship with anybody and let this clear out of my system. Davina phoned and asked about the Estelle situation so I was as truthful as I could possibly be. I'm just trying to clear the decks of emotional attachments and give myself a bit of space. Ulrika goes on holiday on Tuesday and I would like to know if she wants to get back together by then. Davina was asking how I would feel if Ulrika says she needs time. Linsey called me when I was in the middle of an up-and-down mood so I told her I'd call her later. Estelle called me and she was upset on the phone.

20 July

Paul and Caroline came round and we watched a *Jerry Springer* video. I taped a few CDs and tidied them up. Ulrika called and I said to her that I loved her very dearly, but unless something was going to happen I wanted to put this chapter of my life behind me. Estelle put *Scream* on. Ulrika called back and said she couldn't promise anything. She still couldn't promise anything. She said she still couldn't trust me. We cried on the phone. She said she felt trapped, that she couldn't follow what her heart said. I said I had to get on with my life, get on with my training. Had a long conversation with Estelle and she was so upset. More upset than I've ever seen her. She asked if I loved Ulrika and I told her I did. She said: 'Now you know how it feels to be torn apart.'

She asked me how I would feel if I was going out with

Ulrika and Ulrika was on the phone to someone else all the time. That hit home a bit. Estelle said she felt a bit duped coming back from Cyprus early. But I did it with the best of intentions. We decided the best idea was for her to camp here in terms of clothes, but she is going to stay away a few nights a week at her parents' to give me time to get over Ulrika and let me get on with my own life. So Estelle has got her own room here now. Difficult times ahead but I am feeling good. I hope to God I can continue this in the same vein.

21 July

Picture of Ulrika in a couple of the papers going to the cinema in London. I phoned her and she said she was surprised to be hearing from me again. I asked if I could go down and see her. Could sense she was a bit shocked but she said she'd ring me back. She said her heart wanted to see me but not her head. I felt she was making excuses. She said I never listened to her. I didn't want to get into that, so the conversation ended. I told Davina about it and she was playing devil's advocate. One of the papers was saying Ulrika was seeing somebody else. It was some little dickhead, which didn't make me feel a lot better.

Tried to phone Ulrika. Left three messages, just explaining I couldn't get hold of her and all the thoughts going through my head. I don't think she's being honest with me. I've got a feeling somebody is lurking in the background. She says she isn't seeing anybody. I am in love with her, there is no doubt about that. I miss her spirit. I am sitting here on the bed on my tod, which hasn't happened for a long, long time. I am going to tidy up and plod along for the rest of the night. I'm going to phone Davina and find out what the papers said about who Ulrika was seeing. When I can't get hold of Ulrika, I think all sorts of things. It's not my place to think those things, but it doesn't half push my envelope. Maybe her being away in France this week will give me time to get rid of everything. It feels like a giant step not to call her.

Spoke to Ulrika. She said she was frightened about committing to me again. I don't think she really wants to be with me. She said she'd call me back. It's midnight now and she hasn't called. Davina feels I sound worse after I have spoken to Ulrika, which is a shame because I do love the girl. Stayed in tonight and watched *Scream*. I think I should give Ulrika this week to sort herself out without calling her. Maybe she'll call me when she gets back and maybe she won't. If there's love involved, that should conquer all. All I know is that she loves me.

22 July

Pushed myself hard in training. Some supporters by the side of the pitch. One of them had a Collymore shirt on which was great. Showed Alan Thompson around the city. Saw a decent bird in the shopping centre. Gave her the eyes and that. Spoke to Linsey and she came down. She was looking very fit with her cycling shorts on. Had a bit of a kiss and a cuddle. She left. Estelle came over and she was upset because the first thing she heard was me on the phone to Ulrika. We watched *One Flew Over the Cuckoo's Nest*. I am going to try and encourage her to read her copy of *The Happy Book* a bit more. I want her to know she is loved, but in a non-sexual way.

23 July

Football work in the morning. Gaffer pulled me into his office and said he was extremely pleased with the way I was working. He said although there would be obstacles in my way, it was a question of how I would deal with them. He said that if I kept training this way I would play 38 games next season. Took my washing over to my mum's. Sent Ulrika a text message saying I wanted her and loved her. Did some speed work in the afternoon. Came home. Watched a porno. I hate thinking I have let Estelle down but I can't lie to her about Ulrika. I'm concerned about the lack of quality talking time Ulrika and I have on the phone. But faith springs eternal. Linsey rang and wished me goodnight.

24 July

David Unsworth signed today. Walked in the dressing room and there he was. Did some sprints. Some kids were watching and shouting my name. Got home. Told Linsey and her mate to come round. Rang Ulrika. Conversation started well and then deteriorated. She told me about a Ben Elton book her friend Paul had bought her, which narked me. She was asking me too many questions. I have told her enough times that I want her and I want her for the right reasons. She got upset and put the phone down on me. I sent her a text message saying I didn't want anything to do with her and she should get together with Paul. Went out that night. Got back. Ulrika rang. Linsey rang. Can't be doing with the time-wasters. Just want to get on with my life.

26 July

Couple of lads at training asked if I'd seen the papers. Assumed it must be something about Ulrika but it was a story about Fenerbahce bidding £8 million for me. It was only a couple of lines so I knew it was bullshit. Did a weights circuit with Drapes and a few of the lads. Chairman came in and was his crap, talkative-bollocks self. Went and got another tattoo saying 'Strength Through Adversity'. Had a bit of lunch in Chinatown in Birmingham. Bloke came over and wanted me to kiss his girlfriend because it was her birthday. I politely declined. Saw some dykes going into a club and went in and joined them. Had ten birds all around me straight away. Turned out they all played for Birmingham Ladies football team but most of them were Villa fans.

28 July

Feel like I have come a long way since New York. I can honestly say I am happy. Estelle stayed last night. Got up. Had a bit of fruit salad. Went into training. A lot of speculation about whether Yorkie is staying or going. Did a bit of defending and attacking. Scored a few goals. Felt sharp. Did 30-metre doggies. It was hard. Did the team photo. Yorkie's milking all the speculation about him moving to Manchester United. Sitting in front of the cameras on his own. The kit's minging. Got some mail about bank statements which made me a bit panicky. Got to buy a house for Michelle. Finding out whether that's tax deductible. Spoke to Estelle and she was upset. She wouldn't let me know why. She is finding it hard-going not seeing me all the time. I'm in danger of making a rod for my own back because Linsey keeps coming round in short dresses and skirts and it is just too tempting. She is a very tactile person but I have resisted the temptation.

Spoke to Strets [Paul Stretford]. He is doing Kevin Campbell's move to Trabzonspor. Spoke to Davina today and she was on about blokes and said she hadn't had it for a long time. She's a good girl. Rang Ulrika four times and didn't get any answer. The new gym's about to open in Symphony Court and there are a few girls working in the creche opposite. One of them keeps looking over and giving me a little wave and I keep my eyes open for her, but it is all harmless stuff.

I miss Ulrika. I feel okay about it this week because she has been away, but once she comes up here for *Gladiators* next week we'll see how I deal with it then. Feel a bit more relaxed now that Estelle is giving me a bit of space. Just have to make sure that I don't get into a situation with Linsey again. Somebody asked me if I had a goal target for the season and I said 25. First time I have ever set myself a target like that, so that feels like progress.

29 July

Felt a bit nervy when I woke up. Playing Wycombe in pre-season friendly today and Ulrika is due back from holiday. Went to the training ground. Felt bubbly. Knew that Yorkie wasn't playing so it was my opportunity to shine. Had a couple of phone calls from Linsey and Estelle. Had a fax from Nicole in Germany asking if I wanted to go over and see her. Might be difficult. Spoke to Davina. Craving Ulrika, who is going to be in Birmingham in a couple of days. Know I should keep away. Had a bit of a kip on the coach to

Wycombe. A lot of Villa fans there. They gave me a warm welcome. Got barracked by the Wycombe fans, which might be a taste of things to come. They were saying I should be locked up and that I was a retard. It's probably going to be a lot heavier than that in the Premiership.

Set the first goal up for Julian Joachim. Scored the second with a powerful low drive. My runs were good. Felt sharp. Passing was good, movement was good. Gaffer was pleased. Got on the bus. Listened to my Walkman on the way back. Sent text messages to Linsey and Estelle. Phoned Ulrika. Knew she was in France because it was ringing out on a French code. I kept thinking, 'ring her and everything will be all right'. Estelle was there waiting for me when I got back about midnight. She'd made me some sandwiches.

30 July

Had to go to shake hands with the people who sponsored our shirts last year. Drove past the National Indoor Arena and there was a sign outside saying 'Welcome to the Gladiators'. Miss Ulrika a lot. Went out to get the papers to read the match reports from Wycombe. As I drove past the Hyatt I saw a few of the Gladiators all kissing each other in greeting and it made me feel very anxious. Phoned Davina. Told her I was in bits. Went out for a bit of lunch with Thommo at San Carlo in Temple Street in the city centre.

Called Ulrika and she was very terse. Said she was busy. She sounded very cold. Last night, Linsey and Estelle met each other for the first time which was great. Phoned Davina, who told me not to call Ulrika. She said it was obvious Ulrika didn't want to know. Took a sleeping pill. Went to bed with

Estelle. Woke up having a really bad dream about Ulrika with other guys. Called her and told her how much I loved her and that I felt I was right for her. I was very tearful on the phone. In bits, basically. My head's all over the place. She was going to an audition for *Chicago*. I have got to try and keep my perspective and my power. Keep going, Stan. Keep going.

31 July

Told Jim Walker, the physio, about Ulrika being in Birmingham and how I might need some therapy because my regular guy is away. Spoke to Davina who was at a fashion show at Oceana. Had a long conversation with Ulrika. She said she needed time to sort her head out, which is a polite way of saying 'fuck off'. Nicole said that if a woman says she wants time, it means she wants out. Davina thinks the same. It is a shame because I feel it was finished prematurely. Ulrika said she had to go because she had to pack her bags. There is always a reason for her to get off the phone these days. Starting to feel like a pest. Had a great conversation here with Estelle. She's a very intelligent woman when she opens up. I'm fucking down today. Got another game today against Peterborough. Just got to get out there and do the biz.

Bit sloppy in my warm-up. Yorkie scored. Felt a bit tired. It's the brain drain. Went in on goal, went to change to the extra gear, and my thigh went. Stayed down. Steve Harrison came in while I was being strapped up in the physio's room and told me that now was the time to show my strength. Called Ulrika and she was fine. She said she was at home, which I found odd because she was due in Birmingham today.

So I phoned her at home. She answered. The doorbell rang ten minutes into the conversation and she ushered a friend in. It was a bloke, because if it's a woman she greets them by name. She said she'd call me back. I called her back ten minutes later and asked her if it was Paul. She said it wasn't. She said it was a friend she had known for years and she was sitting having a cup of tea.

Had my leg propped up on the settee. Waved at Floss, or whatever she's called, in the offices across the road. Cheers me up. Told a mate of mine in PR to call *The Sun* and tell them that Ulrika has a new boyfriend. I told Davina what I was planning. She said I was being stupid and descending to Ulrika's level. Estelle thought it was a good idea, though. I'm in despair. Ulrika called. We had a conversation for an hour and a half. I said I wanted some dignity but I wanted her to be the only woman in my life. She kept on saying the same things. I've heard it a thousand times. Estelle slammed the phone down because she had heard me. Ulrika called back so I said a wire had come out of the phone. Later, Davina said Ulrika will never want to be with me and everybody else can see it. It's only me who's holding out this forlorn hope.

But I am in love with Ulrika. As long as I am hanging on that cliff edge, even if she has only got one finger left to stamp on, I will keep trying. She hit a real nerve with me when she talked about us having children and a family. Davina thinks it's all over because it's all about her career and I come very low down the list behind fuckers like Chris Evans and Hunter. I want to be the number one in her life and I have got to keep trying as long as there is hope left. I'm down because of my injury, too. It could be a few weeks before I can play again. My brain's mush again. Had a letter from Wendy, who we think is my dad's daughter. She's living in Warwick. Made me think again about what a complete wank stain my dad is. This is a real hard slog for me. Feel quite disillusioned. It's now 12.09. I love you, Ulrika. I love you, Estelle. Thank you, Linsey.

1 August

Asked Linsey to come over. Estelle made a big fuss. She felt her position was being compromised. But they both tried to cheer me up and keep me away from Ulrika. Ulrika called. She said she was going to The Church nightclub which is literally around the corner from my house. I completely lost it. I was freaking out. My brain had gone. I was shouting and screaming because I just could not believe she could be so insensitive. We had a mad conversation. I was sitting in the corner with a pillow over my face, completely distressed that someone I loved and love and that I thought loved me could be so insensitive. She threw everything back in my face. Davina. Estelle.

Linsey was sitting listening to all this and she started crying. She said she'd had enough. She left me here on my own. I begged her to come back and she came back. We sat and watched *Face Off* with Nicolas Cage and John Travolta. Davina told me I should tell Ulrika to fuck off because she was evil and mad. I phoned Ulrika at 1.30 a.m. She answered. I said I would meet her at the bottom of Bridge Street, just outside the Hyatt. I told Linsey, who was on the phone to Estelle. Estelle was on her way over. She was coming in the gates as I walked out of the house. Estelle was begging me not to go, in floods of tears.

Got in the Range Rover, drove down Broad Street and waited for about 10 or 15 minutes. Didn't think she was going to turn up. Then I saw this figure at the top of the road with her unmistakable walk, heading towards me. As she got close to the car I whispered her name, and she turned and gave me that trademark insincere smile. There were a few people around, staggering out of clubs, so she got in the car and I drove round the corner, under the bridge into a car park. We talked and I told her how much I loved her and I was stroking her hand.

She had a baggy jogging-suit top on and jeans. She said she had spoken to her friend Jennifer, and Jennifer had said go and see me. There we were in the corner of a dark car park in Birmingham. I was looking into her eyes. She looked drawn. Her hair was almost shoulder-length. We kissed. I held her. She looked at my tattoos. We kissed some more. I stroked her hair. I put the seats back and we made love to each other. When she came, she cried and said that she loved me.

We talked some more. When I was on top of her, I looked at her for so long. I looked at her eyes and her hair. For all my failings as a man and the ways I've hurt other people along the way, I looked at that woman and felt so much love for her and so much serenity. She said she needed time and that she did love me. When we put the seat back, the back window opened, and we had a little bit of a giggle and she said she felt like a 17-year-old. I dropped her back 30 yards from the hotel and I kissed her on the forehead and told her I loved her.

I saw Linsey and her mum drive past but I don't think they

saw me. I got back and Estelle was sitting out on the patio with a fag, so distressed that I had left her. But I couldn't help myself. I truly couldn't help myself. I said to Estelle, 'come to bed', but she didn't want to get in with me. In the early hours she got in with me. She was shaking because she was having a dream. I was trying to hold her and reassure her because I do love her. The phone rang and it was Linsey and she said she loved me but she couldn't see me do this to myself.

Estelle has been really tranquil this morning. I put *Air Force One* on, and I've been looking over at the gym like an obsessive. Me and Estelle are both like zombies. Two messages on the phone: one from Alan Thompson, and one from Linsey, slagging me off. I'm sitting here in my Villa trackie bottoms. I don't know what direction my life is going in. I thought I had contingency plans but I haven't got the willpower to help myself. I seem to be shelling out a lot of money for therapy and not getting much benefit from it. I'm heading back down towards zero. I'm sinking fast.

People say that when the football's going well, life seems better. But before I can start scoring goals and playing well I have got to make myself strong. I don't think putting myself under the kind of strain and pressure that I will do in the first few weeks of the season is going to be good for me. All sorts of things are going through my mind. Quitting football, living a more simple life. I'm in too deep, but I don't know how to start.

I feel like a freak show. The Man That Beat Ulrika Jonsson Up. I feel that the woman that I love has distanced herself so far from me. We lay in the same bed and shared those experiences for so many months and in so many different places, but she can be so insensitive as to go to a nightclub around the corner and say that she is not going to bother to come and see me. I'm in very deep. I don't know how to find redemption. Maybe it will only be death that gets me out of all this. I don't seem to make too many people happy. I don't seem to make myself happy.

I have been doing this taping for almost a month now. Up. Down. Up. Down. The video tape's on *Stop*. There's an empty bottle of red wine on the table. The patio door's open. I'm still here. An angel just came down the stairs.

4 August

Message from Ulrika asking me how I was. Sounding very lively and chirpy. We arranged to meet up. I had sent her ten bouquets of red roses. She said it took three people to carry them into her room. She's got them displayed round her room. She said she was going to meet Jeremy Guscott and I was a bit distressed because I thought she wasn't going to turn up for the date we had arranged together. Spoke to Nicole and she's in a bad way because her boyfriend's got a new girlfriend. Rang my mum and asked her to order Estelle some roses.

Ulrika rang and said maybe we could meet tomorrow. I said, 'No, I want to see you tonight.' I changed my clothes about ten times to try to impress her and then I thought 'fuck it, just wear what you normally wear'. I was anticipating us coming back to the house so I hid Estelle's clothes, which is terrible. A terrible thing to do. Went to McDonald's for my tea. Went to collect her. She was walking down the road and she looked like the most beautiful woman I had ever seen. She really was my woman. I drove down Broad Street with my woman and took her home. We talked about everything. Paris. How I felt. I showed her the photos from Jamaica and told her how much I loved her. We talked for a couple of hours. We were kissing and touching and hugging and feeling. We went upstairs. Made love in bed. It was beautiful. We talked again. I was a bit tearful and upset. All night I couldn't believe she was there. Every time she moved away she left her hand there for me to hold. I did the same. Woke up and made love again. I looked at her skin and her breasts and her face and her hair. I kissed her and held her. Took her back. I spoke to Davina straight after I had dropped her off. She said Ulrika had made a big commitment by staying the night after everything that had happened in Paris. She said I really just had to value it as much as I could for as long as it lasted. She's right about that. I love Ulrika. I am madly in love with this woman.

5 August

At training we ran around the water park and I was blowing out of my arse. My thigh was hurting. I was worried about my fitness. I was thinking, 'fucking hell, I am losing this fitness already'. I am going to keep plugging away at my long-distance stuff. I'm not going to Spain with the club. Sitting in the phsyio's room with Gareth Southgate and the physio asked us which boxer won the championship and then shit in the ring. No one knew. He said '"Misty Blue the Third" at Crufts.' Pissed ourselves laughing at that.

Got a text message from Estelle thanking me for the flowers. She said they made her cry. Message from Ulrika saying she missed me. That put me on a high. Linsey came round and we went to do some food shopping. She saw a mate of hers who is a big Villa fan. She's got a poster of me on the wall and she says 'I'm not worthy' every time she walks past it. She said to Linsey, 'Are you fucking him?' Linsey said I was only a friend. I am quite happy today. I believe that my woman loves me.

Did a really good workout session today. Forty minutes at pace on the treadmill. Saw the woman next door, Dolores with the big ass, and her husband. Could see all the kids going into the NIA to watch *Gladiators* from my flat. Such a comforting thought to think Ulrika is so close. My mum is 68 today. Bought her some presents and took them up there. I have been through a hell of a lot and maybe I should give myself some credit for still being here. Davina is in Exeter, doing *Streetmate*. I love Ulrika very much and I love Estelle very much, but in entirely different ways. I hope Ulrika decides to see the benefits of me.

6 August

A couple of the boot boys helped me take the roof off my car at the training ground. One of them scratched the wing when he was taking it off but it wasn't his fault. Went down to the garage to look at some Audis and BMWs but I don't like the new shape. I wanted a VL6, which they don't do. Estelle said I have been using her. I hate hurting her. I hate seeing her angry. I was in the land of nod, I was really tired, so she gave me a mouthful before she left. I told her I had to see this thing through with Ulrika.

9 August

Picked Ulrika up after *Gladiators*. Came back to the house. Both tired. The bubbliness wasn't there. Went to bed and made love. But I was tossing and turning and shouting in my sleep. I was wired.

10 August

Dropped Ulrika off in the morning on the way to training. She put her hood up and didn't want to be seen with me in the car, which was disappointing.

Got annoyed with my mum because I'd bought her a mobile phone for her birthday and she couldn't work out how to use it. She said she'd seen my Uncle Don in Cannock for the first time in years and years and he'd belittled her in public, saying stuff about how she had a millionaire for a son but how I didn't want to know her. He's dying from his tumour.

Had to pay £12 for Estelle to use the gym. Going to join her up on Monday. Took Linsey and Estelle to a new club called Hush and paid £45 for the three of us to get in. Had a fucked-up conversation with Ulrika on the mobile on the way back but it wasn't that bad by our standards. Got back to the house and Linsey and Estelle got in the same bed and banged the door shut because they could hear me talking to Ulrika. It's all getting fucked up again. I don't know where it's going. *Gladiators* is finishing in Birmingham tonight. Ulrika's going to be leaving then. I can feel it closing in again. It's getting fucked up. It's getting fucked up. Put on *As Good As It Gets*.

CHAPTER NINE

LEICESTER: SECOND CHANCES

I don't know how I had become so far removed from the essence of the existence I had craved when I was at the beginning of my football career. I don't know how I had got shunted off into that cul-de-sac, so far away from the existence I had envisaged for myself. Everything gets telescoped when you are a footballer. It's like your life only lasts for 15 years.

By the time I joined Leicester in February 2000 I didn't know if I was still capable of playing Premiership football. I had been on the sidelines for so long and gone through so much and seen so many things that made me feel disillusioned about football that I just didn't know if I had the appetite any more. I had never been lacking in belief about my ability, but for the first time, after the battering I had taken, doubts had started to creep in.

Most of all, I needed somebody to trust. I needed to believe there was a manager out there who wouldn't use me as the first excuse to get him out of the shit. Someone who wouldn't turn me into a scapegoat. Someone who wouldn't say one thing to me and then an entirely different thing to the press.

I had become so bitter that I just didn't think such a manager existed any more.

But Martin O'Neill proved me wrong. I wish fervently that I had found him earlier. More to the point, I suppose, I wish he'd found me. He could have saved me. He could have made me. He could have got the best out of me for years. But I never got that chance. I got a glimpse of the promised land. I thought I was going to be able to bask in my Indian summer and that it was going to be better than anything that had gone before. I thought that just when I least expected it, here was a real shot at redemption, a chance to make up for all the frustration I had begun to feel at Liverpool and had been made to endure at Villa. But it was not to be. It was great while it lasted, but too soon all these hopes, all these conceits, were snatched away from me almost before the adventure had begun.

Still, at least I made the right choice when I was given my options of how to escape from Gregory. Bradford had come in for me and they were offering £40,000 a week. That was the deal they gave Benito Carbone six months later. In many ways, it was also the deal that drove them to the brink of extinction. It was double what I was getting at Villa. But once Jonathan Crystal told me Martin O'Neill was interested, there was only one place I wanted to go and it wasn't Valley Parade. I had played against Leicester a few times and I knew they were a strong team. They punched above their weight and I had heard good things about Martin – that he was a fucking great manager, hard but fair.

Jonathan and I went down to London to meet him at the Royal Garden Hotel in Kensington. Leicester were playing

Tottenham the next day. He asked me a few questions about whether I was all right mentally and physically. He also said he hadn't got a lot of time for Gregory, which endeared him to me, obviously. He said he just wanted me to come and enjoy my football. He was very sympathetic.

Actually, he was more interested in Jonathan than me. Jonathan did a lot of work as a criminal barrister and Martin has got this well-known obsession with crime. His idea of a break away from it all is a few days sitting in the public gallery at the Crown Court, watching a bloke get tried for murder. He's a real student of serial killers. He's visited 10 Rillington Place, all that sort of thing. That's what lights his fire.

Anyway, he and Jonathan were soon talking away about James Hanratty and the A6 murders. When Jonathan said he could introduce him to the barrister who was the prosecutor in that case, Martin nearly came in his pants. That was like his wet dream suddenly made reality. The deal to take me to Filbert Street was done. Martin said there was a trip to La Manga coming up that would be a good chance for me to bond with the rest of the lads. I signed for Leicester City the next day.

A lot of people thought it was a marriage made in hell. They assumed hardened, no-nonsense pros like Matty Elliott and Gerry 'Tags' Taggart would dismiss me as some sort of tart, a prima donna who didn't fit in with the ethos of hard work and collective responsibility they had all built together. Funny, but the opposite was true. They were lads who had grafted their way through the lower leagues, but so was I. I got on with those lads better than I had ever got on with any team-mates before or since. I still keep in touch with most of them. They were normal blokes who loved football, which was all I had ever wanted to be. It felt like I was coming home.

I knew Robbie 'Sav' Savage a little bit. When he was at Crewe, my mate Jamie Moralee, who was also at Gresty Road at the time, had brought him down to stay at my place in Cannock for a few nights while he found somewhere permanent to live. He came up to me when I met all the lads in the canteen at the training ground and said how much he had appreciated my kindness.

Most of us hit it off immediately. I liked Matty and Tags instantly. The only one I thought I might have a problem with was Ian Marshall. He was sitting in the canteen, too, reading *The Sun*. When I was introduced to him, he just grunted without looking up from his paper and kept on reading. I never would have expected us to become mates, but after that we got on great, too.

My first day's training was on a Friday and we were due to play Watford on the Saturday. It was a bit of a culture shock. I was used to Villa, where training was very structured and regimented. Plenty of cones and balls everywhere. A routine, an order, a place for everything. Orders being barked. Obedience required. It wasn't like that at Leicester.

On this first day at the training ground in the suburbs, Steve Walford, the first-team coach, came out with a fag in his mouth and a whistle on a string round his neck. He said he wanted us to hurry it up because he needed to be in the pub by midday. I never knew whether he was really going to the pub every time he said that in the weeks and months that followed, but I wouldn't have put it past him. Anyway, that was the kind of light-hearted atmosphere he helped create.

That day, he said we were going to have a five-a-side. 'Right, old 'uns versus young 'uns,' he said, 'go and warm yourself up.' So all the boys are lashing balls into hedges and just having a laugh. I was wondering what the fuck I had got myself into. Next thing, John 'Robbo' Robertson, Martin's number two, came out to watch. He had a fag in his mouth, too.

Robbo always wore a suit, but his tie was invariably halfway down his shirt and he chain-smoked. He would just stand on the touchline, calling out, 'well done, son' or 'brilliant, son'. Nothing negative. Ever. If he wanted to give you a bit of advice, he would come across when the session was over and put his arm around you while you were walking off. And even on that first day, I suddenly began to realise where Leicester had built all their spirit from.

They loved the two coaches for a start. And they all respected Martin. Not everybody liked him. Robbie Savage used to get the hump because Martin was always on at him to win it and give it, not to do too much with the ball. Sav thought he was a better player than that and he got frustrated with Martin at times. But he still respected him. He still recognised what Martin had done for his career and for him as a player.

And me? Within a few weeks of working for Martin I would have walked through walls for him. Just like the rest of the players. If he ever becomes manager of Manchester United or Liverpool, I think those clubs would waltz away with the

Champions League. He is that good. He can get anybody to play for him and he inspires a tremendous loyalty among his players. A loyalty to him and to each other. I can't bear to think what might have been if I could have played for him earlier in my career.

Part of the buzz when you're a kid and you're playing football is the camaraderie, the feeling of one-in, all-in. That all gets diluted when you're a professional. There's the money and the jealousy and the competitiveness between you all. But it's not like that when Martin O'Neill runs a team. He gets rid of all that. He makes it disappear. If he's got a secret, if he's got a gift above all his other gifts, that's it.

I'll give you an example. One of the players who was most friendly to me when I arrived at Leicester was Tony Cottee, and yet he knew that he had more to lose than anybody else when I was signed because I would probably be taking his place up front alongside Emile. And yet Tony didn't think like that, and that was because of Martin. Every single player that I thought would be against me was like a diamond with me. I'd become so cynical by then, I couldn't work it out for a while. But pretty soon I realised it all stemmed from Martin. He's an intelligent man, basically, and a smart coach, too. A myth has grown up around Martin that he doesn't get involved in training and that the players don't see him from day to day until a match rolls around. That wasn't true. He would come out and do his little bits. He let Walford do most of the coaching but he wanted to oversee everything.

Some people have labelled him a long-ball merchant but I've played under long-ball merchants and he wasn't one of them. His Leicester side were just a more combative, practical version of the Villa team I played in. All the training sessions at Leicester were about getting the ball on the ground. People like Muzzy Izzet didn't just lump the ball, they were good footballers. Leicester were a team who could batter you to pulp because they had some big blokes, but they could play you off the park with good football, too. Crucially, in Martin they had a manager who got the best out of the resources he had. He built his team around big players and big characters and he knew which buttons to press on all of us. So the day before we travelled to Watford for my first game, even though I hadn't played for months, Martin said he was going to start me up front with Emile Heskey. He asked me to give him everything I could for an hour and then they would carry me off on a stretcher if need be.

I never played under Brian Clough at Forest, but Martin did, and I imagine that O'Neill was a modern version of the man who brought two European Cups to the City Ground. Mark Crossley told me once that in Cloughie's last season at Forest they had a five-a-side game on a Monday morning, someone scored a cracker and Cloughie said, 'Right, off you pop, see you Thursday.' Martin wasn't quite that laid back but the atmosphere he built was similar.

He would work with individuals, too. On my first Friday he pulled me over with Darren Eadie and a couple of other lads at the end of the session and said he wanted to do a bit of stuff on my sharpness. He gave me loads of shuttle runs to do and I thought it was ridiculous before a game the next day. But when I ran out at Vicarage Road, although my legs were a bit stiff, my muscles were back to knowing what it was all about. Martin is a very perceptive guy. If he doesn't say something himself, he will say it through Robbo or Steve Walford. But it is basically always coming from him.

So at Watford, I hit the post, I hit the bar, I did everything except score. I had a really good game, held the ball up well and clicked with Emile. And I lasted the whole game. It's funny how the few words Martin had said before the game, and the body language he had towards me, can make such a difference. It's the difference between enjoying a game, even though you've been out for a while, and struggling through one where you are supposed to be fit but the pressure's on, and if you score three, somebody like Gregory will say he wants four.

I was delighted with that game at Watford and I already felt at home with Martin and the coaches. I felt part of it. I felt like I was one of the lads already. And so when we flew to Spain a couple of days later for the little break Martin had talked about, I was on cloud nine. There was going to be plenty of golf for the lads who wanted to play and some nice warm-weather training. I've never owned a set of golf clubs in my life and I don't play, but I thought I'd try to be on my best behaviour.

It was mid-afternoon when we got out there and the golfers like Matty Elliott and Neil Lennon went out on the course. We were staying at the Hyatt hotel, where Gazza had famously gone berserk when Glenn Hoddle told him he had left him out of the England squad for the 1998 World Cup. I was rooming with Emile, and most of the early evening he was just chilling out listening to his Walkman and I was lounging on the bed watching the telly. Then, about nine o'clock, we got a call from Matty to say that everyone was in the bar. We wandered down and walked into the bar just as Gary Lineker, Leicester's most famous player, and his brother were walking out.

By that time all the boys were absolutely bladdered. I had only had a couple of beers so I felt very, very sober compared to the rest of them. We all went off to a club a few miles away and stayed there for a while, and when we got back to the hotel bar some time after midnight it was almost empty. There was a bloke and his wife sitting in one corner and two or three couples in the other corner. And then there was us: me, Gerry Taggart, Neil Lennon, Tim Flowers, Ian Marshall and the physio, Mick Yeomans. We were rolling by then, of course, and Ian Marshall was so pissed he started ringing Martin O'Neill's mobile phone. Martin was still back in England, and was planning to come out and join us the next day. He had left Robbo in charge, but by that stage Robbo had gone up to bed. Thankfully, Martin didn't answer his phone but Marshy still insisted on leaving a message. 'Hiya gaffer,' he said, 'we love you and we can't wait to see you tomorrow. All the lads send their love.' Everyone was screaming with laughter but part of me was thinking about how serious and stern Martin could be, too.

Not that I can claim to be an innocent party. By that time, I was sitting next to Mick Yeomans and there was a fire extinguisher just behind me. Neil Lennon got hold of it and touched the nozzle and a bit of powder spurted onto the floor. He said to me, 'Go on, give Mick a bit of a spray.' So I squeezed the nozzle and sprayed him. Mick's bald, and with all the powder on his face he looked like one of those clowns after you've splatted him in the face with a cake. When he opened his eyes, he looked out at us from a mass of white that was the rest of his face.

All the lads were wetting themselves laughing and there was a bit of banter going on. And so I thought 'fuck this'. I got that fire extinguisher and pulled the pin out and as soon as I did that it went off full bore. I got Mick with it a bit more but it started swirling around and it fucked up the whole room. It was like Santa's grotto in that bar by the time I'd finished with that fire extinguisher. Nobody could see anything at all. It was like being in a snowstorm.

Then, suddenly, out of the mist, this short-arsed bloke who must have been about five foot nothing came hurtling towards our group and jumped on Neil Lennon. Lennie was swinging him around and Matty Elliott was wrestling with them both, trying to break it up. It was like something out of the circus. Then another couple came out of the mist, coughing and spluttering and having a go. Eventually, everything calmed down and we all went to bed.

There was a lot of powder around but I didn't really think any more of it. It didn't occur to me that there would be a serious problem, which I suppose is an indictment of my idea of what social responsibility was at that time. It's too easy to lose sight of what's right and wrong sometimes when you're a young millionaire.

The next morning, we met in the reception area with our training kit on and John Robertson came down and announced that we were going home. He said we had to go home; that we had been told to go home. The little bloke who had come out of the mist was apparently one of the most loyal guests the hotel had. He had been a regular there for

30 years and he had given the hotel the classic ultimatum: either the Leicester City team left or he would. Not surprisingly, the hotel chose us.

So we all traipsed out of the hotel and we walked past the bar as we went. I sneaked a glance, long enough to see that white dust had settled on everything. There were about a thousand glasses behind that bar, apparently, and they all had to be cleaned, not to mention the sofas and the carpet and the chairs. Altogether, the cleaning bill would come to about £700.

When we got back to Gatwick it was pandemonium. The press had been tipped off and they were waiting for us in the main terminal, but someone had organised a coach to take us off the tarmac and avoid them all. They were all staring out of the windows at us as we drove past and Muzzy Izzet ducked down behind his seat and stuck two fingers up at them. That was the picture they used with the stories the next day. One of the headlines called us 'Animals' and there was a big inquest about who the two fingers belonged to.

The coach took us back up to the Midlands and straight to a hotel called Sketchley Grange, just where the M6 and the M69 motorways converge. Leicester always used to have club functions there. We were ushered into a conference room where there were about 50 chairs and one long table and it was all in darkness. Out of that darkness, Martin O'Neill emerged and sat down very stony-faced behind the table.

All the lads sat down. I picked a chair halfway back. I was starting to feel very nervous. Then the inquisition started. 'Fucking hell, lads,' Martin said, 'I can't fucking believe this.' He looked at Marshy and asked him if it was him who had called him in the middle of the night. Marshy said it was. 'You haven't done enough in the game, son,' Martin said, 'to fucking call me at three in the morning.'

Then, inevitably, he asked who had set the fire extinguisher off. I had been at the club for all of five days when I put my hand up to admit to that. 'Fucking hell,' Martin said, 'I should have known better. You're a fucking disgrace.' I tried to say that we had just been having a bit of a laugh and then he lost it completely. You need to see him when that happens. He's the funniest man in the world. He was pacing around, beside himself with anger.

The next day, he dragged me into his office at the training ground. All the papers were on his desk. All of them were screaming for me to be sacked. He had highlighted the bits pertinent to me with yellow marker-pen. There was a lot of yellow marker-pen. One of the papers had a picture of me dancing with the missus of one of the blokes in the bar. 'What's your missus going to think of you fucking cavorting with other women?' he said. I thought that was actually the last thing he should have been worrying about. I explained to him that the husband of the woman had actually taken the picture. I said my missus would be cool with it all anyway. He insisted I send her some flowers and an apology, which I did in the end. Then he said that he was giving me an official yellow card and that if anything like that ever happened again then I would be out the door. I got out of his office as quickly as I could, relieved that I was still at the club.

The next game, the following Saturday, was against Sunderland at Filbert Street. They were going well under Peter Reid and I was very nervous because people around the city were already accusing me of being a troublemaker who had wrecked the reputation of the team and sabotaged its spirit. In the midst of it all, it did occur to me that there was an irony here. After all, I'm the guy who's supposed to be a loner, incapable of bonding with team-mates, and now I'd bonded with them so well that I was in even more trouble than usual.

Add to that the fact that the image of the club was of a very well-disciplined unit who didn't have any stars but just solid pros. These men weren't the types to get involved in what was seen as spoiled-brat behaviour. It felt like a very delicate situation. People were even questioning Martin's judgement. But I found that when I was thrust into such a pressured situation, that was when I was likely to respond best.

I'd had a similar scenario unfold before when I'd played for Villa on the Boxing Day after being locked up in Cannock nick in the early hours of Christmas Day, when Michelle had made her allegations about me knocking her out. I got a great reception from the Villa fans that day, but the advantage I had there was that I had been playing for them for some time and I'd scored a few goals. That wasn't the case at Leicester.

The team that started that game against Sunderland was probably one of the best Leicester teams ever, and it was one of Emile's last games, too. They were really at their peak then, and I provided the supporters with the best response possible after La Manga. I scored a hat-trick and we won 5–2.

The Leicester dressing room after that match was a very happy place. It felt like a crisis had passed for all of us. Somebody said we should get fire extinguishers installed in the training ground and let them off every week if that was the effect it had on us. Martin came in and wandered over to me. He just grinned and shook his head. 'You fucker,' he said. Somebody wrote a piece in *The Times* the following Monday about another typical topsy-turvy week in the life of Stanley Victor Collymore.

And it was a bizarre few weeks. The next game I played was against Derby at Pride Park, hardly one of my favourite places because of all my Forest affiliations. Somewhere in the game I played an innocuous pass to Robbie Savage across the pitch. There was no one anywhere near me, but as I passed the ball I lurched forward and all my weight went onto my left leg. I felt this awful pain shoot down my leg and into my ankle. I went down onto the deck and I saw that my toes were pointing the opposite way to where they should have been. My foot had come out of its socket and twisted, and my first reaction was that I needed to get up and run it off. That didn't last long. Matty Elliott came running over and started to ask whether I was all right. Then, midway through his sentence, he put his hands over his eyes, turned away and said 'oh, fucking hell'. With a lot of feeling. That didn't really make me feel any better, obviously. I was panicking anyway, but after that I shat myself.

They brought a stretcher on and they gave me gas, and as I was coming off the pitch I was being applauded by the Leicester fans and I felt so giddy it was like I was tripping. I went to the hospital in an ambulance, still in my kit. That felt like a freak show. My foot was practically hanging off, I was in a lot of pain, and still there were people coming up to me as I was being wheeled in, asking for my autograph.

Once they got me into a cubicle they sat me on the end of a bed and a consultant came in and told me to dangle my leg over the side. He said I had dislocated my foot and suffered a spiral fracture of the tibia. He rubbed his hands together and said that what he was going to do next was going to hurt. He said that before they operated on me to treat the break, they had to put the foot back in its socket. He added that it would only take a split second, and, like an idiot, I looked down and watched him pull my foot down a few centimetres so it seemed as if it was just hanging by skin. Then he twisted it and locked it. I had never felt pain like it before, and thankfully I have never felt pain like it since. I can't describe it. I almost fainted. I was operated on that night; they put a metal plate in it and that was that.

Everybody asked me if I was worried about lapsing back into depression, but I was determined to stay positive and I said I'd be back in six weeks. And I was. I worked really hard with the physios. I did a lot of swimming and biking, and when I was fit again I bought the three physios a TAG Heuer watch each to thank them for everything they had done for me and all the effort they had put in.

I just missed out on the last game of the season. I was desperate to play. I begged Martin to put me back into the side, even onto the bench, but he said that even though he was amazed at the speed of my recovery it was just too soon. The season ended. I went to New York on my own to chill out and do a bit of shopping. That was my end-of-season ritual.

I was sitting in the little deli across the road from the hotel I always stayed in when my mobile rang. It was the Leicester chairman, John Elsom. He told me the club was negotiating with Martin in the hope that he would sign a new contract but there was a lot of speculation linking him with a move to Celtic for the start of the new season. He wanted to know who I would choose to replace him at Leicester if he did decide to go.

I said Steve Walsh and Tony Cottee, because although they didn't have the experience, and although Tony had not been a success at Barnet, they would have been perfect for keeping the dressing-room spirit intact. But most of all I didn't want Martin to go. I spoke to Paul Mace, who was the press officer then, and he was doing his best to be optimistic. But then one day he rang and told me it was bad news. He said: 'Martin's gone.' I was absolutely fucking gutted. It was typical. I had just started something good and now it was over. It wouldn't have mattered who had come in really. It wouldn't have been the same.

There was no resentment towards Martin. Everybody knew he was ambitious. Everybody knew he loved Celtic, and he could hardly be accused of being disloyal to Leicester after everything he had done for the club. But I still desperately wanted to play for him. I got a message to him to let him know it didn't matter to me where he went, I would love to go and play for him again. I knew he had a history of taking players with him when he moved clubs and I hoped he might want to take me to Celtic Park, too. It didn't matter to me where he had gone. If he had moved to Leyton Orient I would have gone there with him. I enjoyed playing for him that much.

For a while it looked as if something might happen. He

called Jonathan Crystal and told him he was planning a pairing of me and Chris Sutton in attack with Henrik Larsson playing just behind us. He said it was all ready to go and we met at a hotel just near where Martin lived in Beaconsfield. He said he was keen for me to come to Celtic. He said he didn't know the board that well yet, but that he could give me a cast-iron guarantee he wanted to take me to Scotland.

And then he went quiet. Jonathan couldn't get through to him and I started to worry. I knew a journalist called Brian Doogan who was a friend of Martin's, and he kept telling me to be patient because the whole thing was just taking longer than expected. But still it stayed quiet. Sutton was signed but I never heard a thing. Nothing ever materialised.

A few months ago, I spoke to Brian and asked him what had happened. He said the Celtic board had blocked the move for me and sanctioned Sutton and John Hartson instead. He said Martin felt bad about it and that was why he hadn't phoned me. The first time I actually saw Martin was at the *BBC Sports Personality of the Year* awards before Christmas. We glossed the whole thing over. He said I was mad to have retired so young but that he liked what I was doing on the radio. We had a good chat. I told him I didn't want to kiss his arse but I did want to thank him for giving me my belief back. It was about trusting somebody. After the Ulrika thing and the depression, if I wasn't playing well or if I was perceived to be being difficult, it was the easiest thing in the world for a manager to turn to that and roll it out as a reason to distance themselves from me. Peter Taylor did that when he took over from Martin and Jim Jefferies did it at Bradford, too.

I trusted Martin because he didn't play any games with me. He is not stupid. He knows how things work. He can play the system, but there is just something about him that makes you take him at his word. He didn't talk in football-speak and bullshit and babble. He could even be a bit brusque sometimes. He operates in a different and unique way to the people he has got round him, but they complement each other brilliantly. That is what makes him stand out.

When he went to Celtic he had pretty much the same personnel as John Barnes and Kenny Dalglish had, and look what he did with them. Look at how he has got the best out of people like Steve Guppy and Sutton. Gups is a great lad but he is very fragile and flaky and he can be the butt of jokes. Martin got him playing. He put his arm round him. He knew what to say to Gups that was different to what he had to say to Gerry Taggart or Neil Lennon. It's man management.

I was disappointed he never rang to tell me from his own lips why the move to Celtic wasn't going to happen. I think he just felt embarrassed. All the newspaper attention up there and my propensity for getting into trouble might not have done him any favours, particularly as he had not been there very long. To get him in the shit in Glasgow would have been heavy duty. It would be harder to weather a storm up there.

But none of it altered the respect I had for him for taking me to Leicester in the first place. After all that happened at Villa, I questioned whether I could play again and he helped me find out that I could. I will always be grateful to him for that. Ultimately, I think he's a selfish man and I respect that in football. He thought I was a good bet but then something else came along and he changed his mind. Can't argue with that.

Not long afterwards, Leicester announced that Peter Taylor had got the manager's job. He was still involved with England at that time and he phoned me up, full of bluster about how he was going to get me back into the national squad under Eriksson. He said all the usual stuff about how he was looking forward to working with me, but I felt really indifferent. In my experience, anyone who talks the talk usually talks bollocks.

We went into training for the first day of pre-season and they had changed it all. The lad Taylor brought in as his first-team coach was a bloke called Steve Butler who had only played in the lower leagues and had just retired. He was okay but he didn't know anything about the Premiership or the players. He was a rookie making his way in the game, but there was none of the enjoyment in training that Steve Walford and Robbo had brought. It just degenerated from there. From day one, it didn't work. Not for me.

The spirit went, too. To try to compensate for Martin's departure, to try to cling on to what he had built, they gave Matty Elliott, Muzzy Izzet, Robbie Savage and Neil Lennon massive contracts. They tried to buy the lads' loyalty to Peter Taylor, but what they didn't realise was that Martin was the glue that had held it all together and it didn't matter how much you paid people because you couldn't re-create Martin's personality. The contracts the board awarded at that time led to a lot of the financial problems Leicester were to suffer thereafter.

Taylor bought badly, too. He signed Ade Akinbiyi and Trevor Benjamin. They were both flops. In fact, Akinbiyi became known as Ade Akin-bad-buy on some of the phone-ins. Taylor brought in a lot of players that just weren't Leicester City players, and even though we did all right at the start of the 2000–2001 season, even though we were actually top of the table for a while, I could sense there was trouble ahead.

Taylor was like John Gregory, Mark 2 all of a sudden. He thought he was God's gift, and for a while he could do no wrong. I told him I wanted to stay at the club and that it had been agreed while Martin was there that we would sit down and renegotiate my contract. John Elsom had agreed that, too. But Peter Taylor said he wasn't interested. That soured it all even further for me because I felt they weren't showing me any loyalty and they were reneging on promises.

Things started to go wrong on the pitch for me, too. I played against Everton and Gazza and I got involved in a bit of a tangle which resulted in me getting a yellow card. The incident was reviewed by an FA disciplinary panel, and after they had seen the video replay they banned me for three games. When I came back I was on the bench and not coming on. It just went downhill fast.

The next thing was that Peter Taylor said I had put weight on and that I wasn't sharp. That was absolute bollocks. I didn't need that. A lot of frustration was building up inside me. I felt let down and I felt a lingering disappointment that what had started off so brightly and promised so much; what had seemed like a fresh start had turned into another stand-off with duplicitous people who couldn't be straight with me or the press.

Against that backdrop I played in a reserve game at Filbert Street and tried to give Trevor Benjamin a bit of advice during the game. He was a raw kid with no football brain and I wanted to try and help him a bit. He was running offside all the time and I pointed out that he might want to try bending his runs, holding the ball up a bit more and generally look around him during the course of the match. He told me to fuck off.

When we got back into the dressing room we squared up. We started punching each other. Everybody scattered. Chairs and tables went flying and it was a real kerfuffle. It only lasted about 15 seconds but it spilled through to the medical room before some of the other lads broke it up. I came back to have another go a couple of minutes later but the lads got in the way again so I gave up on it and went home.

There was a big inquest, and I think by then the club saw it as a great opportunity to get me off the wage bill. When I met with Peter Taylor, I told him that I still wanted to stay. I told him I had been happy under Martin, and, even though I hadn't been happy under him, I didn't want to move. His reply was blunt. He said I didn't have any choice. They had taken statements from people like Matty Elliott and Sav about the fight with Benjamin, and, even though they had said they didn't see anything, the club was talking to its legal people and they were intending to sack me because of what they said was violent conduct.

That same day, Jonathan Crystal phoned. He said Bradford had been in touch. They were still interested. It was time to get out, but I knew the end of my career was coming fast by then. And I couldn't help but fear that a new period of torment lay ahead.

CHAPTER TEN

REAL OVIEDO:
SO THIS IS THE END

My football career died in a fog of other people's broken dreams. I was shunted here and there to a series of clubs floundering around in the shit of relegation and financial meltdown. I became every chairman's favourite last throw of the dice; the shot they made in desperation that was going to save them or seal their fate. I was still only 29 when Peter Taylor ran me out of Leicester, but that felt like the end for me. That was my last chance gone. It was the end of something that had started so well and seemed to have promised a new beginning. *So this is the end, beautiful friend, this is the end.* By the winter of 2000 I didn't see any beauty in football any more. I didn't see friendship or even fraternity. I just saw a wilderness of loneliness and pain. I saw ugliness.

By the end I felt like some sort of fucking circus act. A freak show, actually. That would be more accurate. A travelling salesman peddling a magic potion. Roll up, roll up, and see the mad bloke who's come to save us from the drop and dig us out of our stinking hole. Watch him try, then watch him fail, then watch us beat him with a big stick because he couldn't give us the miracle we asked of him. Watch a footballer diminished.

Watch him denuded of the magic he once had. Watch him pretending he can find it again when he knows, and we all know, that it's not going to happen. Watch the guy who once had the world at his feet thrashing about with Bradford and Real Oviedo: ships that are going down, with everybody scrambling for the fucking lifeboats and not giving a toss whether anybody else makes it or not.

I don't know what I was looking for by then. I don't know why I was still playing. Convention, probably. Footballers aren't supposed to retire when they are 30. Not unless they're injured. Well, I was injured. I was damaged, anyway. It was just that it wasn't the kind of damage that made me limp. I didn't have dodgy knees or creaking ankles or cruciates that had had to be knitted back together. Physically, I was fine. Mentally, I was exhausted with it all. I was fried. I was full of resentment and bitterness and disillusionment about football and what it had done to me.

My first appearance for Bradford was a live Sky game against Leeds at Valley Parade on a Sunday afternoon at the end of October 2000. When he signed me on a free transfer from Leicester, the Bradford chairman, Geoffrey Richmond, called me 'an enormous but legitimate gamble'. Bradford hadn't won for eight games. In fact, they had only won once all season, a 2–0 victory over Chelsea back in the middle of August. The manager, Chris Hutchings, had been told a few days before that he would be sacked if results didn't improve. Richmond was true to his word. Hutchings got the bullet not long after I arrived and they brought in Jim Jefferies from Hearts.

I spent much of the preamble to the match trying to get to

that prick Richard Keys in the studio at the stadium. He'd been slagging me off over something to do with Ulrika. Inevitably, it had to do with Ulrika. So, half an hour or so before the game, I went up to the back of the stand in my kit and started hammering on the studio door and demanding to see him. I don't know if I would have smacked him. I only wanted to give him a piece of my mind but I would have liked the chance to see his arsehole fall out. They locked the door. They wouldn't let me in.

I scored Bradford's goal in a 1–1 draw. Beni Carbone put in a great cross, I peeled off my marker and connected with an overhead kick. It was at the end where the Leeds fans were. That was sweet. It had taken me 21 minutes of my debut to get on the scoresheet. I didn't see it go in, but the reaction of the Bradford fans was a pretty clear sign. Mark Viduka equalised late on for them. I tried to get to Keys after the game, too, but he scarpered before I could get anywhere near him. I have no respect for people like that. They can give it out but they can't take it. When they're confronted by some-one they've criticised, they bottle it. They haven't got the wit or the courage to stand up for what they've said.

I only played six games for Bradford. It was obvious they were going down. They finished bottom by eight points that season, 16 points adrift of safety. There wasn't enough quality there. There were some good lads on the playing staff but a lot of them were at the wrong end of their careers. Jamie Lawrence was there. What a nutter he was. It wasn't so much his brightly coloured hair, it was the way he drove. I followed him down to London once and he was zigzagging from lane to lane at about 120 mph. I think he'd done two years for violent robbery at some point. Lee Sharpe was another one who was past his sell-by date. Stuart McCall was yet another. I always got the impression that McCall was the snout for Jefferies. I think McCall had an idea he'd be in line for the manager's job when Jefferies got fired, but that never happened.

The financial problems at Bradford were crippling. Richmond mismanaged that club badly. They're fucked now, and he's fucked, too. He was declared bankrupt just after he tried to get his fingers in the pie at Leeds. Bradford are so severely skint, they can't even afford to play at Valley Parade any more. Their fans deserve better than that, but when I was there the decline was already well underway. I got a call one night from Jonathan Crystal saying he'd discovered Dan Petrescu, Ashley Ward, Carbone and I were all going to be made available for transfer. I told the boys in the dressing room the next day. McCall told Jefferies, and then Jefferies told me, as if he didn't know I knew. He was supposed to be a no-nonsense, hard-nosed Scot but the truth was he was out of his depth. He should have been more open with me.

I started getting phone calls from all sorts of hucksters and shysters then. I didn't know it at the time but Jefferies had asked an agent called Colin Gordon to try and find a buyer for me. VfB Stuttgart said they were interested but they were struggling at the bottom of the Bundesliga and they couldn't afford my wages. Deportivo La Coruna were supposed to be interested, too, but then I got a call from Colin Gordon saying that Real Oviedo wanted to sign me before Spain's January transfer window closed. They were down near the foot of the Primera Liga but Raddy Antic had just taken over as coach and he saw me as the answer to all their problems. Bradford were so desperate to get rid of me they even waived a fee.

Oviedo had renovated their Estadio Carlos Tartiere so that it looked like a spanking new stadium with a 30,000 all-seater capacity. They were happy, they said, to meet my financial demands. I thought maybe, just maybe, it might work. A fresh start abroad, away from all the bad things and the controversies, away from all the English managers with agendas, away from all the people with preconceived ideas about me, away from the hangers-on and the bull-shitters. I thought that if I controlled it all, if the deal was done right and they didn't mess me about, then this move might just breathe a bit of enthusiasm back into me before it was too late.

I took Jonathan Crystal out to Madrid with me to tie up the deal. I took an accountant from Deloitte Touche, too. I wanted everything to be thorough. I didn't want any room for fuck-ups. I knew that if it wasn't smooth and clean, that it would be the last straw. We sat in that Madrid office for about 12 hours, trying to get it done. It was a two-year deal with an option for a third. They wanted to pay me through some offshore account. They wanted to pay me in some strange currency. In the end, I switched off and let the rest of them get on with it. I had already had a meeting with Raddy. He promised me I would play from the off. I needed games. I spoke to Raddy on the phone again while we were in Madrid and then I signed. When I was unveiled, 6,000 supporters turned up at the stadium.

My first day at training was a culture shock. We trained at an old stadium which was a shithole. The vast majority of the lads spoke Spanish and only Spanish. The squad was full of up-and-coming young Spanish kids who had been chucked in at the deep end because the club had no money. There was a Yugoslav called Paunovic who spoke good English but that was it. It wasn't a cosmopolitan club like Barcelona or Real Madrid. Oviedo was a nice-enough city with a population of about 200,000 people but it was a bit of a backwater. There wasn't much familiarity for me to latch on to. It was Spain's equivalent of Norwich, really, stuck out on a limb in the beautiful Asturias region, halfway between Santander and La Coruna and a long way from either of them, but not far from Spain's northern coast. I would have started taking Spanish lessons but I didn't last long enough for that.

It never felt right. None of the help they had promised me in establishing a new life in Spain materialised. They didn't help me find anywhere to live. They didn't help me set up bank accounts. They didn't put me up in a decent hotel. I know it sounds spoiled but I was used to having my life looked after while I played football. I wasn't used to being independent. I was used to being cosseted. Estelle was pregnant with Mia and I wanted to know about hospitals and clinics if she came out to live with me, but the club didn't give a fuck about that either. They just left me alone to get on with it and I got lower and lower and lower.

The first match after I signed was away to Las Palmas in Gran Canaria. It was a two-hour bus journey to the airport and a two-hour flight. Door to door, it was more than seven hours. Antic put me on the bench. I came on for the last 20 minutes. A seven-hour journey for 20 minutes in a 1–1 draw. Fucking joke. I swapped shirts with Vinny Samways afterwards. He was the only other Englishman playing in the Primera Liga then, and he was surrounded by English ex-pats in the Canaries. I didn't really want that kind of existence but I thought it would be nice to hear some English voices now and again. He said he thought I'd like it in Spain. I thought he was wrong. Oviedo was already beginning to feel like the other end of the earth for me.

I was left out of the next game because Antic decided I should stay behind in Oviedo and work on my fitness. I didn't care. It was away to Real Zaragoza, which meant a six-hour coach journey. I didn't fancy that. My first home game was the following week against Osasuna where Sammy Lee and Michael Robinson had both played. There were loads of Union Jacks slung up around the Carlos Tartiere and I felt really chuffed. Oviedo had their first full house for ages and the stage seemed set. I came on for the last 15 minutes with the scores level at 1–1. We conceded two goals straight away, and we lost 1–3. Nice start in front of the home fans.

I felt sapped by the whole thing already. When I had gone to Forest and they had been in trouble at the start of my first season, I was bursting to help. I knew I could lift them out of it. I felt I could do it on my own. But by the time I got to Oviedo I had been bounced from club to club and I just didn't have the strength to do it. I blamed myself for the defeat to Osasuna. I blamed myself for everything. I had got to the point where unless I went out and scored a hat-trick and was man-of-the-match it would send me into a spin. The

Left: Model professional: David James takes to the catwalk as part of his work for Armani.

Below: Me and Mark Bright heading for a fancy dress party. I hope it was fancy dress.

Above: Sophie's choice: we had a brief fling after the Brit awards ceremony.

Right: Sara Cox: she told Chris Evans her nickname for me was Stan the Can.

Top and above left: Scoring the winner in the Game of the Decade: probably my best moment in football. Newcastle defender Philippe Albert is plunged into despair as I begin the celebrations.

Above right: Liverpool captain John Barnes and me in our infamous white suits before the 1996 FA Cup Final.

Top: Rising above it all: but for once I couldn't score against United and we lost 1–0. Gary Pallister must have hated playing against me but this time he kept me out.

Middle: A rare outing for England: I only got three caps. If I had been playing today, I would have had 40.

Left: Glenn Hoddle welcomed me after I was cleansed by Eileen Drewery but we soon lapsed into bad karma.

I liked Terry Venables but I never really felt he gave me the chance I deserved.

Playing the beautiful game against Brazil: I suppose that was the peak of my brief England career.

Not a prayer: nothing went right for me or Brian Little after he signed me for Villa. He was sacked a few months later.

Me and Ulrika: whatever she says now, you can see in her eyes that we were happy once.

Hell on earth: the Scottish pub in Paris where my life fell apart when I hit Ulrika on the eve of the 1998 World Cup.

Ulrika leaving her house in Cookham Dean soon after Paris: the rain on her car window made it look as if her face was bruised.

Calm down, calm down: Liverpool fans wound me up after I was sent off playing against them for Villa. So I wound them up, too.

My nemesis John Gregory shouting the odds as usual. He said depression shouldn't afflict the rich.

Good times among the bad: a rare moment of joy in a Villa shirt as I celebrate a goal with Ian Taylor.

Martin O'Neill gives me daggers as I face the music over the fire extinguisher incident at La Manga.

Back on track: a few days after facing the music for my jape in La Manga, I scored a hat-trick for Leicester against Sunderland.

Last hurrah: this spectacular overhead kick for Bradford against Leeds was my career's last starburst.

Left: Kirsty Gallagher was an incredibly sexual and sensual woman but I could not commit myself to her.

Below: On parade: Real Oviedo fans give me a great welcome but the honeymoon came to an abrupt end.

On the sofa: with chat show queen Vanessa Feltz. We spent 24 hours locked in a London penthouse for a reality TV show.

standards I set myself were so high, I was always heading for a fall. I started telling people back in England that I was going to retire. Some of them had heard it before from me, but this time I knew it was for real.

The next game was against Celta Vigo away. We were due to be paid a couple of days before the match. Paunovic laughed when I asked him about that. He said they never got their wages on time. That sent a wave of dread through me. I was miserable as it was. If I wasn't even going to get paid correctly then it all seemed utterly pointless. Inevitably, when the money came through it was the wrong amount and in the wrong currency. I felt shattered by that. It was a bit of an overreaction but that was just the state I was in. It seemed as if everything was going wrong.

I played the last 15 minutes in Vigo, a city that really is at the end of the earth. Cape Finisterre, which means land's end, is a few miles away from the dilapidated Estadio Municipal de Balaidos where I played my last game of football. I don't remember much about that final quarter of an hour. It is not framed in sepia in my mind. I had a couple of touches, then the final whistle blew and it was over. I walked back towards the flight of steps that led down to the changing rooms. I was just thinking 'that's it'. I didn't turn to take in one last vista of the site of my final game. There was no sentiment. I didn't want to build it into some final farewell to football. I didn't care enough any more to do that. I just walked back towards those steps, towards the vast expanse of the Atlantic Ocean beyond, and disappeared under the ground.

I knew I was finished. I was weary. I was punch-drunk. This was the last shot at it and it wasn't happening. There was no point trying to flog it. No point dragging out this agony and going on to yet another club struggling at the arse end of another table. I wasn't being bought to help clubs win things any more. I was a sop for teams staring at oblivion; one last pointless extravagance before they disappeared under the ground, too. A person to turn on when the shit started flying and the excuses and the time ran out for good.

I kept imagining being stuck in Oviedo and out of the team. Them accusing me of being overweight. Putting me on diets. Turning me back into that freak show. That was the worst scenario in my mind. I knew that would send me over the edge. People have said to me since that I should have sat it out and invented a persistent hamstring strain. Just milked it for the money. But the money didn't have any meaning to me then. Until then, I had always clung to the idea that if I was playing football, that could be my salvation. I didn't want to sit there and cheat for two and a half years. The consequences for my state of mind just weren't worth it.

Estelle was pregnant and I kept thinking of all the things that might happen to my family at home if I tried to toss off two more years in Spain. What goes around, comes around. That kind of thing. In those final days in Spain I tormented myself with black imaginings of the various tragedies that might befall the people I loved if I was away for so long. And as it happened, Estelle suffered from pre-eclampsia in the latter stages of her pregnancy and nearly died in childbirth. I might not have been there if I'd still been playing for Oviedo.

So I was glad I went home. Glad I packed my bags after that game at Celta Vigo and headed for the airport. Oviedo went down. Bradford City went down. They're both in freefall even now. Both fucked. Maybe I should have stuck it out at Leicester for a bit longer. Maybe I should have taken 12 months out after it went sour there. But when you're in an environment that is all you have ever known, you don't know how to get out so you just carry on and carry on until you run into a brick wall. Well, I ran into mine in Spain. And when I hit it, I didn't get up again for three years.

When I returned from my Oviedo misadventure I slept for the next three years. When I look back on my life after football, that is what it amounts to. A lot of sleep. Flattened by bouts of severe depression, I spent a lot of time in bed. But then, little by little, especially after I began working for Five Live, it began to feel as though I was getting my life on track again. However, what I couldn't foresee was that my predilections away from football would catapult me back into a blizzard of screaming tabloid front-page headlines.

CHAPTER ELEVEN

2004: DOGGIN'

In the damp and apologetic English spring of 2004, the British press and its readers lost themselves in an orgiastic banquet of moralising about the sexual peccadilloes of the millionaire footballers who raced about in their midst in their red Ferraris and their giant Sport Utility Vehicles. Football and sexual deviancy, or at least sexual impropriety, came close to merging in the public mind as the newspapers abandoned themselves to what the American novelist Philip Roth once described in his book, *The Human Stain*, as 'an ecstasy of sanctimony'.

What a phrase that is. What a perfect phrase to describe the scared, trembling little minds who rush to judgement when they catch somebody doing something they, the self-appointed moral arbiters of our society, have decided is a threat to the lie that there is some norm of behaviour out there that the silent majority adhere to. They expose only a few, so that the many may tut and shake their heads and give thanks that their own sins are not considered worthy of censure and ridicule and humiliation because they are not famous enough to invite opprobrium.

As March turned into April, David Beckham, the man who

had been sculpted by the media into a doting husband and a perfect father, whose image was as white and as soft and as comforting as one of his flowing linen shirts, who was supposed to be so perfect the idea of him ever even fancying a woman other than his wife was anathema to the brain-dead *OK!* generation, became the subject of a series of outraged revelations that suggested he had been unfaithful. A former personal assistant called Rebecca Loos came out of the woodwork and said they had had an affair. Then another woman did the same a week later. And they both said that Beckham's marriage to the former Spice Girl Victoria Adams was far from the idyll we had been asked to believe in. Far from being one long, glamorous bout of high living and wild sex, it was suggested that what little passion remained in their relationship belonged to the growing antipathy they felt for one another.

And we were supposed to be surprised by this? We were supposed to think that two people effectively leading separate lives at opposite ends of Europe, loaded with the pressures of demanding jobs and two small children, were going to live happily ever after? Perhaps it was a comforting thought for some people. Perhaps it was important to them that the icon of a generation was seen to be immune to reality and weakness. Perhaps the establishment wanted it that way as they battled the fear that constantly wells up inside them that society is on the verge of breaking down because of the moral turpitude that has gripped the young.

The *Daily Mail* had been informing its readers for some weeks by then that Beckham was a bad father. This is the same *Daily Mail* that is edited by a man called Paul Dacre. I read an interview with him once in which he spoke movingly of how grateful he was that he had an understanding wife who did not complain because he spent so much time away in London, a slave to his work, and had so little time for his family. And yet the *Daily Mail* is supposed to be the bastion of the family; that is supposed to be its guiding principle. Its conservatism is based on the idea that the family is the most crucial unit in society. Yet its editor, by his own admission, chooses not to spend time with his family because he is too busy overseeing articles about David Beckham being a bad father.

How can a man be at once so relentlessly brutal and so completely flawed by his lack of self-knowledge. Although, come to think of it, that is probably Dacre's secret. I'm sure he would be amused by the idea of taking criticism from Stan Collymore, but I am no more flawed than he is and I have caused a good deal less pain to far fewer people than he has through the columns of his newspaper.

Soon after Beckham's dalliances had come to light, the *Daily Mail* ran a back-page picture of a giant flag that some Real Madrid fans, angry at recent poor results and scandals involving highly paid players, had hung up on the fencing surrounding their training ground. 'For you, whores and money,' it read. 'For us, indignation and repression.' The *Mail* loved that. That's why they gave it such prominence, because that was their target readership in a nutshell. Indignation and repression. Put that together with the ecstasy of sanctimony and you have captured the mindset of middle England in a few choice words. Footballers are the people they love to hate. Below all the superficial love of the *Fever Pitch* generation, a deep, bitter resentment about the wages footballers earn is always there, just itching to be triggered by stories like Beckham's.

What men like Dacre are petrified of is the idea that people are not the way they're supposed to be. Everybody has their weaknesses, their secret desires, their failings, their temptations. Some repress them better than others, that's all. Some never crack, although most do. Some never see what's below the surface in our society. Some just don't want to look. I think of our society differently. I think of the opening scene in the David Lynch film *Blue Velvet* when the man watering his immaculate front lawn behind his white picket fence somewhere in middle America collapses with a heart attack, and, as he lies there on the grass, the camera goes down low as if it is among the blades of grass and we see the worms and the insects crawling around in the turf.

It isn't just Beckham. Obviously, it isn't just Beckham. A few weeks before the Rebecca Loos story broke, a group of Leicester City footballers, some of them old mates of mine, were implicated in rape allegations arising out of an incident at the same La Manga hotel where I had let off that fire extinguisher five years earlier. Several of them were incarcerated in a Spanish jail. In England, the press screamed out its collective disgust before it even knew if any of the players would be charged, let alone whether they would be found innocent or guilty if it ever came to trial.

Which it didn't. As it happened, most of the players were released within 24 hours. The Spanish legal system deemed that only three – Paul Dickov, Keith Gillespie and Frank Sinclair – had a case to answer, and they even retracted that decision within a couple of weeks. The three lads all protested their innocence, legitimate doubts were raised about the evidence given by the women concerned and their motives, and three months later the Leicester players had been cleared of any wrongdoing. And yet in England they had already been caricatured as scum.

In this same fevered patch of inquisitorial indignation, that swampy mix of prurience and piety, I fell foul of this persecuting spirit, too. Two reporters from *The Sun*, Neil Syson and a woman I only ever knew as Lucy, had discovered that I had been going to country car-parks and watching couples having sex in their cars. Sometimes I joined in the sex. Sometimes I had sex with the husband's wife. I had found out about this phenomenon on the Internet. It was called 'dogging'.

The Sun splashed what it called my shame on its front page. I talked to the *Daily Mirror* to try to limit the damage and it did the same. It took me by surprise that I was still capable of commanding such a reaction, even in the tabloid press. I had been in retirement for several years, and even though I was still in the public mind because of the summarising I did for BBC radio on Five Live, I was hardly in the front line any more. I don't really know if any small part of me was gratified by being thrust into the limelight again, having reporters clambering over hedges at my house again and sitting outside in their cars. I don't want to admit that to myself. I don't think it's true.

That's just the reality of modern celebrity. Celebrity endures for celebrity's sake, even when the celebrity stops doing what he or she was famous for. As a footballer I had crossed the line from football into entertainment, and once you cross the line it is very hard to step back into anonymity again, however far removed you are from what you once did. Because of who I am, because I have a tendency to find myself in trouble, I will be followed by the media until I die.

The same thing applies to Paul Gascoigne and certainly to David Beckham. They will never be allowed to rest. Every time misfortune crosses their path or they make a mistake or they let their family down, it will be reported. Perhaps that is the price we all pay for earning vast amounts of money for playing a game. We are rich men and perhaps we deserve to be scrutinised, but sometimes it would be nice if they called off the dogs, just for a year or two.

What I did admit to myself was that I was a sex addict. Deep down, I knew that already. The counsellors at The Priory had told me that while I was being treated for depression a few years earlier. It is rooted in my background and the love and attention my mother gave me, I'm sure. I'm always looking for that. I'm always asking women if they love me, if they really love me, almost as soon as I've met them. I need emotional reassurance all the time and I need obvious, instant affection. It's part of my Borderline Personality Disorder.

I should have tried to address it earlier. There were no specific groups for sex addicts at the Priory when I was there the first time. I did go as far as going to a sex addicts' meeting somewhere off the Charing Cross Road. It felt like a splinter group. It felt like the Continuity IRA wing of addiction. There were people there talking about how they used to go up to Hampstead Heath and sniff used condoms. There were people talking about how they couldn't walk past a prostitute without having to shag her. There were people who were addicted to porn, to the extent that they couldn't just watch it on the Net for an hour or so like other people, they had to watch it 16 hours a day. I came out of it feeling pretty normal but I should have persisted.

When the dogging scandal broke, the BBC was indecent in its haste to distance itself from me. I found it pathetic. The corporation disowned me. It released a statement saying I had only been an occasional contributor anyway and there were no plans to use me again in the near future. Funny that, because I was supposed to be going to Bulgaria the next day to act as a summariser for Five Live. I had plenty of matches lined up in the next few weeks for them, too. Not any more, it seemed.

I was even due to attend a meeting later that week with Peter Salmon, the head of BBC Sport, to discuss increasing my contributions to programmes, something I was impatient to progress. That meeting was also cancelled. Very quickly, I became a non-person at the BBC, although I did get some letters from colleagues there expressing their sadness at the way the corporation had acted.

The BBC's moral horror over my behaviour made me think of the passage in *The Human Stain* where Roth excoriates the media for its pursuit of President Clinton over his dalliance with Monica Lewinsky. 'The righteous, grandstanding creeps, crazy to blame, deplore and punish were everywhere,' Roth wrote. Later, he wrote about how that was the summer 'when the moral obligation to explain to one's children about adult life was abrogated in favour of maintaining in them every illusion about adult life, when the smallness of people was simply crushing'.

Was what I had done really so reprehensible that I deserved to be sacked? Was having sex in a car park with other consenting adults such a terrible sin? Forgive me, but I thought that people had been having sex in cars in car parks and country lanes ever since cars started driving down country lanes. I hadn't done anything illegal and, apart from the huge distress I had caused my own wife, I hadn't hurt any of the strangers I had become involved with.

But we are still in deep denial about sex and deceit in England. And so the BBC decided that I should be sacked for what I did, whereas Peter Salmon, who had had an affair with the former *Coronation Street* actress Sarah Lancashire that ended his relationship and broke up a family with children, was judged to be beyond reproach. In the same way, I was not aware of any suggestion that the Five Live breakfast presenter, Victoria Derbyshire, was disciplined in any way for conducting an affair with BBC producer Mark Sandell, the husband of her fellow presenter, Fi Glover. Fi was so broken by that affair that she left the station and Five Live lost its most talented presenter. Nor was I aware that Steve Cram had been reprimanded in his role as a BBC athletics presenter for walking out on his wife and children for another woman.

I'm not condemning Peter Salmon or Victoria Derbyshire or Steve Cram for what they did. I would be a fool indeed if I was to start throwing stones from my glass house. They are just human beings, normal human beings with normal weaknesses. What I'm asking is why was I singled out for punishment when what they did had far more of a profound and damaging effect on the lives of adults and several children than anything I did in the dead of night in car parks across the Midlands. Why are some infidelities accepted and brushed swiftly under the carpet while others are judged to belong to some dangerous twilight world that might bring the wrath of the moral majority down upon the BBC?

The more you think about that, the more depressing it is. There was clearly an assumption within the BBC hierarchy that its listeners would have been so disgusted by what I had done that they would desert Five Live in droves if the corporation had the temerity to continue to employ me as a summariser at football matches. But these are the same listeners that are getting divorced in record numbers, that are having more casual affairs than ever before. And yet the BBC are worried that these people will judge me. Why? So I could be, for a fleeting moment, the scapegoat for a nation's secret guilt; so they could camouflage their secrets and their lies with their contempt for my depravity.

It reminds me of something I heard the great golfer, Arnold Palmer, say just before the US Masters in that same spring. This 73-year-old sporting legend and American hero was asked a question about the trials and tribulations of the former Open and US PGA champion, John Daly, a man four times married and battling openly with a host of addictions and troubles. Palmer said first and firmly that Daly was a friend of his. And then he said he believed people felt uncomfortable about Daly's problems because he was far closer to the model of an average American than anyone cared to admit.

It's the same with me. Do you really think I'm that

different? Do you really think I'm that bad? Do you really think I'm that perverted? I'm not saying dogging is something I want to be involved in any more. In an ideal world I wouldn't be spending my time in car parks at night, but there were certain strains in my life that led me into those situations. I've also had more sexual partners than most people but that's mainly as a product of the money I have earned and the attention I attracted as a Premiership footballer. Apart from the quantity, I'm no different to an average Joe in terms of sexual fantasies and taking advantage of opportunities when they present themselves.

Be honest with yourself. How many blokes do you hear talking about how they'd love to watch a couple of lesbians going at it. Plenty. How many blokes would love to get involved in a threesome. How many blokes go on and on about anal sex with women. It's the type of thing that provokes guffaws of recognition in pub conversations. It's true. It's out there. We know it, but when someone is exposed for doing it they're called a fetishist or a pervert and the moral majority feign their disgust.

Perhaps you'd be surprised if you saw the people who frequent the dogging car-parks. Perhaps you'd be surprised if you saw their cars, too. It's not White Van Man heading up there after a night at the pub and a vindaloo for an easy shag. In my experience, most people who go dogging are professionals. Most of them drive Mercedes or Range Rovers. Most of them wouldn't dream of going to a nightclub to try to cop off with someone. They go dogging as a couple because it gives them a feeling of retaining control in a marriage that may have developed a problem.

I know what it was that led me to get involved. It was opening a letter from Real Oviedo just before Christmas 2001 that informed me the club was going to sue me for £7 million. I got incredibly down about it, as you would. I told Estelle and she was panicky, too. It sent me into a real spiral. For the first time, I didn't really have the buzz of football, and especially scoring a goal, to send my mind racing into happier territory. I needed something to give me that buzz and I found it one night at a remote country car-park in Warwickshire called Barr Beacon.

One of my mates had told me about dogging a few months earlier. The initial impression I had was that it would be people going up to Cannock Chase in their cars for a shag, and blokes coming out of the bushes to watch them with their dicks in their hands. That was just a fable. I looked it up on the Internet and found that it was actually a highly organised pursuit. I was astonished at how many Internet sites there were that were devoted to it, and how many places they identified around the country as dogging venues.

About that time there were a couple of pieces in the national media about it. They called it a new craze. They mentioned Barr Beacon as one of the prime spots for it, so one night I drove up there in my Range Rover and thought I'd have a look at what was going on. I drew the car up alongside another one and saw that there were two blokes sitting in the front seats and two women in the back. All around us there were about 20 other cars stationary with their lights on.

Suddenly, a man came out of the shadows and the inside light went on in the car next to me. The bloke walked right up to their car and a door opened. It was obvious he was getting sucked off by one of the women in the back seat, so I hopped out and wandered around to the other side of the car and had a bit of a fiddle with the other woman. The two husbands were just sitting in the front seat watching.

When I went away, my heart was in my mouth. It had given me a huge adrenaline rush. It was a combination of the fear of people recognising me, and the fear of doing something that I shouldn't be doing. There was a real thrill in getting a glimpse of this strange new world, this midnight world I had never known existed and that was fraught with danger and excitement and a bizarre feeling of adventure that had disappeared from my life since I stopped playing football.

I went up to Barr Beacon a few more times soon afterwards. I had a television in my car by then so I would go up there on nights when there was live football showing or playing on the radio. Mostly I would sit up there watching the football with a McDonald's and a large Diet Coke and just take in the cars coming and going. Most of the time, nothing happened. Occasionally I would see a couple shagging in their car.

Over the next couple of years I got into a pattern of going up there when something was making me anxious. It could have been a bill or a row with Estelle. Anything. In that period I shagged two different women up at Barr Beacon. One of the them, who looked good enough to be a model from Spearmint Rhino, on two separate occasions. Both of them in my Range Rover. Both times, the respective husbands got out of their cars, paced around a bit, made sure no one else was approaching. You think they're going to be watching but they just went off and had a cigarette. The bloke with the model wife came back and stared for a little while but then he disappeared again.

The sex was pretty unfulfilling, but that was not what it was about for me. That was not what gave me the buzz. For me, the addictive nature of dogging was nothing to do with the promise of sex. It was the thrill of anticipating whether there would be anything happening. Seeing couples and other blokes taking chances in this alien environment was what gave me a thrill. Just imagining on the way up there what I might find when I arrived gave me a buzz. I imagined I might find an orgy going on in a car. If I got there and there were no other cars there, I would tease myself with the thought that one would pitch up any minute. It was the subterfuge of it and the voyeurism. It was the old British thing of 'what the neighbour saw'.

That is why it is a British phenomenon. Those who are businessmen by day heading for the hills in the evening because they don't feel they have another outlet for their urges that they can be open about. Our old friends embarrassment and convention push us into having sex with strangers in car parks because our society, unlike other European cultures, is too uptight to acknowledge the acceptability of infidelity.

If it had just been about having sex I would have gone to a nightclub and pulled a bird in there. It would have been a lot easier. Rocking up to a car park in the dead of night and shagging a bloke's wife was all well and good but that wasn't my *raison d'être*. If it had been, I would have turned up a lot more frequently and shagged a lot more husbands' wives. But the nature of the thrill was a lot more complex than that.

Barr Beacon, for instance, is high up on top of a hill. There are three car parks up there, which makes it such a dogging hot-spot. Two are a mile apart and the other, which is called 'the Airport' because it used to be an aerodrome, is three miles away. One of them gives you a view for miles around so at night you can see the lights of other cars coming slowly up the hill towards the car park. And your heart is in your throat. And you are sitting there and it is dark and you might be the only one there.

You see the lights coming and you think maybe this car is going to come up and sidle alongside your car. And that perhaps, when it does, there will be a couple in it and they might stop, and the husband might be rumping her or somebody else might come out of their fucking car and get involved. You buzz off that far more than shagging a bird. If I wanted to shag a bird I could go out and do that for fun.

Some of those car parks are like an underworld. They're like a scene from film noir. There are sometimes a couple of hundred cars in these car parks. There might be 40 or 50 couples looking for something to happen. You are watching in your rear-view mirror and suddenly headlights will come on or a car will do a quick U-turn and other cars will be darting off all over the place. That's what did it for me: the mystery and the possibilities and the danger.

Perhaps part of me wanted to get caught. I have thought about that possibility. I mean, I was going to these car parks in a Range Rover with a personalised numberplate: SVC 1 tended to give the game away really. Things weren't going very well between Estelle and me, and maybe I was looking for an excuse to get out of the relationship. If that was the case, it worked a treat. I suppose it is even possible that in some way I missed the oxygen of publicity that used to be my daily staple. Even though I had come to hate the publicity, I suppose deep down I might have craved another dose of the limelight.

Some time towards the end of February I got another letter from Oviedo saying they had initiated the process of attempting to recover £300,000, which they said I owed them for walking out on what remained of my contract. I am an excessive worrier at the best of times, but in the previous 12 months I had been attempting to deal with any problems that arose in a proper and normal fashion, not just panic about them. I hadn't been letting things get me down. I had approached all the administrative things I had to do methodically and calmly.

But this was a big chunk of money. This was different. This was a hammer blow because I had been led to believe that everything had been sorted out. I was told that Oviedo's financial problems had descended into such chaos that they would go into administration and that would probably be the end of their attempt to pursue me. I didn't want to tell Estelle about it either because she had got so down the previous time Oviedo looked as if they were coming after me.

I don't cope with anxiety well. You can call that spoiled if you want, or immature, but it's the way I am. I get it from my mum. She's very circumspect and wise now, but when I was a kid she panicked about anything and everything. If you see panic recurring as a coping mechanism in the only person you have got in your world, it is obvious you are going to replicate that in your own reaction to periods of stress.

I felt anxiety and fear being transmitted to me through my mum all the time when I was a child, even when the issue was nothing to do with me. When it did involve me it was a million times worse. Once, on the way home from school when I was ten or eleven, my mates and I were lobbing stones at each other. I chucked one and it bounced up off the pavement and cracked a pane of glass in somebody's front door. The woman was standing at the window watching us and she rang the police. She told them it was a black kid. Well, in Cannock there was only one kid that was going to be. I remember standing at the curtains in our front room, getting myself into an absolute frenzy of worry and panic about the police arriving. I was shaking so much I could have shaken myself to death. When the police arrived they said they were going to take me away. My mum was hysterical, and I was hysterical because she was hysterical.

I have never been able to deal well with crises. I always lose it. When I was in my twenties I used girls as a means of trying to alleviate stress. I tried to lose myself in them. But two out of every ten would go to the newspapers with kiss-and-tell stories and suddenly there you are on a merry-go-round of stress. I know problems should be dealt with in a more orderly, calm fashion, and when the latest Oviedo letter came through I thought I would ring Simon Kennedy, my agent, and get him to sort out a meeting with Gordon Taylor, the Chief Executive of the PFA, the players' union, and do it all rationally and efficiently. That thought-process lasted for about two hours until it unravelled like the threads on a jumper and I descended into panic.

When I lose it, I don't run round like a chicken who has

just had its head severed. But inside, I'm panicking. When the letter from Oviedo came, I found myself looking at my daughter Mia playing and thinking that we might not have this house 12 months down the line and she might have to grow up without it. A problem turns into something of apocalyptical proportions. By going up to a car park, you get out of the house and you get your own space. You have your McDonald's, your comfort food, and you have a cigarette. Then a couple comes along and starts shagging and it takes your mind away from everything. You're buzzing and you're no longer in that weird, tortured zone where you are torment-ing yourself with strange imaginings of the horrors that may lie ahead. But then, when you get home, that buzzing makes you feel sick. You are sitting in bed, buzzing your tits off, but by then the Oviedo thing is coming back to you. It is still there. And then you just want to go to bed and stay there forever, and never have to come out and face reality again.

So when the Oviedo letter arrived I was like a cat on hot bricks all through that week. Estelle kept asking me what was wrong and I kept bottling it up. I got to the stage where the inordinate stress of it all was becoming a problem. I should have known to check myself into the Priory really, because I was getting to the point addicts call 'acting out'. At that point, an alcoholic would just go on a bender and a cocaine addict would do line after line, and somebody with a food disorder would eat and eat until they were sick. The thing that links them all is that what they are doing improves their mood in the short-term by taking the stress away with a buzz. You don't get a sustained feeling of well-being from it. I knew that, but when I got back home after doing a stint for Five

Live on Saturday afternoon, Estelle was shattered because she had had a couple of rough nights with Mia and she said I could go out if I wanted to. I made up some bullshit excuse about going over to see a mate in Sutton Coldfield, checked the Internet, saw some entries from couples who said they were going to be in the car park in Cannock Chase and headed up there.

Cannock Chase is not renowned as one of the better dogging venues. From my house, you drive a couple of miles up the road, past the German military cemetery, and you come to two car parks. I drove into the first one and there was nobody there so I thought I might as well go home. But I was still hooked by that image of a car arriving with its lights dimmed so I drove over to the second car-park, which is called Anson's Bank. As I was going in, a couple in another Range Rover were on their way out. I parked up and started eating my McDonald's.

Then the other Range Rover drove back in. It was like a game of cat and mouse. They parked up next to me and we wound our windows down and started chatting. The woman, who was attractive and busty, said her and her husband were both new to dogging. They had been coming up to Cannock Chase every night for the last three weeks hoping to get involved, but the only person they had encountered was a transvestite who was lurking about in the darkness. I asked her what sort of deal she was looking for and she said they were interested in getting it on with another couple.

So I gave them the rundown on the rules and regulations of dogging. I told them about how you turn your interior lights on and off if you are a couple and you are looking for another couple. The other way is to flash your main beam to show you are available. I told them people would approach looking for sex, and if they weren't interested they should just say so. It's not the kind of pastime where some bloke turns up looking for a quick shag. Dogging people don't look kindly on that. They said they weren't sure whether they were looking for a single bloke but we swapped mobile numbers anyway.

The next night I spent the early part of the evening watching the telly with Estelle, but inside I was panicking again about the Oviedo thing and I needed a buzz to get away from it. I needed it right there and then. This time I told Estelle I was meeting up with my agent, but I went back up to Anson's Bank and the same couple were there again. The woman had reclined her seat and she seemed a bit unnerved because there had been a lot of single guys around. They said they wanted to go to Barr Beacon the following Tuesday so I said they could follow me if they wanted to.

Unbeknown to me, our conversation was being recorded by the reporters from *The Sun*. The couple's car was flanked by the reporters on one side and me on the other. There were other cars dotted about that must have had listening devices fitted in them. I know that because our conversation was repeated verbatim to this other couple later when they were trying to get them to tell their story about their meetings with me. I should have realised something was amiss because it is unusual to find so many cars in close proximity, but you are buzzing so much you don't give a fuck.

When we had swapped mobile numbers it crossed my mind that it was dangerous. It crossed my mind they might be press. I mean, they obviously weren't Cath and Bob from Leeds with her in stockings and suspenders. They were obviously professional people and we had been talking for nearly an hour, but they could have been trying to trap me. As it happened, I didn't need to worry about them. It was what happened next, when their Range Rover pulled away, that proved my undoing.

I turned my engine on and manoeuvred the car around to the other side of the couple in the next car. The girl (Lucy) was 25 or so and attractive. The bloke was a small, ugly fucker who looked like some sort of jaded old rep straight out of *Glengarry Glen Ross*. I opened my car door and she opened hers so that they were near-enough touching. She put her legs out of the car and I stood right next to her and leaned in to talk to her. *The Sun* ran a picture of that a couple of days later.

At that point, the ugly bloke leaned over and said they were both new to all this and could I explain what the etiquette was. She said they were looking for another couple. So, like a dickhead, I went through all the same details I'd explained to the other couple. And this time I fabricated a couple of things, too. I told them that sometimes, when I was in London, I met a girlfriend and took her along dogging, too. That was absolutely untrue but it is a lot easier to be accepted in the dogging world if you are part of a couple and I thought that might make me more accessible, more safe, for this woman. I suspect it was uncannily similar to the occasion when Lawrence Dallaglio told undercover reporters from the *News of the World* that he had been a drug dealer in his youth. He wanted to impress them and assimilate. I wanted to impress Lucy and the ugly bloke.

They asked me a few more questions, eking as much copy as they could out of me. Then the ugly bloke said he wanted to see the girl with another guy. We exchanged mobile numbers and he asked me what my name was. I told them it wasn't really done to give out names and addresses, for obvious reasons. Sometimes you can get the odd freak following you home or making a nuisance of himself. It's rare but it happens. Anyway, I had other reasons. I thought I was being circumspect at last.

The small bloke said, 'I'll be John then.' I said I'd be John, too. They asked me if there were any other dogging haunts locally, so we drove back towards Cannock and I stuck my hand up out of my sun roof and pointed out a couple of car parks. When we'd left Anson's Bank I'd noticed that a couple of other cars had pulled away as well. In hindsight, that should have made it pretty obvious what was going on. But I still didn't twig it.

I didn't go home because I was buzzing so much. I went back to the car park. It was about 11 p.m. by then. Everyone had gone because some kids had started a fire and the fire brigade had been called. I texted the ugly bloke to see if he and Lucy were still around, but they didn't text me back. Eventually I went home and I was so pumped up I couldn't go to sleep. I stayed up until about three and then I didn't get up until about four in the afternoon. That was dangerous. That was the pattern I got into when I was depressed: taking to my bed; struggling to get up to face the day; falling into the grip of it again.

When I eventually dragged myself out of bed and out of the house there was a text message from the small bloke waiting for me. He apologised for not returning my text earlier but he said they had had problems arranging a babysitter. What a beautiful fucking line that was. He said that Lucy would love to meet me again but they weren't sure whether they wanted to participate with me or whether they just wanted people to watch them shagging.

I replied with another text. 'Would love to be intimate with Lucy,' I think it said. There was no vulgarity in it. Then, about 10 p.m., I got one last text from the ugly bloke. 'Lucy really needs a fuck,' it said. 'John not present. Call asap.' They must have known they had me by then but that was the first time I thought that something didn't ring true. Women just don't go dogging on their own. Single guys and couples, yes. You'd be surprised how many blokes want to see their wives shagged. But I have never, ever seen a single woman in a dogging area.

I called John and asked him why he wasn't around later. He said he was working but Lucy was still planning to head up there on her own. I said I'd be there about 8 p.m. He said this: 'Eight o'clock's fine, and by the way, Stan Collymore, I'm Neil Syson from *The Sun* newspaper. We have dialogue and photos of you engaged in dogging activities.' I switched my phone straight off and for a few minutes I felt real panic and fear.

For several months, the thought of more communications arriving from Oviedo had dominated my life. Every time something came through the letterbox I felt real fear. Now I felt it again, but there was something different about this. Because, somehow, mixed in with the fear was some relief because I realised it would be out in the open at last.

I felt guilty about it all, too. Of course I did. I also felt embarrassed about what lay ahead. Most of the couples I had chatted to during the dogging nights had got grown-up kids, and for them part of the deal was that they at least knew what the other was doing. It was not as if the husband would let the wife go off to a club by herself and pick up a guy and go back to his place to shag him. It sounds confusing, but dogging is – for a lot of couples – about clinging to the remnants of control in their marriage as much as anything else.

I think I had been pretending, because so many of the people I met in these car parks appeared to be perfectly normal, unremarkable, down-to-earth people, that I wasn't really doing anything out of the ordinary. But, essentially, it was something I didn't really want to do because I was putting myself in harm's way. After I had taken that final call from Neil Syson, I felt how I imagined George Best must have felt when he was photographed drinking again in that pub in Surrey after he had had his liver transplant.

The drive home made me calm because I knew that for me this was the moment that would make me stop dogging. The public would not have been so appalled if somebody had said they had seen me swigging whisky out of a bottle wrapped in a brown paper bag while I lay in the gutter. But this was my addiction. This was what I did to change my mood. It was just that shagging another bloke's wife in a car park is deemed more shocking than drinking yourself into a stupor every night or snorting cocaine up your nose.

I got back home and told Estelle I had been caught. I told her I had been up at Cannock Chase, and I told her some of what I had been doing. She started crying. She said she had

had a feeling something had been terribly wrong for the past few weeks because I had become so quiet and withdrawn. I thought it was perhaps a good idea to put my side of the story across to try to limit the damage *The Sun* was going to do, even if it was only marginal. So I went to meet Simon, my agent. In a car park, actually. And I spoke to a girl from the *Daily Mirror*.

When I got back home, Estelle was exhausted. She had slept badly again the night before because Mia hadn't had a good night. So I went and lay by Mia for half an hour and started to realise what effect this habit that I had become obsessed by was going to have on everyone close to me. I phoned Michelle, warned her what was coming and told her to be careful with Tom at school because he might get teased.

I phoned Vanessa Feltz, who I had become friendly with during some reality TV show where we were locked in a London penthouse for 24 hours, and we talked for about an hour. She's a great listener and she was really helpful. I realised that I needed to deal with this in the right way. I should have dealt with it the last time I was in the Priory but I sidestepped it. I had tried to kid myself that I wasn't a sex addict, but now I was going to have to do something about it. So I drove down to London and checked myself into the Priory.

They put me in the same room I had been in when I attempted to do the addiction course the first time I was in there. I lasted a day that time before I checked myself out, thinking it wasn't for me. Now I realised that maybe I should have stayed. I did not deserve the disgust that was about to be aimed at me by the media and, tacitly, by the BBC, but

I knew that hanging out in car parks at night wasn't really what I wanted to be doing, and it certainly wasn't going to help me raise my children or protect them from ignominy and comment.

I spent most of the first day at the Priory in bed. Dead to the world. Hiding underneath my duvet and blocking everything out. I was just glad to be in a place where nobody could get to me. Later on I phoned Estelle and told her I wanted to come home and see Mia. 'Don't use Mia as an excuse,' she said. 'Mia didn't seem to bother you the other night when you drove up there to the Chase.' She said that if I came back home she would be gone. And she said she would make sure she humiliated me by driving away in the full glare of the press people waiting outside. She told me that I had humiliated her.

I knew that, but I suppose I wanted her to be an understanding wife who could try to come to terms with my addictions. I know that sounds like an awful lot to ask. I know it sounds self-centred, but what we should have been doing was talking about how we moved on from there. About me getting out of this cycle of self-harm and us becoming a family again. But she just said the fact that I had been doing what I'd been doing made me incapable of taking care of her and Mia.

Estelle just saw the dogging as me being unfaithful again, when the reality was that it was a fucked-up coping mechanism. It made me understand why Paul Merson, who has suffered with addictions from gambling to alcohol and cocaine, felt he couldn't keep coming back home to a wife who told him what a fucking tit he was for being an alcoholic.

There is no point harking back to the fact that someone was in the gutter six weeks ago, because that was six weeks ago. You have to move on. There is no point throwing sticks and stones; there is no point throwing stuff back in my face. I needed her to be stronger than that.

On 7 March, almost a week after the dogging scandal had broken and I had spent two days in the Priory talking to counsellors, and after I had spoken again to Davina, I circulated a text message. 'I am sending this to everyone I regard as a friend,' I keyed in. 'I have thought long and hard about it. I am a sex and love addict. I always have been and I always will be. I am going to face it. I am going to go through a 12-step programme to enable myself not to use again. As my friend, I'm pointing you towards Sex and Love Addicts Anonymous, which can be found on the Internet, so you can understand what it is, how it affects me and my friends and my family. It doesn't mean I'm bad, a freak, or morally corrupt, just an addict, plain and simple.' I signed off by saying I was 'Stan Collymore, addict and very capable human being'.

Estelle had left by the time I got back. She didn't answer any of her numbers. I didn't know where she was. Eventually, I tracked her down and tried to reason with her. I tried to be honest with her. I said that if we stripped every person down to the bare bones of what they are about, we would have a very different idea of our society than the one we have now. It's not the good life. It's real life.

It didn't seem to have quite the desired effect. She didn't want to know. She instructed lawyers. She filed for divorce.

CHAPTER TWELVE

LIFE BEYOND FOOTBALL

I had enjoyed my work for Five Live, but after the dogging that was taken away and I started drowning in problems again. Estelle left and moved back in with her parents, but that had been coming for a while anyway. When I first went into the Priory in January 1999, my counsellor told me that part of my problem stemmed from the fact that I wasn't in love with Estelle. I loved her but I wasn't in love with her. We split up for a while and then got back together. It was the comfort of a habit, I suppose. Easier to stay together than to break up.

Estelle grew more and more exasperated with me in the months after I quit football. We had a new baby. Mia suffered a lot from colic. They were both tired a lot of the time, and yet I spent more time in bed than either of them. Of course, I was happy we had a lovely daughter, but her arrival and the agonised feelings that were swirling around inside my mind tortured me when I knew I should have been revelling in the uncomplicated joy of helping to look after a beautiful little girl. For me, though, it wasn't that simple. It's never that fucking simple.

I wrestle with my feelings every day now. I hate sitting playing on the carpet with Mia and feeling nothing where I should be feeling love and happiness. For maybe one in 60 days I feel every laugh and every giggle. But at my worst times it's like I know where I should laugh, I know where I should giggle. I know where to be smiley and I do it because I know it's expected, that it's the normal way for a father to behave towards his toddler daughter. I do it. I smile in all the right places. But I can't feel it. What's the fucking point in that? What's the point in pretending? I can't feel things. I can't feel outrageous laughter or outrageous pain. I feel fuck all.

Mia was born in July 2001. As she grew up, Estelle went back to work in the tanning salon her dad bought for her sister a few years back. Her parents looked after Mia until Estelle came out of work in mid-afternoon. I wasn't doing anything else. I wasn't working. I wasn't playing football. She probably thought I should have looked after Mia. I could have been a house husband, but I didn't do anything. Estelle would arrive back home and I would still be in bed. I should have been helping but I couldn't fucking do it. I couldn't physically do it. I didn't have the energy. I was empty. There was nothing inside.

It's not that I don't care for her. I want to be there for her. I want the best for her. I love Mia more than anything. I have pictures of her in the car. I play with her all the time. I took her to a Center Parcs near Eindhoven with my mum for a few days in May. I want to be close to her. Me and Tom have got a bond but he's getting older now and standing on his own two feet. But Mia's really taken to me. And yet I still couldn't fucking do it. Still couldn't look after her. I tried to explain it to Estelle. I didn't have the energy to get up, to wash my face, to wipe my arse, to have a bath, never mind have the added responsibility of changing nappies and then sitting downstairs with a gurgling little baby and not feeling it.

So I thought 'What's the fucking point?' It may sound selfish but it's just a practical solution. I do feel really guilty about it but I don't physically feel the guilt. I know I should be feeling guilty – I think that's what I mean. Nowadays we play and we get on fine, but I am having to analyse constantly whether it is an excellent day, a medium day or a bad day. That's my life. My life feels like one big fucking tease. I have got beautiful kids and a lot to be thankful for but I don't feel any of it at all. I feel numb. I can't feel what I know I'm supposed to feel.

I feel flat for most of the time. I can still remember what it's like to love and to be excited about something, but most of the time it's just a memory. The best book about depression is called *Malignant Sadness* by Louis Wolpert. He calls it a cancer of the soul. He says it detaches you. You know what love and sadness are but you are left in a vacuum of searching. You look at your kid and you should be happy but you're not. Add that to all the other fucked-up strains of everything that leads to and you just start looking forward to a frontal lobotomy. As the years go on, I would imagine there are only so many places you can take your brain, only so many times you can analyse this and that, before it just goes off the Richter scale and you do end up in a nutty hospital rocking back and forth and gabbling on about Greta Garbo.

So, yes, I do still think about suicide. I know that whatever happens to me, my kids and my family, the mothers of my children, they will all move on. Yes, it wouldn't be very nice and there would be a lot of hurt and a lot of upset and a lot of questions, but the human psyche is such that it will always move on. They will grow up to be 20-year-old kids and they will be okay. The only thing I think is that if anything does happen to me they will not be getting that balance of having two parents, and that might fuck them up just like it fucked me up. That is the only thing I can think of that would stop me from doing it.

I'm not afraid of death. I think about it a lot, even at the age of 33. I do struggle with the idea of people close to me dying. I've never even been to visit the grave of my sister, Andrea. She was more of an auntie figure to me and she died when I was on the verge of moving to Forest. She was only in her mid-forties. She had cancer of the palate. The last time I saw her was at her home and she was just like a stick. It was horrible. I have quite vivid dreams about her, as she was. Maybe that's the best way. I don't know why I've never been to the grave. For me, there has been no finality to my sister's death. I haven't got any closure about it.

I didn't go to her funeral either. I had a holiday booked to Cancun. It was the summer I was moving from Southend to Forest, and I sat down with my mum after Andrea died. I said I wasn't being insensitive but the football season had just finished, I had a lot going on with Forest coming in for me, and I asked her whether she would like me to stay for the funeral or go away with my mates. She said she'd prefer me to go on holiday. She said I'd just be moping around. So I went on holiday. I missed the funeral. My mum's view was very practical; she knew I had a big season coming up. That was the last lads' holiday I went on.

But I'm not afraid to confront my own death. I flirt with death. Sometimes I want to embrace it. After the dogging scandal broke and the public criticism started again and the BBC sacked me and Estelle left me and I couldn't see Mia and I had so much time on my hands again and I took to my bed. Again and the questions started darting through my brain and I got manic and I was agitated and upset and confused and I couldn't sleep no matter how long I lay down and my friends told me to go for a swim and that would make it all right and my life seemed pointless and everything I had hoped for felt out of reach, I set off at first light for a farmer's field with a tow rope in my boot and death beckoning me down the road.

I headed for a place called Penkridge, a few miles away from Cannock. I swerved into a field. The sky was blue by then but it had been raining so the track was muddy. It was great fun bombing along that track in a Range Rover, sliding the car around from side to side and seeing a big oak tree looming up in front, stark and solitary and beautiful against the clear sky. I was at rock bottom again, lower than I had ever been when I was at the Priory, lower than I ever thought I could be, sure in my own mind that this time there really was only one way out of it all.

I sent about ten people a text message. It was simple. It just said: 'That's it, I've had enough.' I took a Dictaphone with me. I didn't want to write anything for Estelle or my mum. I thought I'd put it down on dictaphone. I was speaking into it as I was driving along, trying to explain. As I turned into the field I noticed a crow hanging from a tree with a noose round its neck. That was macabre. A dead crow and dark intentions in my mind. An omen. I could hear *X-Files* music playing in my head.

The sun was coming up. I got out of the car and looped the rope around a good thick branch on the tree. I hooked it over a branch that was about 20-foot high up the trunk. I didn't know how to climb it, but I had learned how to make a hangman's noose from the Internet. There are loads of websites like that, giving you advice on how to do it. Lots of little nuggets in there, like if you use a gun, point it to the base of your head, otherwise you just blow your face off. I used to read them years ago and I used to think they were funny. But not any more. Then my mobile phone rang. It was messages. I listened to them. Don't know why; shouldn't have done, really.

The first one was from a friend who's a policewoman. She wanted me to call her. She said she was at my house. My mum and Estelle were there, too. She said there was a helicopter flying around looking for me and squad cars were out searching for my car. I had a moment then like you see on films where the foreground suddenly comes into focus. I shat myself. I sat in the car for a couple of minutes. Mostly I was just thinking that I didn't want to be nicked. I put the rope back in the car and drove around a bit, intending to clear my head and then go back.

I drove back towards Cannock and thought 'fuck it, I'll go and see who's at home'. When I walked in there were two bobbies standing in the hall. They looked a bit surprised. One of them asked if I was all right. I nodded and went upstairs. I sank down onto the toilet seat and started crying.

I haven't cried like that since I was a kid. I just broke my heart for about 20 minutes. The police came and asked if there was anything they could do. I said I was fine. They went away. My mum came up and held me. She was in floods of tears, too.

I don't know why I didn't do it. I was hellbent on doing it that morning. I wasn't coming back. If I had not listened to the policewomen's message and panicked a bit about the thought of a helicopter being out then I would have gone ahead. It was the thought of the press as much as anything. I didn't want to be stuck in a field with ten press people standing around.

I don't look back now and feel relieved I didn't do it. I don't feel any sense of a reprieve or a second chance. I know it looks like a classic cry for help, but there is going to be a time when it is not going to be a fucking cry for help, believe me. I know that for a fact. I can't keep going through what I'm going through. My illness is such that I actively look for chaotic things and chaotic relationships to feed some fucked-up view of my life. As my mum wept, she told me I couldn't do it because it would hurt her so much. I said: 'Mum, don't cry to make me feel guilty. When I went out there I was so single-minded that anybody crying wasn't going to make a sod's worth of difference.' When I said that to my mum I think she realised that I was at rock bottom and there were no kind words anybody could say to make it better. That was what made it scary. There was nothing anyone could say or do.

And so we're back to my life as a tease. I've got everything, but I've got nothing. I've got two wonderful kids. I've got a lovely house in my home town. I've got a loving mum. I've got money in the bank. I can afford to go away when I want to. I still get paid good money for going on chat shows and talking about my life and about football. I know it's not a bad life, and I know a lot of people probably think like John Gregory and wonder why I should be even close to thinking about suicide. Well, it's not about money, or possessions, or even your kids. It's about the mess of tangled wires in my mind.

I was driving through part of Walsall recently, a part that's a shithole. I saw people with haunted looks on their faces trudging through the driving rain. I'm cruising past in my nice big car with its heated seats and I thought, 'Fucking hell, how can you moan, Stan, with what they're contending with?' But that woman standing in the queue at the bus stop, trying to keep out of the downpour, might have a pile of bills she can't pay, but because of her mental make-up she might still be able to say that the glass is half-full, not half-empty.

I envy that. I envy that so much. What afflicts me knows no age, colour or circumstances. I beat myself up enough without thinking too much about Gregory's line about depression being a woman living at the top of a council block. I know people who have not got a pot to piss in and they are as happy as fuck. I know a girl with cancer who says she never feels down. They're tearing part of her uterus out and she still seems like one of the happiest people I know. She has what everyone calls a sunny disposition. Things don't seem to get her down. Perhaps she's just stronger than me. She obviously has more mental resilience. Much, much more. She has real misfortune to contend with and yet she's still a light to others. And, for so much of the time, I am sunk in misery.

Sometimes I get shafts of light, too. When they happen, I remember them. About ten years ago I was driving back from France and I was almost at the hoverport in Calais and I felt this crunching in my brain that was almost like a physical sensation. Suddenly I was back to normal. I rolled back 15 years. I felt good about myself. Somebody paid me a compliment. Thanks. I felt it. My brain worked. I sent everybody a text telling everybody how good I felt. The next day, sure enough, I was flat again.

I do have some optimism for the future. Given a fair wind. On the good days there is hope. There are a lot of tools I have in my favour. My physical fitness will probably help stave off mental collapse for a while. I'm trying to wean myself off the Effexor. I've been taking antidepressants for too long. I need to try to come off them, and then try and see where I am. Bare. Fit. As healthy as I can be. See where it takes me. Look after my own garden, or whatever Voltaire attributes to his hero at the end of *Candide*.

I think: 'Do yourself a bit of a favour, Stan, don't analyse all this shit, just go to the gym. Try and fill your day with things that will give you positive benefit. It won't change you as a person but at least it may offer you some respite.' Because otherwise I will drive my car to the gym, telling myself over and over again that it has to be a hard session and that I have to achieve a certain set of goals. By the time I get there I am already flaked out mentally. Already exhausted. So I have to tell myself it's okay if I do a lighter session.

After the suicide attempt at Penkridge, and after crying like I had never cried before, something put my life back into 3D again. I thought, 'You know what, fuck it, you've tried everything else and it hasn't worked, just try taking every second as it comes, have some sort of order and structure in your life, gradually get back into work and try and be positive about it and see if it works. The only alternative is to sleep 18 hours a day, eventually get suicidal and sooner or later something will give. So get back to basics. Eat your food. Go to the gym. Eat your food. Go to sleep. Have less things to think about. See if you can function that way.'

I wonder whether I'm going to get the chance to do the things I want to do. I wonder whether anybody's ever going to let me forget Ulrika. I wonder if anybody's ever going to let me forget the dogging. Ulrika's got a column in the *News of the World*, and she likes using it to remind everyone that she thinks I'm a monster. I don't know, maybe things will change. Today it's 'Stan Collymore: Dogger'. But look at some of the transformations that have taken place. Look at someone like George Foreman. Always the bad guy in his heyday, always the epitome of moodiness and aggression. Look at him now: fucking Big Daddy Grill Man grinning from ear to ear; Preacher Man and all that shit.

Whether that could happen to me, I don't know. I'm only 33. I get satisfaction from other things now. It gives me a thrill when a lad like Lee Hendrie or Darren Byfield rings me for advice. That makes me feel like I can contribute something. It makes me feel that I can help other people and that I can start to give things back to the game I love. I'd still like to be a manager one day. I would stack my love of the game, my knowledge of the game and my enthusiasm for the game up alongside anybody else's and be absolutely confident I would not suffer by comparison.

The game and the business surrounding it has changed even since I retired. A lot of people are jumping on it as a business now. It's like the music industry since *Pop Idol*. Music's full of chintzy charlatans that give real musicians the raving hump. I feel a bit bitter about that because there's still a part of me that wants to go out and play. I suppose that as long as I am physically capable of playing, in the back of my mind I think I might go back.

I still feel bitter about certain people in football, like Ray Train and John Gregory and Peter Taylor and Jim Jefferies. I feel bitter that football doesn't seem capable of getting the best out of such different personalities as Alan Shearer and Stan Collymore. Football coaches should be trained to cope with both ends of the spectrum. Sometimes the perfect pro only has one-tenth of the ability of a Collymore or a Gascoigne. What do you want? Ten Alan Shearers, one of whom is the real deal and scores goals for fun, and the rest who are just solid and uninspired?

Today, there is an army of players coming through who are athletic but nothing spectacular. I grew up watching Zico and Eder and Platini and I got off on that. You look at today's breed and they are all ripped and athletic when they take their shirts off and that is the way the game has gone. I hear stuff now about Alex Ferguson running background checks on players before he signs them and it makes me think we are heading towards an era of the domination of the automaton. Thank God for people who slip through the net like Cristiano Ronaldo.

Managers and coaches that I played for were the heads of multi-million-pound businesses. So how could they be allowed not to get the best out of one of their prime assets? Managers and coaches should have to go through proper managerial courses, not just get their coaching badge as an afterthought. They need man-management skills. Think how good Glenn Hoddle might have been as a coach if he could manage his players instead of antagonising them. Let's move on. I mean, ten years ago people tried to get you fit by doing ten-mile cross-country runs and wading through rivers, and now everyone knows that is bollocks.

I worry about my son, Tom, because he is starting to make his way in the game and I think he has got a chance of making it. He plays for a junior team called Cannock Town and West Brom have been asking after him. Now that would be funny: Stan Collymore's lad playing for West Brom. Tom had his eighth birthday party at Molineux this year. They had a penalty shoot-out against Wolfie the Wolf and he tucked his away sweetly.

I have tried to have a heart-to-heart with him because all he wants to be is a footballer. I told him it might be difficult. I told him that out of 100,000 people in Cannock, I was the only one who ever made it to the Premiership. Don't laugh, but I told him he had to work harder than everybody else, and tackle and chase harder than everyone else, and then he might have a chance. I see a lot of myself in him and I don't want him to make the mistakes I made. I never had a male guiding force to tell me I needed to supplement my ability with hard work. He talks a lot in class like I did, and I am trying to impress on him that he will need what they are trying to teach him in school if football doesn't work out for him. He knows he's good, but I want to temper that with a bit of humility. I want to guide him through the obstacles I couldn't get past myself.

I know that essentially he is a very bright kid and he gets bored when he is not being challenged with something. He desperately wants to be a footballer, but if he is anything like me and he's a bit stubborn and he doesn't like people taking the piss, does that mean he is not going to be able to become a professional footballer because the model is an unquestioning, relentless, straightforward, solid pro like Alan Shearer?

I think everybody should have a chance. I think it's too late for me to come back now, although I'd never say never. One of the things I've always wanted to do is act, and now should be an ideal time. I want to make headway. I want to get through the first door. In 20 years' time I would like to be thought of as much for doing four or five different projects as for my football. I want to be in constant contact with my kids. I want to show them things I have seen. I want to be in a normal, settled, happy, functioning relationship. I need somebody that is very knowledgeable about themselves and their feelings, but I know that it's going to be difficult for them to deal with me on a day-to-day basis.

There are a lot of question marks, a lot of doubts. If I didn't have what I know I've got under my bonnet, I would give up. But I feel that as long as I have still got things I want to achieve and that are well within my grasp, then the road will take plenty of turns. If I get there I have this vision of relaxing, exhaling and saying 'fucking cracked it at last'. I have spent three years in bed. I had always planned to have an indefinite period of time to wind down, catch my breath, mull over things, but I have got to the stage now where on my good days I am thinking 'come on, let's get going'.

Other days, things aren't quite so rosy. Sunday, 9 May was one of those. I'd been trying to get hold of Estelle for a few days, ringing her on one of the three fucking mobiles that she maintains. My estranged wife; so estranged that I didn't know where she was and therefore didn't know where my daughter was. None of her mobiles were switched on, which pissed me off because we had an agreement that I would be able to get in contact with her so I could speak to Mia.

So on Sunday evening, about 7 p.m., I went round to her parents' house to see if she was there. Her Mini Cooper, which she had bought when she sold the Jeep I bought her, was in the drive so I assumed she was in. I phoned her mum on my mobile but she said Estelle was still out and they were expecting her back any minute. She said Estelle had said I couldn't see Mia unless she was there, which also pissed me off. So I parked my car around the corner and waited. I switched the television on in the car, but after about ten minutes a BMW with blacked-out windows pulled up and Estelle got out. It was being driven by a Rastafarian bloke with dreadlocks. I said, 'Who the fuck's that?' She said, 'A friend.' She got stroppy. She said, 'I'm allowed to have friends, you know.'

I didn't really give a fuck about the guy, although nobody likes to have their nose rubbed in that sort of shit. No one likes to think of their wife committing adultery with somebody else, particularly as she has always gone on about how she would never do that. She has always beaten me with that stick. I even thought about getting a private investigator to follow her around, but what's the point of being confronted with it when you already know. I would have had more respect for her if she had said she wanted to talk to me about us going our separate ways and her seeing other people, but she never did it like that. I'm not really sure if I can trust her with Mia. I don't want her seeing a lot of different blokes and it affecting our daughter.

Michelle has never done that with me. I went round to her house once and there were a pair of work boots in the hall. I went into the living room and I heard this kind of rustling outside, and when I went back into the hall the work boots had gone. Michelle has never rubbed my nose in it if she is seeing other blokes. I know she has had other boyfriends in the years since we split but I couldn't tell you the name of a single one of them.

What annoyed me more than seeing this bloke dropping Estelle off was that this was the first time Mia had seen either of her parents since I dropped her off at Estelle's parents that Friday. Estelle had been off on some tryst to Southport, apparently. I wanted to take Mia home but she started crying for her mum, which was understandable because she had been missing her. That made me even more wound up and agitated, so I gave her back to Estelle and told her she was a fucking joke of a mum.

Estelle's dad was hovering around pretending to do a bit of DIY with a hammer and a chisel. As the row developed he wandered out with this fucking hammer and stood on the doorstep. It was only a tiny little thing. I don't know if he thought I should be scared by it but he was hardly going to cave my head in with it. I told him that if he came near me with that hammer I'd wrap it round his fucking head. Then her brother, Simon, came down the stairs. I'd given him a little pop on the nose once before when he came round to the house while Estelle and I were having a row. He's a fat bastard who still lives at home with his parents. I said: 'Fucking hell, here comes the fucking cavalry.'

He was all right, to be fair. He said a few reasonable things and they closed the door. I was so angry. I could see Mia crying her eyes out by the bay window at the front of the house. I tried to kick the lights in on the Mini, then I waved at Mia and tried to calm her down. Then I just kicked in the passenger-side window and fucked off out of there.

Estelle called the police and said she wanted to press charges. The next day, I drove down to London and had a few conversations with Estelle and her family. Her dad came on trying to play the hard man at one point and I just told him he was a pathetic little man. They claimed after that that I had threatened to burn the house down and to kill Estelle, which I categorically deny. Later on I had some reasonable conversations with her, and she said that when I got back up to Cannock I could go round and pick Mia up. She was also saying by then that she would be willing to retract the statement she had made to the police. I got back home about 9 p.m., but by then Estelle had decided it wouldn't be a good idea if I had Mia after all.

I walked back into my house, opened a few letters and then there was a knock on the door. I opened it and there was a big lummox of a skinhead copper standing there, who was pretty keen to get into the house. He kept talking about 'threats to kill' in a very melodramatic way and asked me to accompany him and his mate to the police station in Cannock. So I went down there with them and they put me in a cell. I wasn't bothered. I quite fancied a kip by that stage, actually. I asked them for a blanket and I lay down and started dosing. After a bit, they came in and asked me if I wanted a cup of tea. There were a couple of other jailbirds in there. They'd let one of the others out, too, and he was sitting down at a table tucking in to some fish and chips. I fancied a bit of that but they just gave me a cup of tea. My brief arrived about midnight, then the police asked me a lot of questions about the details of my exchanges with Estelle and her family. I got out of there at about a quarter to four.

I went to court in Stafford on 17 May. I thought about sticking some Post-its to my suit jacket saying 'Fuck the Fascist Murdoch Press', that sort of thing. That was an idea I'd got from Morrissey, but I thought that might not go down too well with the magistrates. I was charged with threatening to kill Estelle, causing criminal damage, a public-order offence and issuing a threat to destroy property by fire. I wanted to fight it out at a Crown Court, but when I met my brief he told me Estelle was willing to do a deal. It meant she wouldn't have to take the stand at a Crown Court trial and therefore that none of her shady mates from Birmingham would have to be subpoenaed. That disappointed me, but I thought it was worth settling it for Mia's sake. I stood in the dock in Courtroom Number One at South Staffordshire Magistrates' Court and took the deal. The charges were dropped and I was bound over to keep the peace for 12 months in the sum of £500. No criminal record. No nothing.

I suppose I was happy about that, but I never thought it should have come to court. It was a row. There was no violence. There were no threats. When I walked out of the court building there was a Scouser leaning out of one of the first-floor windows yelling 'Nice one, Stanley'. Outside the court, a reporter called Robin Powell from Central TV asked me whether I was sorry. 'Sorry for what?' I said.

At the time, I felt horribly bitter towards Estelle. At the time, I thought I wished her and her family nothing but ill-will for the rest of their lives. That was another line I got off Morissey. But time salves all those kinds of wounds. I know I was stupid to feel that way and I regret it now. Now, I just hope we can build some kind of civil relationship for the sake of Mia. What I would like most of all is if Estelle and I could become best friends. Which is what we should have been all along. We do love each other but we weren't meant to be man and wife.

I'm going to try and put some distance between us for a while. Give each of us a bit of breathing space. A bit of time to recover. A bit of time to let the anger and the hurt subside. I've been spending a lot more time in Miami recently. I've got friends there and I love the city and South Beach and Ocean Drive. I love the clubs and the sunshine and the lifestyle and the lack of scrutiny that I can wallow in there.

In the summer, I even struck up a friendship with OJ Simpson, who has a house there. He was sitting at an outdoor restaurant with some friends in Coral Gables and he called me over. He said he knew who I was. I thought he was okay. There were some poor kids pestering him for stuff and he gave them $20 each and told them to go and buy themselves some clothes from the Gap round the corner. He invited us round to his house for lunch. We got on well.

I would like to spend a lot more time in the States. It's where I see my future. A year from now, my ideal would be to be enrolled in acting school in Miami or New York and beginning the long road to carving out a new career in films. I know what I'm good at and not good at and I know I could act. I've got a lot to draw on. You know that by now. That's where I'm headed. I'm ready to start again now.

I know my kids will be all right. I want to see them as much as they can but in Michelle and Estelle they both have good mothers who I know will care for them well. Mia's going to grow up a Collymore. There's nothing Estelle can do about that. It's in the genes. I can see it in Tom already and I can see it in Mia, too. Tom's got football talent like me. I can already see he likes doing things his own way. He's stubborn like me. They're both going to be Collymores and if I can set myself up in the States, I'll come back all the time and they can come out for holidays.

That's the optimistic version. That's the happy ending. That's what I still hope for when things are going well, like they are now. The darker version? If things go wrong, the flip-side plays like this: I'm going to join Fathers 4 Justice. Make a protest one day. Climb a tall building in a Batman suit. Stan Collymore in a fucking Batman suit on top of Canary Wharf. I could see the night come falling from the sky up there. And night falls fast in my unquiet mind.

CHAPTER THIRTEEN

FROM FARMHANDS
TO SCUMBAGS

Towards the end of 2004, I finally found myself in that place where celebrities go to die, the reality TV show. I've always thought of them as some sort of purgatory, full of screaming, half-naked men and women up to their tits in witchetty grubs and scorpions or puking up fish eyes. Some of them are a Hades for failures and freaks. Their central insult seems to be to attempt to compound the misery of washed-up entertainers by punishing them for no longer being in a band or a football team. It's almost as if it's the public's particularly sadistic way of getting its own back on celebs for having lived the glamorous kind of life they imagine they wanted to lead.

At least being on *The Farm* kept me occupied. I revelled in the work, which surprised a lot of people. I even finally got to be a manager. Even if it was only Farm Manager. I loved the responsibility of that. It was when I walked out of the show, some time around the end of October, that my life started to race south again and the demons resumed their rattlings in my skull. In early 2005 I fled to France, thinking about ending it all again. By that stage, I was being monitored daily by crisis teams from Staffordshire mental health authority. Let's just say divorce hasn't been good to me.

In a bizarre way, it was like a sanctuary being on that Wiltshire farm with Farmer Ryan, Vanilla Ice, Rebecca Loos and the rest of them. At least it was ordered. At least there was a routine. At least I wasn't spending my days in bed. I spent most of the January that followed *The Farm* in bed, thinking about topping myself. I'd torn down the Christmas tree in my mum's house at the end of December, fuelled by a mixture of panic and rage. The divorce meant I was consumed by money worries again and I found it hard being alone without my wife and kids. At least when I was on *The Farm*, I didn't really have time to think.

It was last July when Channel Five first approached me to see if I wanted to be one of the farmhands. I had been offered a spot on one of the editions of *I'm a Celebrity Get Me Out of Here*. It was the one with Johnny Rotten, Jordan, Peter Andre and Kerry McFadden, who ended up winning it. I didn't fancy it so I turned it down. My old mate Razor Ruddock stepped in for me. He didn't seem to enjoy it very much. I think the lack of food got to him. He needed one of those packages containing a bacon butty that he'd produced in the canteen at Liverpool's training ground. But he couldn't get off this particular treadmill. He got voted off early.

I didn't want to do a reality show for the sake of it. I didn't want to sit on a couch and talk about me all day. But when I saw the format for *The Farm*, I thought it would be a laugh. I didn't know any of the other people. Not Jeff Brazier, who went on to win it, not Rob Van Winkle, better known as Vanilla Ice, not Lady Victoria Hervey, not Debbie McGee or

Paul Daniels, not Terry Christian, not Margi Clarke and not Rebecca Loos. I was a bit sceptical about Rebecca because of course I knew about the allegations of her affair with David Beckham and I realised what the producers would have in mind about her and me, but I decided to go with it anyway. I didn't have anything against any of them.

I thought I might be able to learn a few things about myself. I wanted to take it seriously. I was pleased when we got there and found it was a proper working farm. It was obvious immediately that it was for real and it was going to be hard work. I was happy about that. I didn't really have any agenda about raising my profile. There was the money I was being paid to appear, obviously, but apart from that I just wanted to do what I was told to do as well as I possibly could. I never thought I'd say this, but I just wanted to see if I could be a good farmer.

For most of the 10 days I was in there, I loved it. I was comfortable. I had just come back from spending two or three weeks in Miami and that really rejuvenated me. September and October were always my favourite months of the year because it was the time when you were just getting into your stride in the new football season. It was beautiful being on that farm at that time with the sun coming up at dawn. It was idyllic.

It reminded me of being an apprentice again. Except there was no Ray Train there. It was like what being an apprentice should have been. It was sweeping up, mucking out the pigs, checking the cows, doing the manual work. It was stuff that had to be done. I knew that if it was neglected, the animals would get distressed and that's why it annoyed me when some people just sat on their fat arses and let the rest of us get on with it.

I liked most of the other so-called celebrities who were in there with me. I know a lot of the coverage focused on how close I was supposed to be getting to Rebecca and we did have a decent flirt with each other. But there was no way anything was ever going to happen between us because I had been down that road before. I knew what Rebecca wanted. She wanted fame, above everything else, and to get involved in a proper relationship with her would have meant Stan and Ulrika mark two.

Rebecca isn't a bad person. But she is desperate to be famous. All the others were there because they had done something with their lives. Rob was a pop singer, I had been a footballer, Margi was an actress, Jeff was a television presenter, but Rebecca was only in there because she claimed to have shagged the England football captain. Apart from that, she had been a PA. And I think she felt that on *The Farm*. She felt the pressure to try and get herself noticed and establish her personality so that she could try and move on from being someone who had been fucked by a famous footballer.

She was okay. She put the effort in. She worked. And I thought the furore about her collecting the sperm from a pig and the allegations of the show being akin to bestiality were pathetic. It was a set up that she was chosen for that because the producers of the programme knew it would get massive publicity if the woman who allegedly has had an affair with David Beckham is seen on television pulling off a pig. But the fact remains that it's just part of life. You have to do what Rebecca did to collect sperm from a pig. You have to collect sperm from a pig to create enough new pigs to satisfy the demand for bacon and allow a farmer to earn his money.

People said afterwards that I got suckered by Rebecca because I believed her flirting. But I was playing along with the TV romance thing. People at home love all of that. The easiest thing in the world for Rebecca to do was to make a bee line for another footballer. There was nothing going on between us in there. Now and again, a couple of us would go into the toilet together because it was the one place in the farmhouse where you were allowed to take your microphone off without the Big Brother voice telling you to put it back on again. We went in there for a few chats. Nothing more.

I never got close to shagging her. Nothing like that. Everyone swapped numbers at the end and I know there was a lot of speculation about whether Rebecca and I were going to get together. I spent quite a bit of time with her at the post-show party in a West End night club but I enjoyed Lady V's company more, to be honest. She was the most down to earth person of all of them. For a couple of weeks after the show ended, I was getting texts from Rebecca asking whether I wanted to go to the cinema with her. One of them said, 'I felt something for you while we were in there'. I didn't reply to them.

The whole idea was ridiculous. I knew that if I'd agreed to go out with her, we would have rocked up at the cinema and there would have been 50 photographers waiting outside. It would have been Ulrika all over again. Even though I'm just an ex-footballer, going out with me in real life would have kept Rebecca in the public eye a little longer. It would have extended her precious 15 minutes of fame. I'd been used like that once before and it nearly destroyed me. So I had no intention of even getting close to being drawn into a relationship with someone who could have been a carbon copy.

I had a bit of a laugh and a joke and a flirt with her but that was it. There was no way I was going to get into a relationship. No way. I had learned from the Ulrika thing and I actually felt good about myself that I wasn't rushing into the same trap again. Ulrika and Rebecca are actually very similar types of people. They draw blokes to them like moths to a flame. They charm the pants off blokes but it is all designed for a purpose.

Thankfully, most of the relationships on *The Farm* were a lot less complicated than that. I got on well with everyone really. Perhaps people were surprised by that. Lady V was the smartest. I liked Jeff Brazier best. He reminded me of when I was an apprentice. There was always a chirpy Cockney apprentice just like Jeff at a football club. Always irrepressible with sparkling eyes. When I was a 19-year-old at Crystal Palace, there was a guy called Andy Woodman, who's a big mate of Gareth Southgate, and he was like that. My mate Jamie Moralee was similar, too.

Of course, I had my rucks with Rob. They make me laugh just thinking about them. He was all an act. He was all bravado. I threatened to take him out and batter him once when he got a bit fresh but he soon backed down. He said that if he didn't have the flu, he would have gone outside with me to beat my ass. Well, he might have been a rapper but I wasn't exactly quaking in my boots. But he was all right. I liked him. It was just that he was a lazy twat.

In the end, that laziness made him unbearable. And I felt

it was starting to make a mockery of the whole experiment. I was taking it seriously. He wasn't. And it got to the point where he was taking the piss. Towards the end, when there were less people there and we really needed his help, he would say he was just off for a toilet break and he would be gone for an hour. For me, it quickly became a case of everybody pitches in or fuck it.

I don't think Rob ever intended to take it seriously. He was in it for the publicity. He tried to ride on the back of one of the pigs the first day he was in there. The next day, he threw a glass into the farmyard which smashed into hundreds of shards. We had all been to talks given by animal rights people about how we must treat the animals with respect. We all knew the do's and don't's and I just felt that for him to do something that was so obviously dangerous to the animals showed that he had no idea of what was required and absolutely no respect for anybody else on the farm. If I had done that, I would have been chucked off straight away.

The rows with Rob started to take it out of me and after 10 days I grew increasingly disillusioned with it. We had all had a few chats about things while we were in there and some people were absolutely honest about the fact that they were there to further their careers. That was never my bag. I just wanted to do the farming well and have a few beers. I just wanted to take pride in something. When I was an apprentice at Walsall, I worked hard. I would sweep a whole stadium. Over the course of my career, my contribution to my team in terms of goals and assists was as much as anybody else's.

Look at somebody like Jimmy Floyd Hasselbaink and your snapshot image of him is probably of a guy throwing his hands up in the air in despair or indignation or resignation and that was what I was like. But it doesn't mean we weren't contributing as players. I enjoyed working on the farm because it was something I could get my teeth into. The hard work aspect of it was never a problem at all for me. People seemed to be surprised that I worked so hard and took it so seriously because they have built up this image of me as a lazy shirker but I have always been a hard worker. My mum was a grafter. She worked all the hours god sent to bring me up by herself.

When I had had enough, I just told the production team very calmly that I was going and I told them the reasons why. It was basically because the work was not getting done because Rob would not help us do the work. Things were getting neglected and I didn't think that was acceptable. The production people tried to persuade me not to go but I had made my mind up and that was it. There was no fuss about it.

I walked out after 10 days because we had split into two groups of people. One group wanted to do the work and have a laugh as well, and the other had just turned into parodies of themselves who didn't give a shit. I stuck with the show for as long as it remained what the producers had promised it would be. Once it started to veer away from that, once some people started being indulged and excused, it got to me so much that I had to quit. Our ways just parted.

Soon after I was persuaded to do a telephone interview on the *Richard & Judy Show*, ostensibly to promote my auto-biography. It was only when I was put through to the pro-gramme live that I realised I had been set up. They announced they were running a poll asking their viewers whether they thought I had deserved to be beaten up or not. Well, 95% of them said 'yes'. What a great constituency that is. Then Richard started talking about how ungallant I had been for talking about my affair with Kirsty Gallagher in the book and their panel of Amanda Platell and Nick Ferrari started weighing in, too.

I asked them if they'd read it. Amanda Platell said she wouldn't read it because it was 'scum'. That was her argument screwed really. As for Nick Ferrari, a couple of years ago the Broadcasting Standards Commission upheld a complaint about his attitude to asylum seekers. He's just a shock jock bullshit merchant. They didn't give me a chance to say anything. It was a set-up and I was the victim again. And that was the tip of the iceberg because it was clear that a lot of people felt the same way. Because I had once hit Ulrika Jonsson, seven long years ago, there seemed to be this feeling out there that what goes around comes around. They liked the idea of me as the biter bit.

They didn't give me the chance to speak. The laughing hyenas cut me off before I could reply to their pathetic inanities. Richard was the worst. What a fucking hypocrite he is. The show was supposed to be about how people's lives could be tarnished by media coverage. I wanted to ask him how he had felt when he was charged with being a shoplifter. 'Let's do another viewer's poll,' I wanted to say, 'about whether people still believe you've got light fingers, even though you were acquitted.' I didn't get the opportunity.

That felt like the last straw. Winter seemed to be closing in very fast all of a sudden and so I went home and hid. The last couple of years, the winter weather in England has affected me quite badly. It never got to me when I was a footballer, because playing kept me on my toes and kept my mind off the cold. But now I've got time on my hands, and for large swathes of last December I'd get up so late that it would be dark. I would be going days and days on end without seeing sunlight.

There are still a few last details that need to be sorted out as far as the divorce goes. Estelle and I speak a couple of times a week, usually about Mia. I know there has been a lot of hurt and pain for Estelle in all of this. Hopefully, as time goes by, we can put that out of the way because all we both really want is to take care of Mia's welfare. At Christmas, there was just me and my mum at home. It just all knocked the wind out of my sails and I couldn't cope.

January was worse. I had an awful, awful January. I was very low and constantly suicidal. I was monitored daily by the local mental health people in Staffordshire. I didn't get out of bed in January basically. I have never been so close to suicide. I went up to Stafford Hospital a few times in the new year because I was so desperate. I rocked up at the outpatients unit once at 3am and told them I didn't think I could make it through the night without help because I was worried I was going to commit suicide. I went to the psychiatric hospital one night, too. They alerted the local mental health unit and they were fantastic. They started coming on a daily basis. They sent a crisis team and they were brilliant. They just came every day and chatted. What they do, basically, is just be there. It sounds sad. It *is* sad. I'm eternally grateful to them.

I sparked a nationwide alert one time this winter because I

felt so low I left a note for my mum asking her to take care of things while I was away and took off. I drove to France and of course everyone was frantic about me. I went across the Channel on the ferry and just drove around. I don't even know where I went. I was just dazed and confused. Even thinking about how low I was then upsets me. I could not get my head around things. Eventually, I came back to Dover and the police stopped me when I came out of the tunnel and asked me to get myself home because there was a crisis team waiting for me. *The Sun* found out about it eventually but I seemed finally to have exhausted even their capacity for cruelty. They only wasted a few paragraphs on me this time.

The divorce was caving my head in. I needed to escape. I got back from France and suddenly I was alone again. So I took off for Miami. I've got friends there, I enjoy their company, and we spend a lot of time together. I went over at the beginning of March, intending to stay for a week, and ended up staying for two months. Since the end of January, I've only been in England for four days. Sunshine in Miami makes a difference. It keeps me away from those long days in bed and just pottering around by myself at home.

I took myself off to Thailand for a couple of weeks, too. In some vague sort of way, I wanted to see if there was anything I could do to help after the tsunami. But they ended up helping me. I remember looking at these Thai people who had lost everything. I looked at them and looked at them because they were still smiling. They had retained a peace about them that I could not quite get. I've never felt that. I looked at them in the wreckage of their lives and I envied them.

I came back from Thailand, landed at Heathrow and went

straight into central London to do a screen test for the sequel to the film *Basic Instinct*. It's called *Risk Addiction*, which seems kind of suitable given the way I've run my life the last couple of years. The director, Michael Caton-Jones, had read in a Hollywood magazine that I wanted to get involved in acting and he's a big football fan so he thought he'd give me a try. I read the part in front of him and the casting director. It's only half a dozen lines. I thought I was a bit wooden. I didn't think I'd get it. I thought a proper actor would come in off the street and read it like Olivier. I found out two weeks later that I had got it.

I'm in the opening scenes. I get killed off before the credits have even rolled. And guess what, I'm having sex in a car. The papers loved that when they got hold of it. Especially as the person I'm having sex with is Sharon Stone, or her character, Catherine Trammell. I was really proud of myself when they rang to tell me I'd got it. I haven't had too many reasons to feel optimistic about my future in the past couple of years. Things seem to have been spiralling out of control. Partly because of the way I have behaved, more and more people seem to have been abandoning me.

But somehow this holds out the hope of a fresh beginning. I know I've got a chance now to find another world to give me the adrenaline buzz I crave. I may not have a big part in this movie but I'm determined to eke everything out of it that I can. I want to get advice from as many people as I can. If they say I ought to go to acting school, I'll go. This is a chance to move on. This is a chance to drag myself back into the daylight. Perhaps it can be the beginning of a new life. I feel like the old one is pretty much worn out.

CAREER RECORD

Born: 22.01.71
Birthplace: Cannock, Staffs.
International honours: Three England caps.

CLUBS AND PLAYING RECORDS (all competitions).
Crystal Palace (1991–92): 25 appearances, 2 goals
Southend United (1992–93): 33 appearances, 18 goals
Nottingham Forest (1993–95): 78 appearances, 50 goals
Liverpool (1995–97): 81 appearances, 35 goals
Aston Villa (1997–2000): 61 appearances, 15 goals
Fulham (loan, 1999): 9 appearances, 1 goal
Leicester City (2000): 12 appearances, 5 goals
Bradford City (2000–1): 8 appearances, 2 goals
Real Oviedo (2001): 3 appearances
TOTAL: 310 appearances, 128 goals

CRYSTAL PALACE
Signed: 4 January, 1991 (£100,000 from Stafford Rangers)
Debut: February 16, 1991 v Queens Park Rangers (h) 0–0.

1990–91
Division One

Feb 16	h	Queens Park Rangers (sub)	0–0
Apr 13	h	Aston Villa (sub)	0–0

Apr 17	h	Tottenham Hotspur (sub)	1–0
Apr 20	h	Everton (sub)	0–0
Apr 23	a	Liverpool (sub)	0–3
May 4	a	Wimbledon (sub)	3–0

1991–92
Division One

Sept 17	h	West Ham United (sub)	2–3	
Sept 28	h	Queens Park Rangers (sub)	2–2	1 goal
Oct 1	h	Leeds United (sub)	1–0	
Oct 5	a	Sheffield Wednesday (sub)	1–4	
Nov 16	h	Southampton (sub)	1–0	
Nov 30	h	Manchester United (sub)	1–3	
Mar 11	a	Southampton (sub)	0–1	
Mar 21	h	Aston Villa	0–0	
Mar 28	a	Notts County	2–3	
Apr 4	h	Everton	2–0	
Apr 11	a	Arsenal	1–4	
April 18	h	Oldham Athletic (sub)	0–0	

Rumbelows (League) Cup
Second round (2)

| Oct 8 | h | Hartlepool United | 6–1 | 1 goal |

Third round (1st R)

| Nov 19 | h | Birmingham City (sub) | 1–1 | |

Third round (2nd R)

| Dec 3 | h | Birmingham City (sub) | 2–1 | |

1992–93
Premiership

| Sept 26 | h | Southampton (sub) | 1–2 |
| Oct 17 | h | Manchester City (sub) | 0–0 |

Coca-Cola (League Cup)
Second round (1)

| Sept 22 | h | Lincoln City | 3–1 |

Second round (2)

Oct 6   a   Lincoln City (sub)   1–1

SOUTHEND UNITED

Signed: November 20, 1992 (£150,000)
Debut: November 21, 1992 v Notts County (h) 3–1

1992–93
Division One

Nov 21	h	Notts County	3–1	2 goals
Nov 28	h	Sunderland	0–1	
Dec 5	a	Millwall	1–1	
Dec 12	a	West Ham United	0–2	
Dec 19	h	Barnsley	3–0	2 goals
Dec 26	h	Watford	1–2	
Dec 28	a	Bristol Rovers	2–0	1 goal
Jan 9	a	Portsmouth	0–2	
Jan 16	h	Derby County	0–0	
Jan 20	h	Newcastle United	1–1	
Jan 27	h	Birmingham City	4–0	1 goal
Jan 30	a	Peterborough United	0–1	
Feb 10	h	Bristol City	1–1	1 goal
Feb 21	h	Brentford	3–0	1 goal
Feb 27	a	Wolves	1–1	
Mar 6	h	Charlton Athletic	0–2	
Mar 10	h	Swindon Town	1–1	
Mar 13	a	Oxford United	1–0	1 goal
Mar 21	h	Millwall	3–3	1 goal
Mar 23	a	Notts County	0–4	
Mar 26	h	Tranmere Rovers	1–2	
Apr 3	a	Sunderland	4–2	1 goal
Apr 7	h	West Ham United	1–0	
Apr 10	a	Watford	0–0	
Apr 14	h	Bristol Rovers	3–0	2 goals
Apr 17	a	Barnsley	1–3	1 goal
Apr 20	a	Leicester City	1–4	

Apr 23	h	Grimsby Town	1–0	1 goal
May 1	a	Cambridge United	1–3	
May 8	h	Luton Town	2–1	

FA Cup
Third round

Jan 13	h	Millwall	1–0	1 goal

Fourth round

Jan 23	a	Huddersfield Town	2–1	2 goals

Fifth round

Feb 13	a	Sheffield Wednesday	0–2	

NOTTINGHAM FOREST
Signed: July 5, 1993 (£2 million)
Debut: August 24, 1993 v Crystal Palace (a) 0–2

1993–94
Division One

Aug 24	a	Crystal Palace	0–2	
Sept 11	a	Barnsley	0–1	
Sept 19	h	Stoke City	2–3	
Sept 26	a	Bolton Wanderers	3–4	2 goals
Oct 2	h	Portsmouth	1–1	
Oct 16	h	Tranmere Rovers	2–1	1 goal
Oct 24	a	Leicester City	0–1	
Oct 30	h	Notts County	1–0	1 goal
Nov 3	h	Millwall	1–3	
Nov 6	a	Birmingham City	3–0	1 goal
Nov 10	a	Wolves	1–1	1 goal
Nov 21	a	West Bromwich Albion	2–0	2 goals
Nov 27	a	Sunderland	3–2	2 goals
Dec 4	h	Birmingham City	1–0	
Dec 19	h	Southend United	2–0	
Dec 27	h	Middlesbrough	1–1	1 goal
Dec 28	a	Bristol City	4–1	2 goals
Jan 1	h	Charlton Athletic	1–1	

Jan 3	a	Watford	2–1	
Mar 19	h	Bolton Wanderers (sub)	3–2	1 goal
Mar 26	a	Portsmouth	1–2	1 goal
Mar 30	h	Watford	2–1	
Apr 17	a	Millwall	2–2	1 goal
Apr 24	h	West Bromwich Albion	2–1	
Apr 27	a	Derby County	2–0	
Apr 30	a	Peterborough United	3–2	2 goals
May 3	a	Grimsby Town	0–0	
May 8	h	Sunderland	2–2	1 goal

Coca-Cola (League) Cup
Second round (1)

| Sept 21 | a | Wrexham | 3–3 | 3 goals |

Second round (2)

| Oct 6 | h | Wrexham | 3–1 | 1 goal |

Third round

| Oct 27 | h | West Ham United | 2–1 | 1 goal |

Fourth round (R)

| Dec 15 | | Manchester City | 2–1 | |

Fifth round (R)

| Jan 29 | a | Tranmere Rovers | 0–2 | |

Anglo Italian Cup
Preliminary competition

| Sept 8 | a | Derby County | 2–3 | |
| Sept 15 | h | Notts County | 1–1 | 1 goal |

1994–95
Premiership

Aug 22	h	Manchester United	1–1	1 goal
Aug 27	h	Leicester City	1–0	1 goal
Aug 30	a	Everton	2–1	
Sept 10	h	Sheffield Wednesday	4–1	
Sept 17	a	Southampton	1–1	1 goal
Sept 24	a	Tottenham Hotspur	4–2	

Oct 2	h	Queens Park Rangers	3–2	1 goal
Oct 8	a	Manchester City	3–3	1 goal
Oct 17	h	Wimbledon	3–1	1 goal
Oct 22	a	Aston Villa	2–0	
Nov 7	h	Newcastle United	0–0	
Nov 19	h	Chelsea	0–1	
Nov 25	a	Leeds United	0–1	
Dec 3	h	Arsenal	2–2	
Dec 10	h	Ipswich Town	4–1	1 goal
Dec 17	a	Manchester United	2–1	1 goal
Dec 26	a	Coventry City	0–0	
Dec 27	h	Norwich City	1–0	
Dec 31	a	West Ham United	1–3	
Jan 14	a	Blackburn Rovers	0–3	
Jan 21	h	Aston Villa	1–2	1 goal
Jan 25	a	Chelsea	2–0	2 goals
Feb 4	h	Liverpool	1–1	1 goal
Feb 11	a	Newcastle United	1–2	
Feb 26	a	Queens Park Rangers	1–1	
Mar 4	h	Tottenham Hotspur	2–2	
Mar 8	h	Everton	2–1	1 goal
Mar 11	a	Leicester City	4–2	1 goal
Mar 18	h	Southampton	3–0	1 goal
Mar 22	h	Leeds United	3–0	1 goal
Apr 1	a	Sheffield Wednesday	7–1	2 goals
Apr 8	h	West Ham United	1–1	1 goal
Apr 12	a	Norwich City	1–0	
Apr 17	h	Coventry City	2–0	1 goal
Apr 29	a	Crystal Palace	2–1	1 goal
May 6	h	Manchester City	1–0	1 goal
May 13	a	Wimbledon	2–2	

FA Cup
Third round

| Jan 7 | h | Plymouth Argyle | 2–0 | 1 goal |

Fourth round

| Jan 28 | h | Crystal Palace | 1–2 | |

Coca-Cola (League) Cup
Second round (1)

| Sept 21 | h | Hereford United | 2–1 | 2 goals |

Second round (2)

| Oct 4 | a | Hereford United | 0–0 | |

Third round

| Oct 26 | a | Wolves | 3–2 | |

Fourth round

| Nov 30 | h | Millwall | 0–2 | |

LIVERPOOL

Signed: July 1, 1995 (£8.5millon, British record fee at time)
Debut: August 19, 1995 v Sheffield Wednesday (h) 1–0

1995–96
Premiership

Aug 19	h	Sheffield Wednesday	1–0	1 goal
Aug 21	a	Leeds United	0–1	
Sept 9	a	Wimbledon	0–1	
Sept 16	h	Blackburn Rovers	3–0	1 goal
Sept 23	h	Bolton Wanderers	5–2	
Oct 14	h	Coventry City	0–0	
Nov 4	a	Newcastle United (sub)	1–2	
Nov 22	a	West Ham United	0–0	
Nov 25	a	Middlesbrough	1–2	
Dec 2	h	Southampton	1–1	1 goal
Dec 9	a	Bolton Wanderers	1–0	1 goal
Dec 17	h	Manchester United	2–0	
Dec 23	h	Arsenal	3–1	
Dec 30	a	Chelsea	2–2	
Jan 1	h	Nottingham Forest	4–2	1 goal
Jan 13	a	Sheffield Wednesday	1–1	
Jan 20	h	Leeds United	5–0	1 goal

Jan 31	a	Aston Villa	2–0	1 goal
Feb 3	h	Tottenham	0–0	
Feb 11	a	Queens Park Rangers	2–1	
Feb 24	a	Blackburn Rovers	3–2	2 goals
Mar 3	h	Aston Villa	3–0	
Mar 13	h	Wimbledon	2–2	1 goal
Mar 16	h	Chelsea	2–0	
Mar 23	a	Nottingham Forest	0–1	
Apr 3	h	Newcastle United	4–3	2 goals
Apr 6	a	Coventry City	0–1	
Apr 8	h	West Ham United	2–0	1 goal
Apr 16	a	Everton	1–1	
Apr 27	h	Middlesbrough	1–0	1 goal
May 1	a	Arsenal	0–0	

FA Cup
Third round

Jan 6	h	Rochdale	7–0	3 goals

Fourth round

Feb 18	a	Shrewsbury Town	4–0	1 goal

Fifth round

Feb 28	h	Charlton Athletic	2–1	1 goal

Sixth round

Mar 10	a	Leeds United	0–0	
Mar 20	h	Leeds United (R)	3–0	

Semi-finals at Old Trafford

Mar 31	–	Aston Villa	3–0	

Final at Wembley

May 11	–	Manchester United	0–1	

Coca-Cola (League) Cup
Second round (1)

Sept 20	h	Sunderland	2–0	

Second round (2)

Oct 4	a	Sunderland (sub)	1–0	

Third round
Oct 25   h   Manchester City (sub)   4–0
Fourth round
Nov 29   h   Newcastle United   0–1

UEFA Cup
First round (1)
Sept 12 a   Spartak Vladikavkaz   2–1
Second round (2)
Oct 31   h   Brondby (sub)   0–1.

1996–97
Premiership
Aug 17   a   Middlesbrough   3–3
Aug 19   h   Arsenal   2–0
Aug 24   h   Sunderland   0–0
Sept 4   a   Coventry City   1–0
Sept 7   h   Southampton   2–1   1 goal
Sept 15 a   Leicester City   3–0
Sept 29 a   West Ham United   2–1   1 goal
Oct 12   a   Manchester United   0–1
Nov 3   a   Blackburn Rovers (sub)   0–3
Nov 20   h   Everton (sub)   1–1
Nov 23   h   Wimbledon   1–1   1 goal
Dec 14   h   Middlesbrough   5–1
Dec 17   h   Nottingham Forest   4–2   2 goals
Dec 23   a   Newcastle United   1–1
Dec 26   h   Leicester City   1–1   1 goal
Dec 29   a   Southampton   1–0
Jan 1   a   Chelsea   0–1
Jan 11   h   West Ham United (sub)   0–0
Jan 18   h   Aston Villa   3–0   1 goal
Feb 1   a   Derby County   1–0   1 goal
Feb 19   h   Leeds United   4–0   2 goals
Feb 22   h   Blackburn Rovers   0–0
Mar 2   a   Aston Villa   0–1

Mar 15	a	Nottingham Forest (sub)	1–1	
Mar 24	a	Arsenal	2–1	1 goal
Apr 6	h	Coventry City	1–2	
Apr 19	h	Manchester United (sub)	1–3	
May 3	h	Tottenham	2–1	1 goal
May 6	a	Wimbledon	1–2	
May 11	a	Sheffield Wednesday	1–1	

FA Cup
Third round

Jan 4	h	Burnley	1–0	1 goal

Fourth round

Jan 26	a	Chelsea	2–4	1 goal

Cup Winners' Cup
First round (1)

Sept 12	a	MyPa-47	1–0	

First round (2)

Sept 26	h	MyPa-47	3–1	1 goal

Quarter-finals (2)

Mar 20	h	SK Brann (sub)	3–0	1 goal

Semi-finals (1)

Apr 10	a	Paris St-Germain	0–3	

Semi-finals (2)

Apr 24	h	Paris St-Germain	2–0	

ASTON VILLA
Signed: May 13, 1997 (£7million)
Debut: August 9, 1997 v Leicester City (a) 0–1

1997–98
Premiership

Aug 9	a	Leicester City	0–1	
Aug 13	h	Blackburn Rovers	0–4	
Aug 23	a	Newcastle United	0–1	
Aug 27	a	Tottenham	2–3	1 goal

Aug 30	h	Leeds United	1–0	
Sept 13	a	Barnsley	3–0	
Sept 20	h	Derby County	2–1	
Sept 22	a	Liverpool	0–3	
Sept 27	h	Sheffield Wednesday	2–2	
Oct 4	a	Bolton Wanderers	1–0	
Nov 22	h	Everton	2–1	
Nov 29	a	West Ham United	1–2	
Dec 6	h	Coventry City	3–0	1 goal
Dec 15	a	Manchester United	0–1	
Dec 20	h	Southampton	1–1	
Dec 26	h	Tottenham	4–1	2 goals
Jan 10	h	Leicester City	1–1	
Jan 17	a	Blackburn Rovers	0–5	
Feb 1	h	Newcastle United	0–1	
Feb 7	a	Derby County	1–0	
Feb 18	h	Manchester United	0–2	
Feb 21	a	Wimbledon	1–2	
Feb 28	h	Liverpool	2–1	2 goals
Apr 25	h	Bolton Wanderers (sub)	1–3	
May 10	h	Arsenal (sub)	1–0	

FA Cup
Third round

Jan 3	a	Portsmouth	2–2	

Third round (R)

Jan 14	h	Portsmouth	1–0	

Fourth round

Jan 24	h	West Bromwich Albion	4–0	1 goal

Fifth round

Feb 14	h	Coventry City	0–1	

Coca-Cola (League) Cup
Third round

Oct 15	a	West Ham United	0–3	

UEFA Cup
First round (1)

Sept 16	a	Bordeaux	0–0

First round (2)

Sept 30	h	Bordeaux	1–0

Second round (1)

Oct 21	a	Athletic Bilbao	0–0

Third round (1)

Nov 25	a	Steaua Bucharest	1–2

Third round (2)

Dec 9	h	Steaua Bucharest	2–0

Quarter-finals (1)

Mar 3	a	Atletico Madrid	0–1

Quarter-finals (2)

Mar 17	h	Atletico Madrid (sub)	2–1	1 goal

1998–99
Premiership

Aug 29	a	Sheffield Wednesday	1–0	
Sept 26	h	Derby County (sub)	1–0	
Oct 3	a	Coventry City	2–1	
Oct 17	a	West Ham Utd.	0–0	
Oct 24	h	Leicester City	1–1	
Nov 7	h	Tottenham	3–2	1 goal
Nov 14	a	Southampton	4–1	
Nov 21	h	Liverpool	2–4	
Dec 9	a	Chelsea (sub)	1–2	
Dec 13	h	Arsenal (sub)	3–2	
Dec 21	a	Charlton Athletic	1–0	
Dec 26	a	Blackburn Rovers (sub)	1–2	
Dec 28	h	Sheffield Wednesday (sub)	2–1	
Jan 18	h	Everton (sub)	3–0	
Feb 17	h	Leeds United (sub)	1–2	
Feb 21	a	Wimbledon (sub)	0–0	
Feb 27	h	Coventry City (sub)	1–4	
Mar 10	a	Derby County	1–2	

| Mar 13 | a | Tottenham | 0–1 | |
| Mar 21 | h | Chelsea | 0–3 | |

FA Cup
Third round

| Jan 2 | h | Hull City | 3–0 | 2 goals |

UEFA Cup
First round (2)

| Sept 29 | a | Stromsgodset | 3–0 | 3 goals |

Second round (1)

| Oct 20 | a | Celta Vigo | 1–0 | |

Second round (2)

| Nov 3 | h | Celta Vigo | 1–3 | 1 goal |

FULHAM

Signed: July 19, 1999 (Loan)
Debut: August 7, 1999 v Birmingham City (a), 2–2

1999–2000
Divison One

Aug 7	a	Birmingham City	2–2	
Aug 14	h	Manchester City	0–0	
Aug 21	a	Grimsby Town	1–1	
Sept 11	a	Port Vale (sub)	2–0	
Sept 25	h	Crewe Alexandra (sub)	3–0	
Oct 2	a	Norwich City (sub)	2–1	

Worthington (League) Cup
First round (1)

| Aug 10 | a | Northampton Town | 2–1 | |

Second round (1)

| Sept 14 | a | Norwich City | 4–0 | |

Third round

| Oct 12 | a | West Bromwich Albion | 2–1 | 1 goal |

LEICESTER CITY
Signed: February 10, 2000 (Free)
Debut: February 12, 2000 v Watford (a), 1–1

1999–2000
Premiership

Feb 12	a	Watford	1–1	
Mar 5	h	Sunderland	5–2	3 goals
Mar 11	a	Wimbledon	1–2	
Mar 18	h	Manchester United	0–2	
Mar 26	h	Leeds United	2–1	1 goal
Apr 2	a	Derby County	0–2	

2000–01
Premiership

Aug 19	h	Aston Villa	0–0	
Sept 6	h	Ipswich Town (sub)	2–1	
Sept 9	h	Southampton (sub)	1–0	
Sept 17	a	Chelsea (sub)	2–0	1 goal
Sept 24	h	Everton (sub)	1–1	

UEFA Cup
First Round (1)

Sept 14	h	Red Star (sub)	1–1	

BRADFORD CITY (2000–01)
Signed: October 26, 2000 (Free)
Debut: October 29, 2000 v Leeds (h), 1–1

2000–01
Premiership

Oct 29	h	Leeds United	1–1	1 goal
Nov 11	h	Everton	0–1	
Nov 18	a	Derby County	0–2	
Nov 25	a	Middlesbrough (sub)	2–2	
Dec 2	h	Coventry City	2–1	1 goal

| Dec 9 | h | Tottenham | 3–3 |
| Jan 1 | a | Leicester City | 2–1 |

Worthington (League) Cup
Third round

| Nov 1 | a | Newcastle Utd. | 3–4 |

OVIEDO (2000–01)
Signed: January 30, 2001 (free)
Debut: February 4, 2001 v Las Palmas (a) 0–1

2000–01
Primera Liga

Feb 4	a	Las Palmas (sub)	0–1
Feb 11	h	Villarreal (sub)	1–3
Mar 4	a	Celta Vigo(sub)	0–1

ENGLAND APPEARANCES
1994–95
Umbro Cup

| June 3 | Wembley | Japan | 2–1 |
| June 11 | Wembley | Brazil (sub) | 1–3 |

1997–98
World Cup Qualifier

| Sept 10 | Wembley | Moldova (sub) | 4–0 |

INDEX